# BELONGING BEYOND BORDERS

# Latin American and Caribbean Series

Hendrik Kraay, Series Editor
ISSN 1498-2366 (PRINT), ISSN 1925-9638 (ONLINE)

This series sheds light on historical and cultural topics in Latin America and the Caribbean by publishing works that challenge the canon in history, literature, and postcolonial studies. It seeks to print cutting-edge studies and research that redefine our understanding of historical and current issues in Latin America and the Caribbean.

No. 1 · *Waking the Dictator: Veracruz, the Struggle for Federalism and the Mexican Revolution* Karl B. Koth

No. 2 · *The Spirit of Hidalgo: The Mexican Revolution in Coahuila* Suzanne B. Pasztor · Copublished with Michigan State University Press

No. 3 · *Clerical Ideology in a Revolutionary Age: The Guadalajara Church and the Idea of the Mexican Nation, 1788–1853* Brian F. Connaughton, translated by Mark Allan Healey · Copublished with University Press of Colorado

No. 4 · *Monuments of Progress: Modernization and Public Health in Mexico City, 1876–1910* Claudia Agostoni · Copublished with University Press of Colorado

No. 5 · *Madness in Buenos Aires: Patients, Psychiatrists and the Argentine State, 1880–1983* Jonathan Ablard · Copublished with Ohio University Press

No. 6 · *Patrons, Partisans, and Palace Intrigues: The Court Society of Colonial Mexico, 1702–1710* Christoph Rosenmüller

No. 7 · *From Many, One: Indians, Peasants, Borders, and Education in Callista Mexico, 1924–1935* Andrae Marak

No. 8 · *Violence in Argentine Literature and Film (1989–2005)* Edited by Carolina Rocha and Elizabeth Montes Garcés

No. 9 · *Latin American Cinemas: Local Views and Transnational Connections* Edited by Nayibe Bermúdez Barrios

No. 10 · *Creativity and Science in Contemporary Argentine Literature: Between Romanticism and Formalism* Joanna Page

No. 11 · *Textual Exposures: Photography in Twentieth Century Spanish American Narrative Fiction* Dan Russek

No. 12 · *Whose Man in Havana? Adventures from the Far Side of Diplomacy* John W. Graham

No. 13 · *Journalism in a Small Place: Making Caribbean News Relevant, Comprehensive, and Independent* Juliette Storr

No. 14 · *The Road to Armageddon: Paraguay versus the Triple Alliance, 1866–70* Thomas L. Whigham

No. 15 · *The Politics of Violence in Latin America* Edited by Pablo Policzer

No. 16 · *Belonging Beyond Borders: Cosmopolitan Affiliations in Contemporary Spanish American Literature* Annik Bilodeau

 **UNIVERSITY OF CALGARY**
Press

# BELONGING BEYOND BORDERS

## ANNIK BILODEAU

Cosmopolitan Affiliations in
Contemporary Spanish American Literature

Latin American and
Caribbean Series
ISSN 1498-2366 (Print)
ISSN 1925-9638 (Online)

 **UNIVERSITY OF CALGARY**
FACULTY OF ARTS
Latin American Research Centre

© 2021 Annik Bilodeau

University of Calgary Press
2500 University Drive NW
Calgary, Alberta
Canada T2N 1N4
press.ucalgary.ca

This book is available as an ebook which is licensed under a Creative Commons license. The publisher should be contacted for any commercial use which falls outside the terms of that license.

Every effort has been made to trace copyright holders and to obtain their permission for the use of copyright material. The publisher apologizes for any errors or omissions and would be grateful if notified of any corrections that should be incorporated in future reprints or editions of this book.

Excerpts appear in this book from the following works and editions:
Derechos Reservados © ELENA PONIATOWSKA, *Los rituales del caos*, Ediciones Era, México, 2013.
Vargas Llosa, Mario. *La Tía Julia y el escribidor*. 1977. Alfaguara, 2000.
Vargas Llosa, Mario. *El Paraíso en la otra esquina*. Alfaguara, 2003.
Vargas Llosa, Mario. *El sueño del celta*. Punto de lectura, 2010.
Vargas Llosa, Mario. *Aunt Julia and the Scriptwriter*. Farrar, Straus and Giroux, 1982.
Vargas Llosa, Mario. *The Way to Paradise*. Farrar, Straus and Giroux, 2003.
Vargas Llosa, Mario. *The Dream of the Celt*. Farrar, Straus and Giroux, 2010.
Volpi Escalante, Jorge. *El fin de la locura*. Alfaguara, 2003.
Volpi Escalante, Jorge. *No será la Tierra*. Alfaguara, 2006.
Volpi, Jorge. *Season of Ash*. Open Letter, 2009. Translated from the Spanish by Alfred Mac Adam.

LIBRARY AND ARCHIVES CANADA CATALOGUING IN PUBLICATION

Title: Belonging beyond borders : cosmopolitan affiliations in contemporary Spanish American literature / Annik Bilodeau.
Names: Bilodeau, Annik, author.
Series: Latin American and Caribbean series ; no. 16.
Description: Series statement: Latin American and Caribbean series, ISSN 1498-2366 ; no. 16 | Includes bibliographical references and index.
Identifiers: Canadiana (print) 20200256831 | Canadiana (ebook) 20200257110 | ISBN 9781773851594 (softcover) | ISBN 9781773851600 (Open Access PDF) | ISBN 9781773851617 (Library PDF) | ISBN 9781773851624 (EPUB) | ISBN 9781773851631 (Kindle)
Subjects: LCSH: Spanish American literature—20th century—History and criticism. | LCSH: Spanish American literature—21st century—History and criticism. | LCSH: Cosmopolitanism in literature.
Classification: LCC PQ6073.C67 B55 2020 | DDC 863/.709355—dc23

The University of Calgary Press acknowledges the support of the Government of Alberta through the Alberta Media Fund for our publications. We acknowledge the financial support of the Government of Canada. We acknowledge the financial support of the Canada Council for the Arts for our publishing program.

This book has been published with the help of a grant from the Federation for the Humanities and Social Sciences, through the Awards to Scholarly Publications Program, using funds provided by the Social Sciences and Humanities Research Council of Canada.

 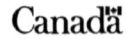 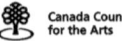

Copyediting by Ryan Perks
Cover photo by Alexander Schimmeck on Unsplash
Cover design, page design, and typesetting by Melina Cusano

# Contents

**Acknowledgments** — VII

**Introduction** — 1
   Spanish America against the World | 8
   Conceptions of Cosmopolitanism and Cosmopolitan Reading | 16
   Rooted Cosmopolitanism in Spanish American Literature | 23

**1 Narrating Transculturation: Elena Poniatowska's *La "Flor de Lis"*** — 27
   A Transcultural Education | 35
   Conclusion | 60

**2 Cosmopolitanism and Nationalism in the Global Era in the Fictions of Mario Vargas Llosa** — 63
   A Literary Evolution Defined by Tensions | 65
      *Politics and Utopia* | 67
      *The Way to (Liberal) Rooted Cosmopolitanism* | 70
      *Liberal Cosmopolitanism* | 72
      *Characters Making History* | 76

Cosmopolitanism and Internationalism in *El Paraíso en la otra esquina* | 79

The Fate of the Cosmopolitan Patriot in *El sueño del celta* | 99

Conclusion | 127

## 3 Cosmopolitanism at the End of History in the Fictions of Jorge Volpi  137

"Mi biblioteca es mi patria" | 140

The Crack | 140

The End of National Narrative | 143

Rejecting Ideological *realismo mágico* | 149

The Global Novel | 155

*El fin de la locura:* Cosmopolitanism and the Global Intellectual | 157

*No será la Tierra:* The Fate of Cosmopolitanism in the Neo-liberal World Order | 182

Conclusion | 198

## Conclusion  209

## Notes  219

## Works Consulted  233

## Index  247

# Acknowledgments

Even though I study cosmopolitanism, it had never occurred to me to build this philosophy into my own writing process. Early on in graduate school, I fell into the trap of believing that academic work, especially in the humanities, was a solitary, lonely endeavour. The irony is not lost on me. Working on *Belonging Beyond Borders* taught me that we are only as good as the community we surround ourselves with. Here's to everyone who helped me bring this book to life!

Over the years, I have benefited from the guidance and wisdom of many colleagues and thinkers who were always very generous with me, who inspired me and helped me polish my ideas, but who were also eager to share their sometimes nightmarish visions of the publication process. And so it was with the understanding that publishing my first monograph would be quite the ordeal—some sort of dreadful but necessary rite of passage—that I sent the manuscript to the Press. Nothing could have been further from the truth! Working with the editorial team at the University of Calgary Press was a challenging but extremely rewarding experience. I am particularly indebted to Brian Scrivener and Helen Hajnoczky for their attentive editorial work and for fostering a supportive publication process from beginning to end, but most of all, for their flexibility with the constraints of my schedule. A very special thank you to Alison Cobra and Melina Cusano, who took my pleading to heart (please, no reference to the globe or flags even though the book is about cosmopolitanism!) and helped make my vision for the cover come to life, and to Ryan Perks for his superb revision and sharp copyediting of the manuscript, and for the many back and forths over the subtleties of the English language. Thank you to Timothy Pearson for his thorough reading of the book and for, in addition to creating the index, providing me with the ultimate critical eye in the last stretch of revisions, finding the typos four other people had missed. Knowing I could rely on everyone's help and strengths has kept me sane this past year.

Several institutions provided funds to make research and writing possible. *Belonging Beyond Borders* draws on research supported by the Social Sciences and Humanities Research Council of Canada. I would also like to thank the Awards to Scholarly Publications Program for their support of this book.

I have been extremely lucky to have in Professor Jorge Carlos Guerrero a PhD supervisor who cared equally about my work and about me as a human being, and treated me as such. Your patience and persistence have shaped me, both in my personal and professional life. I truly value our countless hours of discussion, and, above all, the time you still dedicate to me after all these years.

At the University of Ottawa, Professors Rosalía Cornejo-Parriego and Joerg Esleben each raised tough questions, challenging me to expand my scope and inquiry. Your mentoring in the early stages of this investigation provided me with critical theoretical and methodological tools that framed this project.

I would also like to extend my thanks to the anonymous reviewers for their astute comments. *Belonging Beyond Borders* is stronger because of their thorough reading of the manuscript and many useful suggestions.

This monograph has blossomed thanks to the careful reading and thoughtful insights of many people. I want to express my gratitude to friends and colleagues who were always available to exchange and discuss ideas, and who read parts of the manuscript, many times over . . . sometimes getting to know the claims of my research almost as well as I do.

Nadine Fladd, my writing coach, turned research and writing into a very pleasurable experience—something I now (gasp!) look forward to every day. This book would not have come to fruition without you. Thank you for teaching me to be a better writer and a sharper thinker, for helping me trust myself, and for showing me how to deconstruct patterns, mostly in my writing . . .

Julien Labrosse, you helped me see I had socks all along, and always had my back. You believed in me a lot more than I believed in myself back then, and for that I will be forever indebted to you.

Jamey Cook-Irwin, you were my pair of fresh eyes before I sent the manuscript to the Press. Your not-so-serious in-text comments made an umpteenth revision of the text bearable. A special thank you for wanting to smash the patriarchy like Flora!

May Morpaw, you have been crucial to my growth over the past ten years, and are a model to follow. Your assistance in the last stretch of the editing process and in translating hard, idiomatic passages was instrumental to the swift completion of this book.

Some friends also provided moral comfort, solace, and a break from the mayhem.

Anushka Birju, thank you for being happy that I was happy at every stage of this lengthy process. Your contagious smile—and let's be honest, occasional tough love—were welcome reminders that despite the little voice in my head, I've got this! I now know that anyone who tells me otherwise is welcome to refer to the t-shirt.

Nicole Nolette, thank you for being such an amazing friend and making sure I clocked a few hours of writing every week, even during the worst ones. Your dedication to your work is truly inspiring. Life in Waterloo is better because of your friendship!

I also owe a debt of gratitude (and constant existential doubt) to my colleague, mentor, and friend, Mario Boido. You told me, in the early stages of writing this book, to stop looking for my lost voice, that I never had one to begin with—it was mine to develop. That one comment made a huge difference.

Finally, a very special thank you to my parents, Réjane and Férial, for their steadfast support and understanding over the years. Your unconditional love and encouragement have always been the backbone to all my achievements. Merci de m'avoir enseigné que les seules limites qui existent sont celles que l'on s'impose.

# Introduction

"El Perú soy yo aunque a algunos no les guste" ("I am Peru even if some do not like it"[1]), claimed Mario Vargas Llosa after he was awarded the Nobel Prize for Literature in 2011. And indeed, even if it is a great honour for any nation to have one of its citizens receive such a prestigious distinction, many Peruvians questioned the Nobel Foundation's decision. Vargas Llosa was not—at least in his detractors' eyes—Peruvian enough to be celebrated for an award that news outlets often report with an emphasis on the recipient's nationality. Since he moved to Spain in the 1990s, Vargas Llosa has been seen as removed from his birth nation. There were even multiple calls for the revocation of his Peruvian citizenship, some of them made by the government itself.

If we replace *Perú* with *México* in the above quotation, the criticism levelled at Vargas Llosa could also apply to Elena Poniatowska and Jorge Volpi, the two other writers I analyze in this book. Poniatowska is, and has been for the past forty years or so, a staple of contemporary Mexican narrative. While no one called for the revocation of her citizenship when she was awarded the Premio Cervantes—the highest recognition in Hispanic literature—in 2013, as a young female author in 1960s and '70s Mexico, her aristocratic background and her harsh criticism of the Mexican government after the Tlatelolco massacre made her an outcast in national(ist) literary circles. Volpi, like Vargas Llosa, has faced calls for his citizenship to be revoked—in his case, after the publication *En busca de Klingsor* (*In Search of Klingsor*; 1999), his first work to gain international acclaim. The book's major flaws in Mexican literary critics' eyes? The protagonist is not Mexican, and the plot is not set in Mexico.

These anecdotes highlight how closely the conceptions of literature and national identity are intertwined in Latin America. The three novelists I study in *Belonging Beyond Borders: Cosmopolitan Affiliations in Contemporary Spanish American Literature* are acutely aware of their delicate positioning in the literary tradition. They are cosmopolitans with strong ties to their home nations, positions many critics consider irreconcilable. In spite of this, Vargas Llosa, Poniatowska, and Volpi embraced the tensions engendered by their bodies of work and political positions, and exploited them to serve their intellectual agendas, which promote contacts between cultures through rooted cosmopolitanism. One of the main concerns of *Belonging Beyond Borders* is reconceptualizing cosmopolitanism in order to consider the specific characteristics of Latin America's socio-historical and geopolitical contexts. It traces the shift from the rejection of cosmopolitanism to its emplotment by three contemporary Spanish American authors, and the ways this is reflected in five of their novels. I am particularly interested in how these narratives showcase characters who aspire to be cosmopolitan. The struggle they face in complex political environments and the way they strive to embody rooted cosmopolitanism can provide a template for contemporary readers.

The current political climate, both in Spanish America and around the world, highlights the necessity of discussing cosmopolitanism and its various formulations. Not only are we experiencing globalization at an increasing speed, but the rise of novel and more extreme forms of nationalism makes the study of cosmopolitanism and its new articulations more relevant than ever. In *Belonging Beyond Borders*, I understand cosmopolitanism as a mindset that celebrates diverse affiliations—be they local, national, or global—and I adopt the notion of rooted cosmopolitanism theorized by Anthony Kwame Appiah. Rooted cosmopolitanism—an openness to the world grounded in one's primary affiliation to the nation—illustrates how the individual's relationship to the nation and the world inform their identity, and challenges some of the limitations of early formulations of the concept.

Indeed, despite its pretense of universality, conceptions of cosmopolitanism are not devoid of imperial connotations, and have, since their inception in Ancient Greece, carried a certain Eurocentric and elitist bias. Derived from the extraordinarily ambitious proposition of world citizenship, traditional cosmopolitanism urges us "to recognize the equal, and unconditional, worth of all human beings, a worth grounded in reason and moral capacity, rather than on traits that depend on fortuitous natural or social arrangements" (Nussbaum, "The Worth of Human Dignity" 31). It sets the ground for a universal fraternity and challenges us to reject exclusive loyalties in favour of an allegiance to humanity as a whole while also emphasizing the need to embrace one's community. By definition, the concept seeks to erase the fortuitous arrangements of class, gender, and race. In practice, however, cosmopolitanism struggles to overcome the imperial and elitist connotations it carries. Another critique the concept has faced is the erasure of the local, which is why it has been generally so vocally rejected in the developing world, and more specifically in the context of this project, in Latin America. Despite this rejection and the continent's particular relationship with colonialism, cosmopolitanism is not only reconcilable with Latin American society, but can also be a productive lens through which to analyze its artistic and literary production, as it forces contemporary readers to look outwards and involve the continent in a conversation with global trends.

One of the latest articulations of cosmopolitanism, rooted cosmopolitanism—in which the nation and the world complement each other—is particularly relevant to the study of Latin America. Unlike other forms of cosmopolitanism, rooted cosmopolitanism emphasizes a primary attachment to the nation as a necessary part of expanding one's ethical commitment to one's fellow human beings. Rooted cosmopolitanism is also a call to action, a praxis rather than a philosophy. Appiah posits that cosmopolitanism is the articulation of "universalism plus difference" (*Cosmopolitanism* 202); I take this as a starting point for my attempt to develop a definition of rooted cosmopolitanism that is applicable specifically to Latin America. By adding socio-historical considerations—that is, the articulation of place and time—I ground rooted cosmopolitanism in decolonial Latin American perspectives and overcome some limitations of the concept. Drawing from Walter Mignolo's theories, I also blend the concept of rooted cosmopolitanism with the concept of decoloniality. I argue that both rooted cosmopolitanism and decoloniality are praxes, as opposed to strictly philosophical concepts. Both point to concrete ways to act as a cosmopolitan and/or to develop a cosmopolitan sensibility.

Through fiction, we can better understand the necessity of developing a cosmopolitan sensibility, and take concrete steps toward an ethical cosmopolitan position. Poniatowska, Vargas Llosa, and Volpi are actively engaged in this conversation, and their interventions in Spanish America and abroad can lead readers to re-evaluate how they choose to be citizens of the world and encourage them to develop empathy for their fellow human beings. Other concepts, such as hybridity or *hibridismo*, third space, and glocal, could be used to analyze the narratives I examine in *Belonging Beyond Borders*. While the relevance of these theories and concepts to Latin American cultural studies cannot be overstated, they are mostly descriptive in nature. They express the inherent politicization of one's identity, but they are not an ethical position one can aspire to or a concrete ethical praxis. Unlike rooted cosmopolitanism, these aforementioned concepts are not ways to behave ethically toward other human beings.

Whereas most investigations of cosmopolitanism in Spanish American literature are about the influx of traditions in a given literary work, and are concerned with discerning how artists and writers try to create a universal artistic language, *Belonging Beyond Borders* identifies novels that express political concerns, and reads them as articulating a form of "cosmopolitics." Poniatowska, Vargas Llosa, and Volpi offer a nuanced understanding of citizenship in which the best way to explore globalization, migration, and the rise of new nationalisms is to be a cosmopolitan, albeit a cosmopolitan who is aware of the pitfalls of the position. Unlike canonical cosmopolitan works that were produced either during *Modernismo*—which developed an aesthetic cosmopolitanism through the blending of traditions—or the Boom—which sought to create a universal language and a universal aesthetic expression—the works that form my corpus tackle the political aspects of cosmopolitanism. They are concerned with representing characters who are politically engaging their localities and the world.

Very few studies look at political cosmopolitanism, and those that do tend to cover the eighteenth, nineteenth, and twentieth centuries. In recent years, Fernando Rosenberg and Mariano Siskind have each advanced theories articulated around the notions of "displacement" and *deseo de mundo* ("the desire for the world" or "cosmopolitan desire"). Both researchers have focused on earlier periods to conclude that cosmopolitanism, while always a lingering presence on the continent, has generally been displaced by analogous concepts that emphasize local cultures over foreign ones—transculturation, *hibridismo, antropofagia*—or that cosmopolitanism has always expressed a "desire for the world," an impulse on the part of artists, including writers, to break with the asynchronicity of living at the periphery of the Western world. I agree with these authors' assessment of earlier periods, and take the notions of "displacement" and "desire for the world" as starting points for my analysis of contemporary narratives published between 1988 and 2010: Poniatowska's *La "Flor de Lis"* (*The "Fleur-de-Lys"*; 1988), Vargas Llosa's *El Paraíso en la otra esquina* (*The Way to Paradise*; 2003) and *El sueño del celta* (*The Dream of the Celt*; 2010), and Volpi's *El fin de la locura* (*The End of Madness*; 2003) and *No será la Tierra* (*Season of Ash*; 2006). Studying them together for the first time enables the charting of the evolution from displacement to an overt affirmation of cosmopolitanism and its literary emplotment. *Belonging Beyond Borders* is premised on the identification of a new affirmation of cosmopolitanism in these works—both in the treatment of the concept and in narrative form. I examine these three authors together because each belongs to a different literary generation, has a body of work that spans decades, and publishes openly political works. The evolution of their cosmopolitan position can be seen in their writings. They not only represent the political and philosophical concept, they deploy it as a political tool. These novels are about the practicality of rooted cosmopolitanism, how to take concrete steps to be a good global citizen.

Naturally, these positions on cosmopolitanism have been shaped by evolving historical circumstances. Examining works published both before and after the end of the Cold War allows me to reveal this shift. In the period marked by the hegemony of the nation-state—which, in Spanish America, ends more or less in the late 1970s and '80s—the most relevant concepts with which to discuss issues of cultural identity were miscegenation and transculturation.[2] Writers often produced fictions that revealed the intricacies of these cultural processes, or, conversely, turned them into central themes of their fictions. However, since the late 1980s, the fading importance of the nation-state and the rise of globalization have led to the increased emplotment of cosmopolitanism. The following chapters examine this evolution through the study of the works of three authors. They show that, whereas Poniatowska's novel is a defence of transculturation, both Vargas Llosa's and and Volpi's narratives share a conception of rooted cosmopolitanism. This reflects the limitations of some metaphors of identity in Latin American discourse. Ultimately, these discourses-turned-ideologies failed to achieve emancipatory politics in the region.

Engaging with cosmopolitanism also leads writers to develop new narrative recourses to represent cosmopolitanism in changing cultural, literary, and historical circumstances. My reading is set against national and nationalist literary traditions so as to establish how Spanish American novels explicitly or implicitly represent and create a critical dialogue with various literary genres, and especially with those that have traditionally served to project notions of national identity and history. I show that Poniatowska reworks the codes of the autobiographical novel, Vargas Llosa those of the historical novel, and Jorge Volpi the global novel in order to reflect their vision of a cosmopolitanism grounded in socio-historical circumstances and to critically articulate a global consciousness.

This articulation of a global consciousness is explicit in all three authors' works. My reading of their narratives is predicated on the notion that the representation of travelling and residence across nations always involves the emplotment of cosmopolitanism. For each protagonist, travel or dislocation—either chosen or imposed—is the starting point of his or her identity quest. The characters' dislocation from their primary setting allows them to evolve, and in some cases, to become cosmopolitan. The five texts propose worlds that combine spaces, times, and experiences, and in which cultural and historical specificities are plotted and made to interact. I follow three major lines of inquiry that aim to reveal the political in literary representations of cosmopolitanism: I examine how the emplotment of cosmopolitanism differs in authors from three literary generations; I compare how the conceptions of cosmopolitanism at work in their novels differ, and the impact this has on how the authors inscribe themselves in Spanish American intellectual and literary history; and I assess the rewriting and reframing of literary genres to show how the politics of cosmopolitanism inform aesthetic transformations.

In chapter 1, I explore the displacement of cosmopolitanism in favour of transculturation in Elena Poniatowska's 1988 novel *La "Flor de Lis,"* an autobiographical novel that explores cultural identity in 1950s Mexico through the figure of Mariana, a young, French-born cosmopolitan woman recently arrived in Mexico. In late twentieth-century Spanish

American literature, the first-person narrative, be it testimonial (*testimonio*, autobiography) or fictional (autofiction, autobiographical novel) was the genre of predilection for the representation of memories of trauma and/or the development of an individual's identity. Poniatowska uses it to discuss both the protagonist's evolution and concrete politics of identity, which is rare for this genre. I read the main character's trajectory toward the adoption of a transcultural Mexican identity as marked by tensions between two extremes, the Eurocentric cosmopolitanism of her French family and the exacerbated nationalism of mid-century Mexico. The character's evolution mirrors the adoption of transculturation in the cultural and political discourse of twentieth-century Mexico.

In chapter 2, I consider the importance of liberalism in Mario Vargas Llosa's *El Paraíso en la otra esquina* (2003) and *El sueño del celta* (2010), two historical novels that depict the cosmopolitan and nationalist trajectories of major artists and political figures of the nineteenth and early twentieth centuries. Both explore the dangers of socialist internationalism and nationalism, while ultimately celebrating cosmopolitan patriotism. My reading of *El Paraíso en la otra esquina* shows that the parallel cosmopolitan trajectories of Flora Tristán and Paul Gauguin end tragically due to their ideological shortcomings. My analysis of *El sueño del celta* demonstrates that the novel's protagonist, Roger Casement, who has a similar cosmopolitan trajectory, is redeemed by the narrative voice despite his turn to nationalism because he eventually acknowledges the error of his ways. However, Casement differs from Tristán and Gauguin in that he is represented as a tragic hero who is not blinded by extreme ideologies. He is, rather, a patriot who makes a mistake in trying to reconcile his cosmopolitan philosophy and the plight of his motherland. Whereas the twentieth-century historical novel's main purpose was to question, reassess, or fill the void in official versions of history, debate major political ideas and ideologies, and concentrated on the author's setting, Mario Vargas Llosa rewrites the Latin American historical novel by deterritorializing it through the introduction of figures and histories that transcend the continent, and he uses it to promote his own liberal positions.

In chapter 3, I look at Jorge Volpi's *El fin de la locura* (2003) and *No será la tierra* (2006), two global novels about major intellectual and historical events of the twentieth century. Both are set during the period of radical transformation caused by neo-liberal globalization. While *El fin de la locura* begins in Paris in May 1968 and concludes as the Berlin Wall is about to fall in 1989, *No será la tierra* starts with the Chernobyl disaster of 1986 and uses the fall of the USSR as its backdrop. I argue that these narratives articulate Latin America in a global context by erasing major indicators of identity that are conventions of the Spanish American novel. Indeed, Volpi's narrators, characters, events, and settings are removed from or only partially intertwined with the continent. In *El fin de la locura*, a novel about twentieth-century intellectual history, Volpi represents intellectuals as a global category whose members need to develop an international conscience to fulfill their roles in society. *No será la tierra* is a novel about the emergence of the so-called New World Order and the "end of history" discourse first elaborated by political scientist Francis Fukuyama in the nineties. My analysis highlights how the cosmopolitan aspirations of characters of different nationalities represent modes of universal engagement. The two works also posit rooted cosmopolitanism as a desirable mode of community membership in the global era. Volpi's novels articulate globality, and in so doing reconceptualize the relationship between Spanish America and the world.

## Spanish America against the World

To this day, Spanish America has a particularly contentious relationship with cosmopolitanism dating back to its colonial situation and to the various wars of independence waged between 1810 and 1822. During the nineteenth and early parts of the twentieth century, Spanish American literature was characterized by a tension between nationalism and cosmopolitanism, in a context where the new nations sought to develop their own identities in opposition, first to Spain, and later the United States. Even if the vast majority of writers did not explicitly plot political cosmopolitanism in their works, their cosmopolitan works and positions were nonetheless the object of much criticism and debate. Many of these authors were interested in aesthetic cosmopolitanism and drew from multiple traditions to create a richer literary language; aesthetic cosmopolitanism has always been intensely political. Although they did not necessarily deal with the political implications of cosmopolitanism, their literary peers rejected their worldly position, for it was perceived as diluting the national tradition.

From the birth of the new Latin American nations in the 1800s up to the Boom of the 1960s, there was a clear divide between Latin American authors: either they focused on nation-building processes in their narratives and aligned with government policies, or they reached beyond the confines of their national borders and became pariahs within national literary circles. Across the continent, the debate raged; one was either open to the world and rejected the nation, or looked inwards and rejected the world. This black and white understanding of cosmopolitanism meant that it was almost impossible to have a level-headed conversation about it. Both "nationalist" and "cosmopolitan" were insults of choice, with cosmopolitan authors criticizing their colleagues' supposed close-mindedness and nationalist authors and literary critics calling for the revocation of their peers' citizenship.

For the former group, cosmopolitanism, understood as a productive engagement with global artistic practices, was never about rejecting the nation. It has been at the heart of every artistic and literary movement or school since the nineteenth century, whether we think of *Modernismo* (1888–1910), the *Vanguardias* (1920–30), or more recently, the Boom (1962–72). For many authors, the desire to assert their national identity was not irreconcilable with adopting the best elements from various cultural and literary traditions. For instance, Rubén Darío immersed himself in the French tradition; more than just a poet, he was a cultural translator who tried to make sense of European modernity for the continent. In his classic 1932 essay "El escritor argentino y la tradición" ("The Argentine Writer and Tradition"), Jorge Luis Borges, claiming the world as the repository from which he could draw inspiration, articulated his cosmopolitan position in the following manner: "Todo lo que hagamos con felicidad los escritores argentinos pertenecerá a la tradición argentina . . . no debemos temer y . . . *debemos pensar que nuestro patrimonio es el universo*" (273–4; my emphasis) ("Anything we Argentine writers can do successfully will become part of our Argentine tradition. . . . We should not be alarmed . . . and *we should feel that our patrimony is the universe*"[3]).

Embracing aesthetic cosmopolitanism was a means to address the problems of a continent perceived as lagging behind in terms of culture, intellectual life, and political organization—a term Ángel Rama had dubbed "arritmia temporal" ("temporal arrhythmia"). Artists and writers saw themselves as involved in bridging the gap between Europe and Spanish America, and their work as a way of deconstructing the faulty perception that relegated the continent to the periphery of modernity. This asynchronicity explains why cosmopolitanism has always been at the forefront of artistic and intellectual discussions. This catching up with modernity extended to all areas of intellectual life. It was both aesthetic and political, but never political in the true sense of cosmopolitanism, since it did not involve a reflection about the universal ideas and values of a global community. Criticism of cosmopolitanism was both triggered by the aesthetic proposals authors were making in engaging various literary traditions and by the debates on identity. The mere addition of literary devices and styles was seen as diluting pure national elements, thus sparking debates about authenticity.

Beginning in the late nineteenth century, *Modernismo* was one of the first movements to attempt to bridge the gap between Latin America and Europe. It is, to this day, one of the most cosmopolitan literary movements in Spanish American letters. To their critics, the *Modernistas*' cosmopolitanism was merely aesthethic and thus frivolous, and a strong rejection of their birth nation's culture. Artists were (seemingly) seeking "una identidad internacional . . . artística" ("an international artistic identity") and their work reflected a distancing approach (Grünfeld 35, 36). Literary scholars have long maintained that "a través de su escritura, los poetas modernistas participan en el proceso de creación de una mitología del extranjero" ("through their writing, Modernist poets participate in the creation of a mythology of the foreign"; 37), one that necessarily rejected national aspects in order to emphasize foreign ones. However, a more nuanced assessment of the *Modernistas*' political engagement reveals that in a context in which Spain's hegemony was fading, cosmopolitanism was one of several critical tools to rework the hemispheric dynamic, as well as to establish a stronger *rapport de force* with the growing cultural weight of the United States. Ultimately, the *Modernistas*' openness to and integration of multiple cultures in their work was a tactic to avoid falling prey to cultural neo-colonialism, be it Spanish or American—a demonstration of what Jeff Browitt and Werner Mackenbach call a "cosmopolitismo cultural crítico" ("critical cultural cosmopolitanism"; 7). The liberalization of the "trade in contributions to Spanish American cultural autonomy" ultimately helped artists undermine the Spanish monopoly in that field (Aching 12).

Yet, the Western European culture to which cosmopolitans subscribed meant more than mere cultural products and consumerism. Scholars such as Camila Fojas maintain that such cosmopolitanism was in part a reaction to this crisis of modernity and provided writers and artists with the tools necessary not only to gain a better understanding of their own culture, but also to criticize it through a different paradigm, one that was both political and cultural: "Cosmopolitanism . . . [was] also a political sign of international diplomacy and justice, a sign of world-wide hospitality for the outcast, the exiled, migrants, foreigners, and travellers" (ix). Like Fojas, I see this cosmopolitan ideal as a way to acquire a different cultural framework that added nuance or even rejected nationalist perspectives. Writers not only felt an urge to write ground-breaking poetry, but also a need to create a new literary language, replete with new forms and techniques, that would confine them neither to a specific space nor to their own time frame. Their aesthetic cosmopolitanism was a form of political engagement, a rejection of subordination, and this dimension of their work reveals them as artists engaged in dislodging coloniality, rather than as alienated or self-absorbed, as tradition branded them. Octavio Paz is correct in stating that "Los modernistas no querían ser franceses, querían ser modernos. . . . En labios de Rubén Darío y sus amigos, modernidad y cosmopolitanismo eran términos sinónimos. No fueron anti-americanos, querían una América contemporánea de París y Londres" ("El caracol y la sirena" ["The Siren and the Seashell"] 94–5) ("The Modernists did not want to be French, they wanted to be modern. . . . Modernity and cosmopolitanism were synonymous to Rubén Darío and his friends. They were not anti-Latin American; they wanted a Latin America that would be contemporaneous with Paris and London"[4]). The *Modernistas* had no interest in creating a new cultural dependency on yet another cultural metropole; they wanted to change the Spanish American literary order (Rama, *Rubén Darío* 22).

*Modernismo*'s cosmopolitan impulse is present in the incorporation of the European canon in its production (Rama, *Las máscaras democráticas del Modernismo* [*The Democratic Masks of Modernism*] 173; Fojas 3), which, as was already established, led the nationalists to view their work as a form of cultural amnesia and a conscious avoidance of the past. The cosmopolitans were not national enough to be integrated into a national culture that sought to rally everyone under a single identity: cosmopolitans were oddballs and outcasts, captivated by various foreign cultural metropoles. In sum, they appeared to their critics as lacking an interest in undoing colonial legacies. However, the *Modernistas* aimed to integrate the framework of modernity, so that Latin American cultural identity would be contemporaneous with that of Europe, and in the process rejected its colonial legacy. By doing so, they were able to enter a wider sphere of cultural influence that would later prove useful in defining the Latin American literary canon. Like the authors of the Boom and those of the later Crack movement, the *Modernistas* wanted to work within the Western literary tradition writ large.

The quest for contemporaneity remained at the centre of artistic and literary endeavours of the various vanguard movements that spanned the 1920s. The *Vanguardias* marked a period of literary experimentation, during which numerous manifestos—many attacking Western modernity itself, and exhibiting a certain tension between renewal and tradition—were published across the continent. Every nation had its own form, rooted in its particular experiences.[5] The ultimate objective of these movements was to renew the national artistic vision and literary references, as well as to debate the notions of national and continental identity in a changing geopolitical order. This questioning of tradition and of the function of art happened simultaneously in Europe and Latin America—a first step in reducing the deeply felt sense of *arritmia temporal*.

Whereas the European vanguard tended to be socially and aesthetically radical, the members of the Latin American *Vanguardias* were more moderate, "their function resid[ing] more in the building of cultural and artistic institutions that the European movements strove to destroy" (Rosenberg, "Cultural Theory and the Avant-Gardes" 414). These artists shared national preoccupations and were influenced by the production that had taken place during the celebrations of the centenary of independence a decade before. The alternative modernities that were being proposed by the European vanguard movements were not productive tools in Latin America, since they did not question Latin America's position at the periphery of the Western world (Rosenberg, *The Avant-Garde* 2). These authors thus engaged in a form of critical cosmopolitanism that sought to undo the colonial mindset and create works of art that took into consideration the continent's pre-Hispanic cultures. The Avant-Garde was a turning point in Latin American literature, since, unlike the *Modernistas*, who drew on the French tradition but never really questioned it, the *Vanguardistas* questioned various traditions and the function of art itself in the creation of their cultural identity. One of the major successes of the Avant-Garde was that the authors were able to reconfigure their locus of enunciation: they stopped reproducing "global cultural hierarchies that legitimated different levels of subordination" ("Cultural Theory and the Avant-Gardes" 415), and put Latin America on par with the rest of the world. This critical stance displayed both local and cosmopolitan affiliations, since artists were able to redefine their identity as one that included the best of both the native and the foreign. By incorporating modern values, they were able to acquire tools that would help them undo the colonial mindset, embracing an ideal of "non-Eurocentric, always-situated universalism" (*The Avant-Garde* 40). Their creation of a new modernity was grounded in a more nuanced understanding of their colonial past, as demonstrated, for example, by Brazilian *antropofagia*.

A few decades later, the members of the Boom were also forced into the debate over the authenticity of the Latin American author's identity. It was arguably the last literary movement compelled to engage in the debate over the adoption of aesthetic cosmopolitanism. Most Boom writers thought of their art in universal terms, and some consciously tried to develop a universal aesthetic through the introduction of international art forms such as jazz and photography (Russek 7). Like the *Modernistas*, the Boom writers did not necessarily want to be international; their priority was being modern, and this meant being published in Spain—indeed, this is one of the major criticisms the movement faced.[6] After years of Latin America literary independence, Spain acted once again as the literary metropole, since most publishing houses were located in Europe.[7] Nevertheless, whether they published in Latin America or Spain, their literary language was the same: as Carlos Fuentes observed in *Geografía de la novela* (*Geography of the Novel*; 1993) "A partir de la certeza de esta universalidad del lenguaje, *podemos hablar con rigor de la contemporaneidad del escritor latinoamericano*, quien súbitamente es parte de un presente cultural común" ("Given the certainty of this universality of language, *we can truly speak of the contemporaneity of the Latin American writer*, who suddenly becomes part of a common cultural present"; 34; my emphasis). For the first time in Spanish American literary history, a cultural movement broke with the asynchronicity that had characterized the dynamic between the core and the periphery of the Western world.

This central quest finally bore fruit, thus opening new possibilities for the next generation of writers. This new attitude toward cosmopolitanism coincided with the advent of globalization, with its global ethos and global consciousness. By becoming contemporaneous with their European counterparts, the Latin American writer was faced with "la necesidad de sumarse a la perspectiva del futuro a fin de dirigirse a todos los hombres" ("the need to assimilate the perspective of the future in order to address all mankind") while also remaining a writer "que debía superar varias etapas a fin de integrar una literatura que se dirigiese a los lectores de su comunidad" ("who had to survive several stages in order to integrate a literature that addressed his community of readers"; *La nueva novela* 23). This double process, international yet local, was a treacherous one, and unsurprisingly, many literary critics disapproved of the internationalization of the Spanish American literary market and the ever-growing exposure of their national authors. This supposedly meant that these authors' novels were not continental or national enough, as if living and publishing abroad somehow disconnected them from Latin America. History was repeating itself.

As a matter of fact, the Post-Boom movement (1972–80) arose partly in reaction to the formal experimentation and ambitious continental allegories of the Boom novels. The Post-Boom was a return to realism and to more concrete issues like exile and dislocation, more fitting to the historical circumstances in which these authors were evolving at the height of the Cold War and the emergence of dictatorships across the continent, such as those in Chile under General Pinochet and Argentina under General Videla. The Post-Boom authors completely questioned the work of their predecessors, and ultimately deemed it elitist and reader-unfriendly (Shaw 6). Its excessive cosmopolitanism and universality at the expense of local preoccupations, as well as its emphasis on technique, were also criticized. Post-Boom authors, by virtue of their historical circumstances, were more focused on national issues than universal ones, and they displaced political cosmopolitanism in favour of national narratives.

Later literary movements, especially those emerging in the 1990s, issued manifestos that strove to renovate the novel, and that set aside the historical obsession for which their predecessors were known. For the most part, they wanted to distance themselves from the narratives about identity put forth by both the Boom and the Post-Boom.[8] Rather than a generational movement, the Crack is more of a thematic-formal nature. In 1996, the group penned the "Manifiesto Crack" ("Crack Manifesto"), in which the authors proclaimed themselves a new literary group, exposed their ideas about literature—be it Mexican, Latin American, or global— and traced the genealogy of Mexican literature in order to situate themselves within it. The manifesto also served as a way to break free from national and continental structures. About that same time, Alberto Fuguet and Sergio Gómez published *McOndo*, a collection of short stories, all of which broke with the tradition of *realismo mágico* ("magical realism"). McOndo is also the name of the literary movement that emerged from the publication of Fuguet and Gómez's anthology. The collection appeared as a reaction to the pervasiveness of magical realism, which American and European critics and readers expected of Latin American literature since the 1960s. They presented a *post todo* generation, one that sidelined family values in favour of individualism, and focused on describing the individual realities of the protagonists ("Presentación del país McOndo" ["Presentation of McOndo"]). The so-called McOndo novels are characterized by their realistic settings, which do not exaggerate or emphasize Latin American exoticism. The background of McOndo fictions is more apolitical and individualistic than that showcased in the novels of the Boom, and they set aside the deliberate pursuit of Latin American identity. For the Crack and McOndo movements, the *arritmia temporal* appears to be resolved, such that Latin American authors no longer feel compelled to engage in debates about cosmopolitanism; on the contrary, they seem to feel part of a global system of letters.

## Conceptions of Cosmopolitanism and Cosmopolitan Reading

Even if cosmopolitanism still causes tensions in Spanish America, we are now past a black and white understanding of the concept. Current articulations like rooted cosmopolitanism—as proposed by Anthony Kwame Appiah and Will Kymlicka—expose the limitations of former models and are particularly relevant to the study of the continent, for they deconstruct the dichotomy that pits cosmopolitanism against nationalism, and not only make cosmopolitanism applicable to, but also reconcilable with the Spanish American context. In Appiah and Kymlicka's approach, rooted cosmopolitanism is a celebration of diversity in which cosmopolitans are able to reconcile their love and responsibilities for their birth nation with a universal commitment. With rooted cosmopolitanism, then, one does not need to choose between conflicting allegiances anymore.

In order to understand the specificities of Spanish American cosmopolitanism, we must first look at the origin of the concept and at some of the debates surrounding it. Cosmopolitanism was first brought to the fore by the Greek philosopher Diogenes of Sinope, the founder of the Cynic school. His views emerged from major disappointments with traditional Greek expectations. He "declared himself *a-polis* (without a city), *a-oikos* (homeless) and *kosmo-polites* (a citizen of the universe)" (Goulet-Cazé qtd. in Inglis 13). By living at the margins of society, the Cynics attempted to purge themselves not only of the *polis* itself, but also of social ties of any sort, and they aimed to remove themselves from society to criticize it with a fresh perspective—a rather extreme take on cosmopolitanism, one we can hardly reconcile with our understanding of the world as highly globalized and interconnected. This detachment, which the Cynics deemed essential to their work as critical intellectuals, was often considered out of place in nineteenth- and twentieth-century Latin America, where intellectuals were expected to contribute to the building of national, and often nationalist, states.

Unlike the Cynics, the Stoics maintained that local affiliations could be reconciled with cosmopolitanism (Nussbaum, "The Worth of Human Dignity" 37), and believed that the cosmos itself should be considered a *polis*, albeit one with which we cannot have physical ties. They mapped our affections as a series of concentric circles surrounding each individual, each circle containing different groups of people. While the largest contains the entire human race, subgroups of humanity are in smaller ones; the smaller the circle, the closer one's attachment to the people in it (Bett 539; Nussbaum 37). The objective, then, is to treat every single human being as if they were a member of the smaller circle, not to treat anybody as a stranger, and eventually to collapse circles altogether to erase any "degrees of distance." However necessary it was to treat everyone fairly, the most significant aspect of Stoic cosmopolitanism was the immediate political environment to which a citizen had ties—their roots.

Most common contemporary definitions originate from these views and include the idea of "a posture of worldly sophistication which is naturally contrasted with more provincial or parochial outlooks" (Scheffler 255); treat cosmopolitanism as involving a "reflective distance from one's original or primary cultural affiliations, a broad understanding of other cultures and customs, and a belief in universal humanity" (Anderson qtd. in Goodlad 400); describe the core of cosmopolitanism as "an intellectual and aesthetic openness toward divergent cultural experiences, and an ability to make one's way into other cultures" (Hannerz 200); and/or focus on the cosmopolitan—the person—rather than on the concept. Ulf Hannerz, for instance, thinks of the cosmopolitan "as possessing [a] set of cultural skills . . . a cultural repertoire" (210). Aligned with Scheffler and Hannerz, I argue that cosmopolitanism is a mindset rather than an ideology. I also go one step further by claiming that rooted cosmopolitanism is a praxis, one made of concrete actions toward the Other. Cosmopolitans are not only open to learning about diversity, both in their local environment and on a global scale, but also to extending empathy toward others. As mentioned, this ability to transcend one's local surroundings is what often led in Latin America to the association of cosmopolitan writers and their works with a lack of commitment to and disengagement from the nation.

In order to assess cosmopolitanism in contemporary Spanish American literature, it is crucial to ground the concept in the context of the continent's trajectory on the periphery of the modern Western world, and to consider its history of colonialism and neo-colonialism. I side with contemporary thinkers Kwame Anthony Appiah and Walter Mignolo in their reconceptualization of cosmopolitanism, and blend the concepts they have proposed in order to create a conception of cosmopolitanism that does not deny Latin American specificities. I build on Appiah's theorizations to develop my own working definition of Latin American rooted cosmopolitanism. Appiah posits that cosmopolitanism is the articulation of "universalism plus difference" (*Cosmopolitanism* 202); I take this as a starting point for developing a definition of rooted cosmopolitanism that is applicable specifically to Latin America, by adding socio-historical considerations to Appiah's work. More specifically, I add Mignolo's concept of decoloniality, which I deem highly receptive to rooted cosmopolitanism. They are both praxes, as opposed to strictly philosophical concepts, and are achievable and attainable. By adding the articulation of place and time to Appiah's theories, I ground rooted cosmopolitanism in decolonial Latin American perspectives.

Appiah defines cosmopolitanism as a sentiment, and as an ethical stance regarding world citizenship. In *Cosmopolitanism: Ethics in a World of Strangers*, he proposes that

> there are two strands that intertwine in the notion of cosmopolitanism. One is the idea that we have obligations to others, obligations that stretch beyond those to whom we are related by the ties of kith and kind, or even the more formal ties of a shared citizenship. The other is that we take seriously the value not just of human life but of particular human lives, which means taking an interest in the practices and beliefs that lend them significance. (xv)

Cosmopolitans are "secure in [their] difference, but also open to the difference of others" ("Cosmopolitan Reading" 215). Later on, Appiah expanded on that view by suggesting that cosmopolitanism "commits you to a global conversation, or a set of global conversations, about the things that matter. I count someone as a cosmopolitan if they're willing to engage in that conversation without the hope of making everybody like them" ("Making Sense of Cosmopolitanism"). In "Cosmopolitan Patriots," Appiah expresses his belief that "the cosmopolitan patriot can entertain the possibility of a world in which everyone is a rooted cosmopolitan, attached to a home of one's own, with its own cultural particularities, but taking pleasure from the presence of other, different places that are home to other, different people" (618). Consequently, rooted cosmopolitanism is a celebration of diversity that takes both the nation and the world into account.[9]

In my view, the cosmopolitan par excellence is a person who cares about other human beings, but more crucially, is aware that the specificity of their values and social practices is an integral part of their identity. Cosmopolitans are also conscious that such practices may be different from theirs, but are willing to accept them nonetheless, even if there is a clash between practices. After all, cosmopolitanism is about human beings and whatever practices they choose to enjoy. I maintain that cosmopolitanism ought to be an ideal to which one aspires, not a complete identity one assumes. It advocates difference in the name of universalism. The fact that it promotes cultural difference as the basis of any articulation of a universal community makes rooted cosmopolitanism a particularly apt tool for the study of Spanish American literature. I conceive rooted cosmopolitanism as a conversation among peoples and places, with diversity as its core principle. The nation cannot be the locus of absolute sovereignty anymore. While affirming the enduring and necessary reality of the nation, cultures and states must be constrained by universal moral cosmopolitan commitments. Rooted cosmopolitanism thus redefines our understanding of the relationship between cosmopolitanism and nationalism, and, in the process, subverts the foundations of the traditional binary opposition.

Above all, in my conceptualization I take the term "rooted" to invoke cultural difference—cosmopolitanism is universalism plus difference (Appiah, "Cosmopolitan Reading" 202). I understand cultural difference as the articulation of place and time, subverting the inherent Eurocentrism of cosmopolitanism. As in most of the developing world, Latin America's relationship with cosmopolitanism is closely tied to the notions of nationalism, colonialism, and post-colonialism. Most post-colonial readings of cosmopolitanism thus focus on how the very concept has promoted a Eurocentric view and has been tied to imperialism from its inception. By combining the nation and the world with the history of a given culture, my rearticulation accounts for this flaw. Although post-colonial scholars of cosmopolitanism frequently underline the lack of critical assessment of colonialism and neo-colonialism, a pragmatic approach to the concept provides for a theorization that does not circumvent the complexities of cosmopolitanism and its Eurocentric history. Indeed, I understand cosmopolitanism as a concept that implicitly carries historical considerations. In this regard, I take "rooted" to mean the cultural difference of a given nation across place and time.

Grounding cosmopolitan thought in history is instrumental for assessing its place in Latin American intellectual and literary development. Walter Mignolo examines it in the context of the colonial and neo-colonial histories that characterized Latin America's relationship with Europe and the United States. He considers coloniality to be the darker side of modernity, albeit a constitutive one ("Many Faces of Cosmo-polis" 724). Without coloniality, modernity would not have happened. For Mignolo, the close proximity (two sides of a coin) between modernity and coloniality made it nearly impossible for Latin America to enter the realm of modernity as long as it was bound by its colonial mindset (*The Idea of Latin America*). The impact of colonialism was such that, even long after the Spanish colonizer had left, Latin Americans struggled to modify their epistemic understanding of themselves. A true dialogue among nations—a colonial power and a colony—is improbable as long as the empire retains its superiority. The challenge is to undo the impact of colonization, and for that Mignolo proposes the notion of decolonial cosmopolitanism, conceptualized as devoid of imperial world views, and therefore distinct from some formulations of Western cosmopolitanism in the modern era. Western cosmopolitanism could then be one of many possible cosmopolitanisms, but not the sole option.[10] The conceptual range of terms such as "nationalism" and "cosmopolitanism" vary across place and time, especially given the plurality of social imaginaries of modernity. Despite its premise of universality, cosmopolitanism is the object of discourses that are specific to cultures and their historical circumstances. This multiplicity of incarnations serves to reconcile the concept with Latin America because it allows the continent to transcend the core/periphery dogma, and engage in the cosmopolitan conversation. These post-colonial readings are creating a space for the subaltern to erase the idea of a passive reception of the positive aspects of the Western world by the other. In a sense, post-colonial cosmopolitanism is attempting to reach the ideal within the very concept of cosmopolitanism—that is, a relationship in which there are no subaltern cultures. It seeks to create a relationship based on true equality.

My reading of rooted cosmopolitanism—considering the cultural difference of a given nation across place and time—is thus particularly receptive to Mignolo's notion of decolonial cosmopolitanism. These conceptualizations are not mutually exclusive; on the contrary, both explicitly or implicitly advocate for universal values in the context of the absence of subaltern cultures. This post-colonial perspective can be productively reconciled with Appiah's formulation by instilling the notion of rooted cosmopolitanism with post-colonial and decolonial history. Rooted cosmopolitanism articulates a redefined notion of nationhood and universalism, and grounds that articulation in historical concerns.

Literature is a privileged discourse in which to discuss cosmopolitanism, since the concept of narrative is universal. Even national narratives can resonate with readers that are not necessarily native to a national setting; human experiences are, after all, similar. "Literature creates the world and cosmopolitan bonds," stresses Pheng Cheah, "not only because it enables us to imagine a world through its power of figuration, but also because it arouses in us pleasure and a desire to share this pleasure through universal communication" (*What is a World?* 27). The worlds postulated by literature, in which characters move about in situations similar to ours, face obstacles, and debate ideas, are among the best ways to spread cosmopolitanism, for "literature [plays] an active role in the world's ongoing creation because, through the receptibility it enacts, it is an inexhaustible resource for contesting the world given to us" (35). Literature creates empathy and allows readers to develop solidarity across space and time.

This idea of a narrative, be it national or global, and that of the "narrative imagination" (Nussbaum, "Cultivating Humanity" 44) are two of the cosmopolitans' most important tools. I agree with Appiah that everyone can be a cosmopolitan because every human being understands the concept of narrative—indeed, it is "through their shared exposure to narrations of those events" (*Ethics of Identity* 245) that human beings acquire an understanding of other people's lives, for "the basic human capacity to grasp stories, even strange stories, is also what links us, powerfully, to others, even strange others" (257).[11] Appiah postulates that "our modern solidarity derives from stories in which we participate through synecdoche" (245). In simpler terms, narratives allow us to put ourselves in other people's shoes (Nussbaum, "Cultivating Humanity" 45), and to begin to understand their life and circumstances. We recognize ourselves through others and their stories, and in the end, the solidarity and empathy we develop commit us to others. For Appiah, a

> Cosmopolitan reading presupposes a world in which novels (and music and sculptures and other significant objects) travel between places where they are understood differently, because people are different and welcome to their difference. Cosmopolitan reading is *worthwhile* because there can be common conversations about these standard objects, the novel prominent among them. Cosmopolitan reading is *possible* because those conversations are possible. But what makes the conversations possible is not always shared culture . . . ; not even, as the older humanists imagined, universal principles or values . . . ; nor shared understanding. . . . What is necessary to read novels across gaps of space, time and experience is the capacity to follow a narrative and conjure a world. ("Cosmopolitan Reading" 224)

As a result, a cosmopolitan reading is more than aesthetic cosmopolitanism—taking from multiple traditions—or a cosmopolitan interpretation—deeming a novel cosmopolitan—since it is the very condition of possibility for a cosmopolitan community. The universality of narrative clearly indicates that cosmopolitanism is within reach of every human being. A cosmopolitan reading entails two aspects: narrative is cosmopolitan because it is universal, and as such can reach any human being, and literature is among the best spaces to discuss cosmopolitanism due to its universality. The reading of narratives of diverse nationalities promotes cosmopolitanism since narratives reveal the universality of human experience. These do not need to be cosmopolitan narratives—on the contrary, their cultural specificity allows for the detection of the universal in all humans and therefore reinforces the very idea of cosmopolitanism.

In line with the notion of the cosmopolitan reader who turns fictions into spaces of universality, I identify the emplotment of cosmopolitanism in novels whose worlds are populated with characters who reside in multiple localities, travel across cultural boundaries, and live through global events. The ability to enact a cosmopolitan reading and to empathize with fictional characters is one more skill in cosmopolitans' set of cultural skills. To make the concept of cosmopolitan reading fully applicable to Latin America, I ground it in historical and cultural concerns, much like what I have done with the concept of rooted cosmopolitanism. Of all literary genres, the novel appears as an ideal space to promote cosmopolitanism, since it creates complex worlds that resemble the one in which readers evolve. Readers also play a primary role: it is incumbent on us to produce, through the confirmation of commonalities across cultures, a cosmopolitan reading. Readers, then, are in charge of connecting the dots, turning novels into spaces of universality, getting closer to the cosmopolitan ideal in the process.

## Rooted Cosmopolitanism in Spanish American Literature

As shown above, while nationalism and cosmopolitanism operate hand in hand in Spanish America, they have mostly been seen by literary critics as irreconcilable: one was either a national or a cosmopolitan author. Any examination of literary histories published until very recently reveals that there was no middle ground. On the one hand, the notion of political cosmopolitanism, however vague its uses in Latin America, has been intricately associated with more politically expedient concepts such as miscegenation and modernity, which were perceived as useful tools with which to reinforce national aspirations. On the other, aesthetic cosmopolitanism, invariably understood as receptiveness to a universal artistic and literary tradition, has been at the forefront of efforts to undo colonial legacies. Cosmopolitan artists and works were engaged in an important mission, albeit one not always perceived as such, especially by nationalist critics.

Up to the very early twentieth century, one major problem with the definition of the word "cosmopolitanism" or the concept of the cosmopolitan artist or intellectual in Latin America is that they have been desemanticized to mean diverse things. "Cosmopolitanism" was recurrently associated with luxury, decadence, the imitation of everything foreign, extraterritoriality, and the denial of locality, all tied to elitist and imperial connotations. In my view, this appears to be the major problem of writers deemed cosmopolitan faced when encountering a nationalist critic. This perception correctly echoes the preoccupations of the scholars to which this investigation refers—namely, that cosmopolitanism has mostly been misunderstood in Latin America. Indeed, cosmopolitanism has almost always been exaggerated in the region.

Cosmopolitanism does not need to be understood as dissociated from national concerns. In fact, one of the major flaws seen in the critical reception of cosmopolitan authors in Spanish America is the belief that cosmopolitanism is exclusive and cannot coexist with other ideologies or concepts in the creation of an artistic identity. The proposed notion of rooted cosmopolitanism allows for a more appropriate assessment of this complexity. From this perspective, Spanish American writers and thinkers have never been absolute cosmopolitans; their position, rather, was one of rooted cosmopolitanism.

Moreover, contemporary Latin American intellectuals defined as cosmopolitan, such as Borges or Reyes, while moderate cosmopolitans, were often read as immoderate because their critics worked within the binary framework of cosmopolitanism and nationalism. Borges's profound understanding of the Western canon left a deep mark on his corpus. His full acknowledgement of the world's literary traditions, as well as his cosmopolitan outlook on literature, never led him to a cosmopolitanism that denied the relevance of national difference. This makes him, in my understanding, a rooted cosmopolitan, one who made use of the best elements of what he considered to be the epitome of Western literary culture to showcase his own. Mexican Alfonso Reyes, also criticized for his cosmopolitan openness, claimed that "Podemos ser muy buenos mexicanos pero paralelamente podemos ser universales" ("We can be very good Mexicans but at the same time we can be universal"), underlining the fact that nationalism and cosmopolitanism are not irreconcilable. However, these authors' cosmopolitan positions and the reception of their work were always conditioned by the colonial and neo-colonial trajectories of the continent. Rooted cosmopolitanism was synonymous with inclusivity and diversity for these authors. It allowed them to be national writers while also belonging to the Western canon, two roles that were complementary.

Although they were criticized for their supposed rejection of their nation and continent, Spanish American rooted cosmopolitans never rejected the importance of national belonging—they only framed it on a global scale.

In Latin America, cosmopolitanism has always been explicitly or implicitly associated with the quest to undo the legacies of colonialism. The positions of cosmopolitan authors should be understood as those of rooted cosmopolitans, but the heated intellectual and literary debates of a continent in political turmoil—turmoil that was due partly to foreign interference—impeded this nuanced assessment until only a few decades ago. The advent of the Boom in the early 1960s meant, for most artists and intellectuals, the end of the *arritmia temporal* that had characterized artistic and literary production; and the end of this artistic and intellectual gap coincided with the fading of the nation-state and the advent of globalization. Both of these intellectual and structural transformations have led to a new era in which some Spanish American writers have begun to engage the world on new terms that can now properly be called cosmopolitan.

I intend *Belonging Beyond Borders* as a contribution to Spanish American literary history in two ways. It posits rooted cosmopolitanism as the form that has been embodied by Spanish American authors since the nineteenth century, and combines narrative emplotment of cosmopolitanism with recent theories of cosmopolitanism to explore how Spanish American literary works have served to deconstruct the binary opposition that has pitted nationalism against cosmopolitanism. I read these contemporary Spanish American novels as cosmopolitan fictions or fictions about cosmopolitanism. The novels analyzed in this book specifically plot the politics of cosmopolitanism, and this emplotment affects narrative form. In this regard, these fictions have acquired another function, different from that of their so-called cosmopolitan predecessors, at least according to literary history.

The five narratives can be read with a view to cosmopolitanism as a political and philosophical idea, and to its effect on one's identity. Unlike the previous generations' literary output, these novels are not in search of a universal language. Their main focus remains political. The fact that they are not set in Latin America may make them more accessible to a global readership, but no specific literary technique is used to make them universal, as was the case with *Modernismo*, the *Vanguardias*, or the Boom. This marks a break in the treatment of cosmopolitanism in Spanish American literature. Most Latin American authors referred to as "cosmopolitan" by the mainstream critical tradition have not written cosmopolitan novels in the sense of writing narratives, as Berthold Schoene-Harwood puts it, with the political "purpose and intention . . . to imagine humanity in global coexistence . . . or to conceive of real cosmopolitics as [the] communal tackling" of the world's problems (186). This tackling of the world's problems, as we will see in the chapters that follow, is represented through the selected novels, in which characters show a preoccupation with being world citizens.

# 1

# Narrating Transculturation: Elena Poniatowska's *La "Flor de Lis"*

> *México es de quien nace para conquistarlo.*
> *Yo nací para México. México es mío, yo soy de México.*
>
> (Mexico belongs to whoever conquers it.
> I was born for Mexico. Mexico is mine; I am from Mexico[1]).
>
> —Elena Poniatowska, *Tinísima*

In her acceptance speech for the 2013 Premio Cervantes, the most prestigious literary prize in Hispanic literature, an Elena Poniatowska dressed in Mexican national costume shared her first memories of Mexico. She explained that when she saw a map of the country, she was intrigued by the various "Zona[s] por descubrir" ("Zones yet to be discovered") spread before her eyes. "Este enorme país temible y secreto llamado México," she said, "se extendía moreno y descalzo frente a mi hermana y a mí y nos desafiaba: 'Descúbranme'" ("This huge, fearsome, and secret country called Mexico lay dark and threadbare before my sister and me, daring us: 'Discover me'"; "Discurso Premio Cervantes" 3–4). She claimed that "El idioma era la llave para entrar al mundo indio, el mismo mundo del que habló Octavio Paz . . . cuando dijo que sin el mundo indio no seríamos lo que somos" ("Language was the key to entering the Indigenous world, the world described by Octavio Paz . . . when he said that without the Indian world we would not be who we are"; 4), a reference to Paz's *El laberinto de la soledad* (*The Labyrinth of Solitude*), arguably one of the most influential works on Mexican identity of the twentieth century. In my view, this speech sums up Poniatowska's artistic, intellectual, and personal trajectory. Moreover, it alludes to an understanding of cultural identity that resonates with the work that I analyze in this chapter. *La "Flor de Lis"* (1988) is an autobiographical novel, a *Bildungsroman* that depicts the evolution of its author's identity through Mariana, her literary alter ego.[2]

By combining local, national, and global perspectives, Poniatowska's fiction tackles the tensions at the heart of the conceptualizations of cosmopolitanism in Latin America. While I have used Mariano Siskind's expression *deseo de mundo* ("desire for the world" or "cosmopolitan desire") to describe the desire some authors had, and to some extent still have, to discover and inscribe themselves in the global literary canon, it is my contention that through Mariana, Poniatowska shows what I call a *deseo de México*—that is, a desire or longing to belong to her new country—that compels her to shed her cosmopolitan identity. As she herself stated in a 1997 interview with Walescka Pino-Ojeda, Mariana, although a fictional character, embodies Poniatowska's own desire to belong to Mexico: "Es obviamente el deseo de saber cómo era México y qué era México y eso no lo iba yo a saber sino a través de otras gentes, que además me enriquecieron y me dieron mucho más que lo que podía darme cualquier miembro de mi clase social" ("It is obviously the desire to know how Mexico was and what Mexico was, and I was only going to figure that out through other people, who also enriched me and gave me much more than what any other member of my social class would have been able to do"; "Sobre castas y puentes" 30). She then goes on to describe her love for Mexico as "amor a la gente de México, a la gente que hace, que es la urdimbre, la textura . . . la tela o el telar, la piel de este lugar. . . . Yo creo que ser mexicano no es simplemente pertenecer a un país, cabe más" ("love for the Mexican people, for the people who do, who are the fabric, the texture . . . the material or the skin of this place. . . . I believe that to be Mexican is not simply to belong to a country, it means much more than that"; 32). Through Mariana, Poniatowska was able to explore this love for Mexico and this desire to become Mexican at a time when the historical circumstances—namely, the exacerbated nationalism of mid-century Mexico— did not necessarily facilitate it.

Born on 19 May 1932 in Paris, France, Elena Poniatowska settled in Mexico in 1942, where she went on to become one of the country's most prolific journalists and authors. Always striving to give a voice to the subaltern, she specializes in works that broach social and political issues and that mostly concentrate on women and the poor. However, the fact that she was born abroad to upper-class parents—her father, Jean Joseph Evremond Sperry Poniatowski, was related to the last king of Poland, and her mother, María Dolores Paulette Amor Yturbe, came from a family of wealthy Mexican landowners who fled the country during the 1911 revolution—meant that she has been seen as an outsider for most of her life. When she started her journalistic career in the 1960s, most thought of her as someone who "knew nothing about the country. She was French by birth and was educated in a Catholic school in the United States.... Elena knew about Mexico only what her family talked about, and it was always related to high society" (Schuessler 133). She overcame this perception and eventually published well-recognized testimonials that relate pivotal events in her adopted nation, as well as works of fiction that tackle social and class issues.[3]

La "Flor de Lis" also tackles class and social issues, albeit in a subtler manner than most of Poniatowska's other works. The narrative recounts the life of the duchess Mariana, who must leave France in the early years of the Second World War. She journeys to Mexico with her mother, Luz, and her sister, Sofía, while her father remains in Europe to fight alongside the French troops. Upon arrival, the two sisters must quickly adapt to a way of life far removed from the one they have always known. During the war, the sisters discover a new side to their mother and develop a very close relationship with her: she appears to be freer in Mexico than she ever was in France, and she dedicates more time to her daughters—a drastic change in their lives. The transition from Europe to America is easier for Sofía than for Mariana, as the latter feels marginalized in a society to which she has a profound desire to belong but which continually rejects her. Mariana eventually acquires elements of Mexicanness through the presence of her nanny, Magda, who embodies the popular Mexico that the protagonist longs to make hers. Magda introduces Mariana to *her* Mexico by taking the young protagonist out into the streets, where she becomes acquainted with new aspects of the country. She is also a constant presence in her life, unlike Luz, whose attention wanders from one interest to another.

The close relationship Luz had developed with Mariana and Sofía changes dramatically when Mariana's father returns from the front, and again when her brother Fabián is born. The repeated absence of a maternal figure leaves Mariana in a situation of crisis, which in turn brings Father Teufel—a French priest whose last name means "devil" in German—into her life. Mariana becomes obsessed with the priest; the lessons that he imparts about culture in Mexico and the need to transcend class have a profound impact on the teenager. She remains under his spell until he betrays her trust. The novel concludes with Mariana affirming her love for both her mother and Mexico, the former being in her mind a personification of the latter.

Literary critics have often underlined the autobiographical character of *La "Flor de Lis,"* and have typically focused on the role that exile and dislocation plays in the narrative. For instance, Sara Poot-Herrera highlights that Poniatowska "pone su escritura al servicio de su vida, su vida al pedido de su escritura . . . y dibuja el árbol de su genealogía" ("puts her writing at the service of her life, her life bows to the demands of her writing . . . and she draws her genealogical tree"; 100), whereas María Caballero reads it as a work of autofiction (84), mingling biographical elements with purely fictitious ones. As a matter of fact, one cannot help but see Poniatowska floating just behind the protagonist Mariana. Throughout the narrative, the child's voice and that of the adult intertwine as Mariana recalls the strongest memories of her childhood. Mariana's life—from her birth in France to a mother of Mexican heritage, to her escape from the Second World War, to her arrival in Mexico—runs parallel to the life of the author, who left France at ten years of age and has lived in Mexico ever since. Poniatowska herself has acknowledged in various interviews that "los personajes de *Lilus Kikus* y *La 'Flor de Lis'* son una combinación de varias niñas, ninguna de las dos me refleja totalmente, porque siempre entra el elemento ficción" ("the characters in *Lilus Kikus* and *La 'Flor de Lis'* are a combination of several little girls, neither one of whom represents me completely, because there is always an element of fiction at play"; *Me lo dijo Elena Poniatowska* 29), and she even claimed that the text "está muy ligado a mi niñez y a mi persona" ("is closely tied to my childhood and my own sense of self"; 21).

Few scholars have focused on the philosophical and intellectual positions elaborated in the novel, and it has yet to be read as an allegory for the evolution of the various philosophical positions in Mexico during the second half of the twentieth century. Examining *La "Flor de Lis"* allows me to illustrate the displacement of cosmopolitanism by concepts deemed better suited to the building and cementing of a strong national identity in the context of 1950s Mexico. To provide a more nuanced study of the novel, this chapter examines the various levels of significance present in the book. As noted by Doris Sommer in her canonical *Foundational Fictions*, allegory "invites a double reading of narrative events" (41). I claim that in the case of *La "Flor de Lis,"* "the two parallel levels of signification" (42) are, on the one hand, the evolution of a young French newcomer to Mexico, and, on the other, the veiled criticism of nationalist proposals, as well as of the cosmopolitan elite present at the time. The novel, then, proposes to replace cosmopolitanism with a Mexican culture of transculturation that would be more fitting to the country's history. In my allegorical reading, Mariana embodies Mexican society on the road to accepting a culture of transculturation, and Luz, her mother, the rejection of elitist Latin American cosmopolitanism.

I also read *La "Flor de Lis"* as a work about the increasing prominence of transculturation, after its conceptualization by Ortiz in 1940, in Latin American intellectual discourse, and Paz's notion of Mexican cultural identity as essentially hybrid. The character of Mariana embodies the cultural movement toward the acceptance of transculturation as a fundamental aspect of Mexican identity, since the text develops the idea that such an identity was formed on the basis of harmony between Indigenous and European heritages.

In my reading, Mariana's evolution mirrors that of a Mexico caught between two ideological extremes. After Mexico obtained its independence from Spain in 1821, civilization became synonymous with Europeanization—and more specifically, *afrancesamiento*, or Frenchification. Mexico's political and intellectual elite built the nation in France's image; it became its political, artistic, and intellectual model. It is this mentality inherited from the Porfiriato—the thirty-four years (1876–1911) during which General Porfirio Díaz ruled over Mexico under an "order and progress" doctrine—that Mariana's family embodies, a cosmopolitan culture modelled on that of Europe. However, the cosmopolitanism promoted by the Mexican political elite in the late nineteenth and early twentieth century is an exclusionary cosmopolitanism—an oxymoron—that only considers practices that its proponents deemed civilized, and that rejects the national elements, such as those of Indigenous groups or the popular masses. Unlike the canonical definition of cosmopolitanism, which posits a universal commitment with a global community, notwithstanding race, class, or gender, this exclusionary cosmopolitanism was at best a *cosmopolitismo de fachada*—a cosmopolitanism in name only, more a Eurocentric affirmation. In large part, this rejection of the major part of the Mexican population led to the Mexican Revolution (1911–20), a popular uprising that promoted nationalism as a politics of emancipation from the European model. It, too, reached an extreme: a total rejection of foreign elements and a nativistic celebration of national elements in the nationalist period that followed the Revolution.

Following the Revolution, the nation was in many ways created again, this time in the image of Indigenous peoples. Various well-thought-out and well-crafted artistic initiatives were implemented in an attempt to foment a more inclusive and stronger national identity after the armed struggle that had left the country divided. In the 1920s, José Vasconcelos, then minister of education, sponsored muralism and its proponents, such as Diego Rivera, David Siqueiros, and José Clemente Orozco. Their murals, painted on government buildings so that any passerby could admire and learn from them, glorified Mexico's Indigenous past and promoted the idea of a Mexican identity deeply rooted in its Indigenous ancestry. Given the country's suffering at the hands of Europe and the United States, it became unpatriotic to have strong ties to these imperial nations. To be fully accepted as a member of Mexican society, everyone was expected to celebrate the country's hybrid culture. The concept of the cosmic race also helped cement the rationale that the Mexican *mestizo* had been chosen as the repository of a greater purpose, which led to a strong national feeling. Through these initiatives, Mexico became a centre of modernity in Latin America, where artists and intellectuals from across the globe converged. The ambitious education programs spearheaded by Vasconcelos, along with the industrial policies, the land reforms, and the nationalization of oil companies and railways during a period of economic protectionism, led to what has been dubbed the "Mexican miracle," a period of growth not seen before or since.

In Poniatowska's novel, Mariana must contend with the contradictions and tensions inherent to growing up in a post-revolutionary era. Mariana's Mexico is a country that has not resolved the conflicts between a cosmopolitan elite and a nationalist *pueblo*—both of whom conceive identity and culture in exclusionary terms. It is Mariana who clears a path through the fusion of the two cultures to which she belongs, through hybridity and transculturation.

At this point, it is worth reviewing Ortiz's conceptualization of transculturation. The prevalence of the discourse of transculturation in the second half of the twentieth century in Latin America is embodied by the celebrated work of Cuban anthropologist Fernando Ortiz. Published in 1940, his *Contrapunteo cubano del tabaco y el azúcar* (*Cuban Counterpoint: Tobacco and Sugar*) describes the process of transformation that a society undergoes in acquiring foreign cultural material (97–103). Partially in reaction to prevailing American and European anthropological theories that viewed cultural exchange in terms of dissolution of a given culture, Ortiz coined the term "transculturation" to describe "las complejísimas transmutaciones de culturas" (86) ("the extremely complex transmutations of culture"[4]) to which a society is subjected after coming into contact with another; in particular, he uses the term to refer to a loss or a displacement of culture within a given society as new cultural material is assimilated. Ortiz theorized transculturation as a three-phase process: the loss of one's cultural elements, the incorporation of new cultural elements, and, finally, cultural recomposition. Acculturation describes the social repercussions in the transition from one culture to another, while transculturation refers to the sharing and mixing of cultures and the creation of a new one. Moreover, the Cuban anthropologist understood this word as an act of resistance. Indeed, in his thinking, Ortiz wanted to replace the word "acculturation" with "transculturation," since "the process of transit from one culture to another [is] more powerful" than the mere acceptance of new cultural traits (Millington 260). Acculturation involves the loss of an earlier culture and its assimilation into another, while transculturation is a bridge between cultures, a place where cultures meet and interact. In such a process, social groups never completely lose their own cultural background. Rather, they adjust their vision of the Other and remodel it to fit their ways in order to create new forms. It is this process that Mariana undertakes after she arrives in Mexico.

In this way she embodies Octavio Paz's affirmation that Mexicans are fundamentally hybrid beings, and that only an acceptance of this four-hundred-year legacy of cultural mixing can remedy what Paz deemed the impasse in which Mexico's cultural identity found itself. This work is often discussed in conjunction with transculturation, hybrid cultures, and third space. Paz used the term *hibridismo*, semantically quite similar to the term "transculturation" employed by his Cuban colleague, to refer to the origins of Mexican identity. The concept of *hibridismo* as understood by Paz also differs from that of Nestor García-Canclini in *Culturas híbridas* (*Hybrid Cultures*; 1995), which serves to identify the mixing of elite and popular cultures, whereas Paz identified the mixing of cultures in the context of colonialism. Finally, *hibridismo* can also be tied to Homi Bhabha's notion of third space, developed in his landmark book *The Location of Culture* (1994). Mariana, growing up in Mexico yet living in a French home, can be seen as evolving in a third space. For the purpose of this investigation, I chose to use *hibridismo* and transculturation to refer to Mariana's evolution toward her identity, for I analyze *La "Flor de Lis"* against the historical background of the evolution of Mexican nationalism and the evolution of those very theories, which are linked to the emancipatory politics of the post-revolutionary context. Novel and theory are then related.

In *El laberinto de la soledad* (1950), alluded to in Poniatowska's Premio Cervantes speech, Paz affirms that the identity impasse comes from the fact that throughout history, Mexico's political and intellectual elite have always attempted—often successfully—to deny a culture built on creative interaction during the long process of colonization. Mexicans, fundamentally hybrid beings born of the contact between pre-Colombian and Spanish societies, must accept their nature in order to overcome this identity deadlock. Paz argues that, "Nuestro grito es una expresión de la voluntad mexicana de vivir cerrados al exterior, sí, pero sobre todo, cerrados frente al pasado. En ese grito condenamos nuestro origen y renegamos de nuestro hibridismo" (225) ("We express our desire to live closed off from the outside world and, above all, from the past. In this shout we condemn our origins and deny our hybridism"[5]). As long as Mexicans negated such hybridity, they would be unable to find their true selves.

*El laberinto de la soledad* depicts a mid-century Mexico full of contradictions that has yet to experience the cultural decolonization movement, and whose inhabitants are still at odds with their identity: "El mexicano no quiere ser ni indio ni español. Tampoco quiere descender de ellos. Los niega. . . . El mexicano y la mexicanidad se definen como ruptura y negación" (225) ("The Mexican does not want to be either an Indian or a Spaniard. Nor does he want to be descended from them. He denies them. . . . The Mexican and his Mexicanism must be defined as separation and negation"). The Mexican, then, "se vuelve hijo de la nada. Él empieza en sí mismo" (225) ("becomes the son of Nothingness. His beginnings are in his own self"[6]). For Paz, post-revolutionary Mexico needed to become self-aware and recognize the importance of both cultural traditions. Years later, Paz was still contemplating the nature of his compatriots' identity. In the foreword to *Quetzalcóatl y Guadalupe: The Formation of Mexican National Consciousness*, while reflecting on the inherent contradiction that is the Mexican identity, Paz affirms that "La ambigüedad mestiza duplica la ambigüedad criolla aunque sólo para, en un momento final, negarla: como el criollo, el mestizo no es ni español ni indio; tampoco es un europeo que busca arraigarse: es un producto del suelo americano, el nuevo producto" ("The ambiguity of the mestizo was twice as great as that of the creole, but negated the creole ambiguity in that last analysis. Like the creole, the mestizo is neither Spanish nor Indian, nor is he a European who seeks to put roots down into the American soil; he is a product of that soil, a new man; 46, xvi). In Poniatowska's novel, Mariana, growing up in the 1950s Mexico that Paz describes, personifies this new being, one born of the contact between European and Indigenous Mexican cultures, who has yet to adapt to a new country.

## A Transcultural Education

As a child, Mariana is open to adjusting her vision of Mexicans and Mexicanness and remodelling it to carve out a space for herself. And so, despite her cosmopolitan origins, a French Mariana newly arrived in Mexico progressively assumes a Mexican identity, presented as a negotiation between cosmopolitanism and nationalism. The change of setting—the journey from France to Mexico, and the transition from home to street—is the first step that affects both Mariana and her perspective on life. She begins by developing a cosmopolitan outlook by default, modelled after that of her mother, Luz, and, after experiencing xenophobia in her interactions with the fervently nationalistic popular classes, evolves toward an identity that combines European and American influences. In her struggle to define her identity, Mariana clears a path between the pervasive ideologies of the late 1930s and early 1940s—exacerbated Mexican nationalism and racist Eurocentrism—and finds a middle ground through transculturation. Her transcultural identity, found through her nanny, Magda, and her maternal grandmother, embraces all aspects of her complex cultural heritage.[7]

Throughout La *"Flor de Lis,"* the protagonist constantly adjusts her vision of both her cosmopolitan and Indigenous relatives. Mariana's flight to Mexico with her family marks the beginning of her cosmopolitan overture. The child is surprised to learn that her mother, Luz, is of Mexican descent; indeed, she says that "Sofía y yo no sabíamos que mamá era mexicana" ("Sofía and I did not know that *mamá* was Mexican"; 32). While the child is intrigued by this new discovery, stereotyping and disdain for her immediate family in Latin America mark this awakening. Even before they embark on their journey to Mexico, the sisters are warned that it is a strange and dangerous country: " 'You see children this is Mexico.' La abuela Beth nos enseña en el 'National Geographic Magazine' unas negras de senos colgantes y hueso atravesado en la cabeza. Sonríen, sí, porque van a comernos, son caníbales. 'This is where your mother is taking you' " ("Grandmother Beth shows us in the 'National Geographic Magazine' some Black women with sagging breasts and a bone through the head. They smile, yes, because they are about to eat us, they are cannibals. 'This is where your mother is taking you'"; 27). La abuela Beth, their American aunt, does not know much about Mexico; indeed, she appears to confuse her neighbour to the south with some African countries. Yet, she nonetheless manages to frighten her nieces, and the first image Mariana has of her new country is one of cannibals who want to devour her. The child internalizes this idea of Mexico and cannot help but wonder why their mother is taking them to such a dangerous place.[8] Upon reaching the country, she is bewildered when she cannot find any cannibals. While "En tierra en el aeropuerto de México, [donde] espera nuestra nueva abuela," she wonders, "¿Dónde estarán las del hueso atravesado en la cabeza?" ("On the tarmac of the airport in Mexico City, [where] our new grandmother is waiting for us, she wonders, 'Where could the women with a bone through the head be?'"; 32), once she gets used to the country, she realizes that this image was based on prejudice.

Although her non-Mexican relatives' perception of Mexico is false, Mariana does not recognize this right away, for once there, her family makes a point of maintaining its status as foreign, as such a designation positions them within the upper class. Since the mother expects to return to France once the war is over, she wants her children to retain their cultural ties to Europe. It is these ties to their past that prevent them from completely assimilating into the new culture. While Luz sends Mariana and Sofía to a British school to learn English, they all speak French at home. As for Spanish, they are rarely exposed to the language, for it holds little value in Luz's world view:

> Mamá avisó que iba a meternos a una escuela inglesa; el español ya lo pescaremos en la calle, es más importante el inglés. El español se aprende solo, ni para qué estudiarlo. En el Windsor School nos enseñan a contar en "pounds, shillings and pence" y a transferirlos. Cantamos "God save the Queen" todas las mañanas al empezar las clases.
>
> *Mamá* informed us that she would enrol us in an English school; Spanish would be for later, to be picked up on the streets, English is more important. You will learn Spanish on your own, there is no need to study it. In the Windsor School they teach us to count in "pounds, shillings and pence" and to convert them. We sing "God Save the Queen" every morning at the beginning of class. (33)

Consequently, the school, normally the crucible in which children's identities are shaped, rejects most Mexican elements, and when it does present them, it does so through a Eurocentric prism. The girls are thus exposed to British culture, one that is far from being their own, or even being one they could grow into, simply because it is perceived as more valuable than its Mexican counterpart. Culture, then, becomes a skill, necessary for survival, rather than something one embodies. This is where Mariana's dilemma stems from: she wants to be accepted by Mexico, but is not sufficiently exposed to its culture to assume it properly.

The relationships Mariana's family maintain with other Mexican families are reflective of this same mentality. These families value their European ties over Mexican ones, and consider that their children can only learn how to evolve in the world by spending some time in Europe: "no cabe duda de que el mundo se adquiere en el otro continente, aquí somos todavía muy provincianos" ("there is no doubt that the world is acquired on the other continent, here we are still very provincial"; 50), and associate culture with the elite. This leads them to view anyone who took part in the Mexican Revolution, a popular uprising, as uncultured:

> ¿Te has fijado cuánto la menciona [a Lucecita] el Duque de Otranto en sus columnas? En la del martes contó de un gigantesco ramo de flores que le mandó Ezequiel Padilla, y Marie Thérèse Redo que lo vio en la sala dijo que era una cosota así, desproporcionada, claro que de mal gusto, del gusto de los políticos, del gusto de la Revolución Mexicana que no tiene el menor gusto, qué le vamos a hacer, la cultura no se aprende de un día para el otro.

> Have you noticed how much the Duke of Otranto mentions her [Lucecita] in his columns? On Tuesday he wrote about a gigantic bouquet of flowers that Ezequiel Padilla sent her, and Marie Thérèse Redo, who saw it in the room, said that it was large and tacky, out of all proportion, and of course in bad taste, the taste of politicians, the taste of the Mexican Revolution, which has no taste, what can we do, culture is not something that you acquire overnight. (50)

Once again, as exemplified by Ezequiel Padilla's major faux pas with the flowers, culture is a tool that must be acquired by people who want to be accepted into higher circles. If one does not master it, one is to be ridiculed and set apart. Mariana develops this art of acquiring elite culture, for she was born into that milieu, but it is not this elitist cosmopolitan culture that she wants to embrace.

While Mariana demonstrates interest in learning about Mexico and Mexicans—their social backgrounds notwithstanding—her mother only looks to the European aspects of Mexican life. Luz's attitude toward her country and fellow countrymen reveals her disdain toward the Spanish language: indeed, language and nation are closely aligned in her mind, with Spanish being associated with the lower classes and countries with a colonial or neo-colonial past in Latin America. Those who speak it are therefore inferior to the world she has chosen. Although Mexican, Luz prefers to identify as French. She embodies Fernando Rosenberg's assertion that the rejection of cosmopolitanism as a prism through which to approach Latin America was due to the concept's imperial connotations, connotations that were rejected throughout the continent, where

> La noción de cosmopolitismo está muchas veces asociada con ideas tan desencontradas como las pretensiones universalistas eurocéntricas de la alta cultura, con adscripciones imperiales al nivel de la política, y con el desapego, el desprendimiento, o simplemente la posición irónica, esteticista o hedonista al nivel del sujeto (una vida de lujos y placeres, como dice algún tango, y lo sigue afirmando hoy el nombre del trago). Al cosmopolitismo se lo relaciona con una estudiada distancia, cuando no un menosprecio y falta de sensibilidad, respecto a los problemas locales y/o nacionales.

> The notion of cosmopolitanism is often associated with widely divergent ideas such as the Eurocentric, universalist pretensions of high culture, adherence to imperialist politics, indifference, detachment, and even an ironic aestheticist or hedonistic position (eloquently described in a familiar tango as a life of luxury and pleasure, or reflected even now in the name of the cocktail). Cosmopolitanism is thought to relate to a measured distance, if not contempt

and lack of sensitivity toward local and/or national problems. ("Afecto y política" 468)

Mariana's mother is a shining example of this affirmation: she presents both *una estudiada distancia* ("a measured distance") from the Mexican people and a *menosprecio y falta de sensibilidad* ("contempt and lack of sensitivity") toward them. She epitomizes the idea of betrayal associated with cosmopolitanism, as she chooses to deny her past, rejects tradition, and in times of crisis refuses to accept the transcultural society from which she came, favouring the culture she had adopted in the metropole.

Indeed, Luz embodies such elitism, and displays her disregard for her fellow citizens and local problems during a trip to the countryside. When Sofía suddenly becomes thirsty, Luz, used to a life of plenty, expects a farmer to be able to give the child something to drink:

> Sofía reclama: "Tengo sed." Mamá le dice: "Vamos a conseguirte un vaso de leche." Cuando lo pide, frente a una puerta, la enrebozada hace una larga pausa antes de responderle como si fuera a darle un vahído: "No hay." Mamá patea el suelo con sus botas, cómo que no hay, si ésta es una región ganadera, no hay, no hay, no hay, repite a cada patada, no hay, en este país nunca hay nada, no hay, en cualquier pueblito mugroso donde te detengas en Francia te dan de comer estupendamente y aquí, no hay, no hay, no hay, lo mismo en la miscelánea, en la trapalería, no hay, no hay, ¿para qué abren tiendas entonces si no hay?, lo que pasa es que no quieren atenderte, no hay, no hay. . . . "Pero ¿de qué vive esta gente, qué come, si ni siquiera tiene un vaso de leche?"
>
> Sofía complains: "I am thirsty." *Mamá* tells her: "Let's get you a glass of milk." When she asks, at a door, a woman wearing a *rebozo* takes a long pause before answering, as if she suddenly had a dizzy spell: "There isn't any." *Mamá* stamps the ground with her boots, how come there is none, if this is ranch country, there is nothing, there is nothing, there is nothing, she repeats with every kick, there is

> nothing, in this country there is never anything, there is nothing, in any filthy village where you stop in France they offer you marvellous food to eat and here, there is nothing, there is nothing, there is nothing, it's the same at the corner store, at the hardware store, there is nothing, there is nothing. Why open shops if there is nothing? What happens is that these people do not want to serve you, there is nothing, there is nothing. . . . "But what keeps these people alive, what do they eat, when they do not even have a glass of milk?" (69–70)

Luz becomes upset and acts like a capricious child. Instead of acknowledging that they are riding through a poor region of Mexico, she prefers to convince herself that the farmers are making a conscious decision not to help the wealthy. She projects the disdain she feels for these rural people onto them and paints herself as the victim. She cannot fathom being denied anything. Luz erroneously compares Mexico to France: in her idyllic vision, she imagines that French farmers would have fed strangers knocking at their door. She fails to mention that France is now a war zone in which food is sparse and rationed, and that had she stayed, she would probably have been in a situation similar—or even worse—to that of the Mexican farmers.

Instead, Luz quickly shifts her attention to the Revolution, which she blames for taking everything away from her wealthy family, for the lack of milk, and the utter poverty of the region they are visiting: "Habla de la Revolución; antes con los hacendados, todos tenían de todo, ahora el país está muerto de hambre. . . . Pinche revolución tan pinche, sintetiza mamá" ("She talks of the Revolution; before, with the landowners, everyone had everything, now the country is starving to death. . . . Damn the damned revolution, *mamá* synthesizes"; 70). Before the Revolution, the conditions were not any better for the poorer classes, but the neo-colonial aristocracy ruled the country, and as such, could expect almost anyone to be at their service. Mariana, of a more affable nature, listens to her mother but does not internalize her destructive words. In this regard, Cristina Perilli rightly points out that "La desvalorización de 'la raza' mexicana dentro del discurso familiar produce, como contraparte y respuesta a la búsqueda de pertenencia, el discurso de Mariana que la naturaliza y mitifica" ("the degradation of the Mexican 'race' that occurs within family discourse, triggers, in counterpoint and in response to the search for belonging, Mariana's discourse that naturalizes and mythifies it"; 33). Unbeknownst to her at the time, Luz is helping her daughter to become Mexican.

For Mariana's family, and particularly for her mother, Europe remains the cultural reference, thus preventing the two sisters from truly beginning the process of Mexicanization. Luz makes sure, with help from different strategies—the British school, the piano lessons, their speaking French at home—that the dominant domestic culture remains that of the old continent. Luz hierarchizes and instrumentalizes culture. Mariana discovers that her mother is in fact a product of cultural mutation, typical of the neo-colonial cultural elite of the early twentieth century, the so-called *ciudad letrada*, or lettered city, always turned toward the overseas metropole. Evidently, as it was across all of Latin America at the time, this metropole could not be Spain, but rather France or England, two fundamental benchmarks for Mexico's national education system.

While Luz embodies the elitism that until recently had tainted cosmopolitanism, the concept of transculturation is primordial in the case of Mariana, who, unlike her mother, begins to build a different identity by slowly absorbing elements of her new surroundings, bit by bit. As a result, the adversarial relationship between Mariana and her mother serves as a starting point for the protagonist's acceptance, and her eventual integration or assimilation, of her Mexican roots. As a child, Mariana has not yet assumed the racial prejudices of her mother and remains open to the perception of Mexico held by other authority figures, such as her nanny Magda and her Mexican grandmother. The Mexicanization of the protagonist happens in two phases. Mariana first idealizes her mother, which corresponds to the acclimatization period in her new environment; this leads her to establish a link between mother and motherland. She believes that being accepted by her mother will mean being accepted by Mexico too. Then she wishes to be more Mexican than her mother, in order to be accepted by her peers, most of whom are of a nationalistic mind (Hurley 156). Mariana's contradictory and conflicting desire to finally obtain Luz's maternal love even though it never seems to be within reach pushes her to develop a transcultural identity.

Even if she is quite young, Mariana feels the sting of not being accepted by the Mexican community. This rejection happens even when she is with her grandmother, who has lived in Mexico her whole life. Although she is clearly Mexican, her upper-class status separates her from most of her fellow citizens. For instance, Mariana feels deeply alineated during a church service:

> Casi no hay gente, apenas unos cuantos bultos enrebozados, morenos como las bancas, monitos que se rascan y se persignan, confundidos los ademanes. A veces capto, entre las cortinas del rebozo, el fulgor de una mirada huidiza; la mano vuelta hacia adentro como una garra que se recoge es la de un animal que erró su ataque y tuvo que retraerse. ¿Qué tanto hay dentro de esos rebozos? ¿Cuánta mugre rencorosa, cuánto sudor ácido, cuánta miseria arrebujada en el cuello y en el cabello opaco, grisáceo? Quisiera hablarles, sería fácil acuclillarme junto a una forma doliente, pero aprendí que no me aceptan, me ven en sordina, agazapados entre sus trapos descoloridos y tristes, hacen como que no me entienden, todo su ser erizado de desconfianza. Dice la abuela que es más fácil acercarse a un perro sarnoso. . . . "Dios mío, dime ¿qué les he hecho? ¿Qué les hacemos para que nos rechacen tanto?" Espío sus gestos hieráticos, vergonzantes y sobre todo, esa terrible tranquilidad oscura con la que esperan yertos a que el más allá les dé la señal. ¿Qué esperan? Magda me dijo una vez: "Es que no tienen a nadie." ¿Qué hago entre esas ánimas en pena?

> There is almost no one here, just a few bundles wrapped in *rebozos*, dark as the benches, little monkeys that scratch and cross themselves, mixing the gestures. Sometimes I catch, among the folds of the *rebozo*, the glow of an elusive gaze; the hand turned inward like the retracting claw of an animal that missed its target and had to draw back. What lies there inside those *rebozos*? How much spiteful grime, how much sour sweat, how much misery caked in the neck and

the dull, grey hair? I would like to talk to them, it would be easy to squat next to a mournful shape, but I learned that they do not accept me, they see me in a muffled way, crouched between their sad, faded rags, they pretend not to understand me, their whole being bristling with distrust. *La abuela* says that it is easier to get close to a mangy dog. ... "My God, tell me, what have I done to them? What do we do for them to reject us so much?" I spy on their inscrutable, shameful gestures, and, above all, that terrible dark tranquility with which they wait in stillness for the hereafter to give them the signal. What do they expect? Magda once said: "They don't have anybody." What am I doing among these grieving souls? (*La "Flor de Lis"* 51–2)

Mariana is aware of the divide between her family and most Mexicans, and in church, she wishes she could talk to them—"quisiera hablarles"—and make them see her profound desire to understand them, to accept them, and most of all, to be accepted by them. As a child, she does not feel the need to have such a separation between people because of their socio-economic backgrounds. She does not understand what she did wrong to be rejected in this manner, when in fact her mistake is having been born into what is perceived as the wrong class. She finds solace in Magda telling her she did not, in fact, do anything wrong.

Once Mariana begins to appreciate Mexico, the maternal figure she attempts to emulate pivots from her mother to Magda. Magda is present and shows a consistency in caring for the children, unlike Luz's fleeting love. She ends up having more influence on Mariana's search for identity than her own mother. Mariana loves Magda, and is aware of the many sacrifices she makes to attend to the family—something Luz could not bring herself to do. In Mariana's words, Magda "Es sabia, hace reír, se fija, nunca ha habido en nuestra casa presencia más benéfica" ("is wise, she makes us laugh, she notices, there has never been such a beneficial presence in our home"; 58). However, Mariana does not understand why Magda needs to make all those sacrifices for the family while no one else seems to be doing anything in the house:

> Veo sus manos enrojecidas cambiando los platos de un fregadero a otro; en uno los enjabona, en el otro los enjuaga. Los pone después a escurrir. ¿Por qué no soy yo la que lavo los platos? ¿Por qué no es mamá la que los lava? ¿O la nueva abuela? ¿O para eso Mister Chips? ¿O el abuelo, tantas horas sentado en Francia? ¿Por qué no es Magda la que toma las clases de piano si se ve que a ella se le ilumina el rostro al oír la música que tecleamos con desgano?
>
> I see her red hands moving the dishes from one sink to another; in one she lathers them with soap, in the other she rinses them. Then she puts them up to dry. Why don't I wash the dishes? Why is it not *mamá* who washes them? Or our new grandmother? Or Mister Chips for that matter? Or our grandfather, who spent so many hours sitting in France? Why is it not Magda who is taking piano lessons when it is her face that lights up when she hears the music we play with reluctance? (58–9)

Contact with popular culture allows Mariana to acquire new values and to understand the differences that exist between her family and the rest of society. She questions not only her role in the household, but everyone else's. Mariana regards Magda as more than a maid and a nanny, and is saddened to see how little she cares about herself: "Ella siempre se atiende a lo último. Para ella son los minutos más gastados, los más viejos del día, porque antes, todavía encontró tiempo para venir a contarnos el cuento de las tres hijas del zapaterito pobre" ("She thinks of herself last. To her, these are the most wasted moments, the last minutes of the day, because even before then, she still found time to come and tell us the story of the three daughters of the poor cobbler"; 59). Through Madga, Mariana becomes aware of the privileged place she has in society. Even though her family was financially ruined during the Revolution, they were able to retain their status. Mariana questions this situation.

Through Magda, who represents contact with two groups, the Indigenous and the popular majority of society, Mariana discovers a Mexicanness different from the exotic image to which she was first introduced in Europe.⁹ In fact, the relationship Mariana develops with Magda gradually helps her to assume her Mexican identity. Whereas France, and later her grandmother's house, represent closed spaces where European culture flourishes, Mexico and its streets represent free, open areas where an uninhibited Mariana can develop and learn more about her new country. Moreover, Magda's presence in the house causes this otherwise closed space to become porous, and all are touched by a certain degree of Mexicanness. Mexico, then, acquires a sense of normalcy in the mind of the protagonist, rather than the aura of foreignness that her relatives attribute to it.¹⁰

Through Magda, Mariana discovers and falls in love with the Zócalo, the main square in the heart of Mexico City, where she experiences popular culture. Mariana describes the Zócalo as "esa gran plaza que siempre se [le] atora en la garganta" ("this big plaza that gets stuck in your throat"; 58). She develops a strong love for the plaza and, for the first time in the novel, senses that she is part of her new country. By establishing a connection to one of the most important locations in Mexico, she asserts her metaphorical belonging to the country:

> Amo esta plaza, es mía, es más mía que mi casa, me importa más que mi casa, preferiría perder mi casa. Quisiera bañarla toda entera a grandes cubetadas de agua y escobazos, restregarla con una escobilla y jabón, sacarle espuma, como a un patio viejo, hincarme sobre sus baldosas a puro talle y talle, y cantarle a voz en cuello, como Jorge Negrete, cuando lo oía en el radio gritar así: México lindo y querido si muero lejos de ti que digan que estoy dormido y que me traigan aquí.
>
> I love this plaza, it's mine, it's more mine than my home, I care about it more than my home, I'd rather lose my home. I would like to wash it all with great buckets of water and a sweeping broom, scrub it with a brush and soap, cover it in foam, like an old patio, kneel on its tiles scrubbing nonstop, and singing at the top of my lungs, like Jorge Negrete, when I would hear him on the radio crying out: Beautiful

and dear Mexico if I die far from you let them pretend that
I am asleep and bring me here. (58)

Not only does Magda introduce Mariana to a symbol of Mexicanness, the Zócalo, Magda also enables Mariana to accept the hybrid nature of her identity, thereby allowing her to become Mexican. According to Mary Louise Pratt, "subordinated or marginal groups select and invent from materials transmitted to them by a dominant or metropolitan culture" (6). Mariana can be likened to the marginal groups to which Pratt refers. Even with her status and class privileges—or precisely because of these attributes—in a country full of Mexicans, she is the minority, the one perceived as the outsider. She is the one who has to internalize the cultural materials transmitted to her by the dominant culture of the country where she now lives; her desire to belong makes it necessary. In some sort of reversed pattern, the nanny, the outsider in the French-dominated house, becomes the vessel of the culture through which Mariana will finally attain a sense of belonging.

Adaptation to a new setting remains a treacherous process for Mariana and her sister Sofía. An adult Mariana comments: "Éramos unas niñas desarraigadas, flotábamos en México, qué cuerdita tan frágil la nuestra, ¡cuántos vientos para mecate tan fino!" ("We were two rootless little girls, floating in Mexico, our strings so fragile, such strong winds against such fine rope!"; Poniatowska, *La "Flor de Lis"* 47). Even if it is easier for Sofía to acclimatize, both sisters are like tightrope walkers on a *cuerdita frágil*, a loose cord, and can lose their balance at any moment. This instability reflects the fact that Mariana is aware that her sense of her place in society is not as deep as it could have been had her family remained in Europe. However, unlike her sister, who is able to pass as a native-born citizen of the country, a blond, blue-eyed Mariana is always branded as a stranger. Children and adults alike question her Mexicanness and tell her she does not look the part, calling her a *gringa*. Multiple times, Mariana asks herself, her mother, Magda—anyone who is willing to listen to her—where she belongs. She never seems to get a satisfactory answer. Rather, she is often deemed not Mexican enough, and told that one does not *become* Mexican, one is *born* Mexican:

—Pero tú no eres de México ¿verdad?

—Sí soy.

—Es que no pareces mexicana.

—Ah sí, entonces ¿qué parezco?

—Gringa.

—Pues no soy gringa, soy mexicana.

—¡Ay! ¿A poco? . . .

Busco trabajo de secretaria:

—No vayas a decirles que no naciste mexicana porque ni caso te hacen.

—Si no eres de México, no tienes derecho a opinar.

—¿Por qué? Tengo interés en hacerlo.

—Sí, pero tu opinión no vale.

—¿Por qué?

—Porque no eres mexicana.


You don't look Mexican.

Oh well, so what do I look like?

A *gringa*.

Well, I'm not a *gringa*, I'm Mexican.

Seriously?

I am looking for a secretarial job.

Don't go telling them you weren't born Mexican because they won't pay any attention to you.

If you are not from Mexico, you have no right to comment.

Why? I want to.

Yes, but your opinion is not worth anything.

Why?

Because you're not Mexican. (114)

Mariana is told she does not have a right to express her opinion since she was not born Mexican. Once again, she tries to belong to a society that constantly rejects her, solely on the grounds of her birthplace. She, her mother, and her sister are called terrible names—"Cochinas extranjeras que vienen a chuparnos la sangre" ("foreign pigs that come to bleed us dry"), "pinche emigradas" ("fucking emigrants")—and are told that being Mexican is a birthright: "Los que no han nacido en esta bendita tierra no tienen derecho a participar. Si no les gusta lárguense" ("Those who were not born in this blessed land have no right to participate. If you don't like it, leave"; 75). However, Mariana believes that she is "mexicana porque [su] madre es mexicana; si la nacionalidad de la madre se heredara como la del padre, sería mexicana" ("Mexican because [her] mother is Mexican; if nationality were inherited from one's mother like that of the father, I would be Mexican"; 74). When she is told that she is not from Mexico and cannot be considered Mexican, her reply makes it clear where her allegiance now lies: "Soy de México porque quiero serlo, es mi país" ("I am from Mexico because I want to be, it's my country"; 74). Indeed, even if she was born in France, she wants to be Mexican and to belong to Magda's Mexico. She claims her mother's Mexicanness as her own, more than her mother does, and goes one step further when she affirms that nationality is not necessarily something one is born with, but rather something one chooses. Mariana's decision echoes Martha Nussbaum's claims in *For Love of Country*—namely, that "the accident of where one is born is just that, an accident; any human being might have been born in any nation" (7). In this sense, Mariana behaves like her mother, who identifies solely as French. Even if the world is challenging her, she still chooses to be Mexican.

However, Mariana cannot escape the hybrid nature of her being and her perceived incompleteness. As a teenager, she does not see herself as incomplete; she is made to think she is, which confuses her even more. She commits to being Mexican, but is constantly reminded that she is not, even during the most mundane activities, such as on a trip to the countryside:

> —Ay, Mariana, ¿qué no sabías que las mulas son hijas de yeguas y burros?
>
> —¡Ése es el origen de las mulas!
>
> —Por eso las mulas son estériles.
>
> Sammy comentó:
>
> —Hay cierto tipo de cruzas que no se deben hacer, que no se pueden hacer. . . .
>
> Emilio pronunció la palabra híbrido. Híbrido, híbrido . . . se parece a Librado. . . . Híbrido. Librado, híbrido. El maíz híbrido no se puede sembrar. No agarra.


> "Oh, Mariana, didn't you know that mules are the daughters of mares and donkeys?"

"That is the origin of the mule!"

"That's why mules are sterile."

Sammy commented:

"There are certain types of cross breeding that should not be done, that cannot be done...."

Emilio sounded the word "hybrid." Hybrid, hybrid . . . it's reminiscent of Librado [to liberate, and also the name of one of the novel's characters].... Hybrid. Librado, hybrid. Hybrid corn cannot be sown. It doesn't take root. (Poniatowska, *La "Flor de Lis"* 193)

The final portion of this passage is particularly pertinent: by mixing the voice of the adult with that of the child, it anticipates Mariana's future path. Although both the *mulas* and the *maíz híbrido* are sterile examples of why hybridity ought to be condemned—and thus embody her peers' rejection of *mestizaje*—Mariana disagrees. The voice of the adult recalls Emilio's hard words about hybridity—"Emilio pronunció la palabra híbrido. El maíz híbrido no se puede sembrar. No agarra"—while the child plays with them and makes the word *híbrido*—hybrid—rhyme with Librado, the name of one of the family's horse grooms, which also means "liberated." Hybridity and freedom are then linked in the mind of the protagonist, at least a posteriori. The repetition of the word *híbrido* in Mariana's discourse reflects her condition, and the difficulties Mexico has in embracing this notion of identity. An allegorical reading makes obvious the reference to identity; hybridity, then, is linked to the protagonist's freedom.

Mariana's adolescence, a period of conflict during which her desire to belong is amplified, is accompanied by the affirmation of her Mexicanness. Her friend Casilda puts her finger on Mariana's sense of self and understands that for Mariana, to love is to morph into the loved one (202), which is why her encounter with Father Teufel, a French priest, is worrisome. Teufel is no stranger to Mariana's sudden awareness of class disparity and the importance of embodying one's culture. The priest holds

Marxist beliefs and hopes the young girls he coaches as part of a scout organization will eventually reject their aristocratic heritage, beliefs, and values, and instead personify a new evolution of Mexican society—one that includes the poor and the Indigenous. Teufel is vocal in his criticism of Mexican society, and during a meeting with industrialists, overreacts when discussing these issues:

> –Ustedes comparan al pueblo mexicano con los pueblos de Europa, concretamente con Francia, y sólo en la medida en que México se parezca a Francia, se justificará su pretensión de formar parte de la comunidad de los hombres. Esto es muy grave, señores trasterrados, porque ustedes mismos, aunque ya no viven en Francia, se erigen en civilización y pretenden civilizar a un pueblo que desprecian. ¡Oh no, no protesten, me han atestado su superioridad durante todos los días de mi estancia y conozco bien su acción civilizadora; hacerlos trabajar diez o doce horas en lo que ustedes quieran, regular su natalidad cuando este gran país tiene aún tantas zonas sin poblar, terminar con una religión primitiva y ciega, a su criterio pagana, sólo porque su mezquindad los hace incapaces de comprenderla, seguir aprovechando esa mano de obra sumisa, barata, ignorante, como a ustedes les conviene, porque de lo que se trata es de que no mejoren, no asciendan a ninguna posición de mando! Oh, no me digan que ustedes les han enseñado lo que saben, jamás encajarán los mexicanos pobres dentro de su mundo mientras no se parezcan a ustedes y a su familia.

You compare the Mexican people to the people of Europe, specifically with France, and only to the extent that Mexico resembles France will its claim to be part of the human community be justified. This is very serious, exiled gentlemen, because you yourselves, although you no longer live in France, set yourself up as the embodiment of civilization and pretend to civilize a people you despise. Oh no, don't protest, you have shown me your superiority daily during

> my many days here and I know your civilizing action well; make them work ten or twelve hours a day at whatever you want, control their birth rate when this great country still has so many unpopulated areas, eradicate a primitive and blind religion, in your understanding, a pagan one, just because your greed makes you unable to understand it, continue taking advantage of that submissive, cheap, ignorant workforce, since it suits you, because the objective is to ensure that they do not better themselves, do not ascend to any position of leadership! Oh, don't tell me that you have taught them what you know, poor Mexicans will never fit into your world as long as they don't look like you and your family. (231–2)

Teufel criticizes the upper class and its Eurocentric views, as well as the Mexican industrialists that treat the lower classes badly. He tells them quite bluntly that they "no encarnan civilizadores ni cultura alguna. . . . Ustedes encarnan sus privilegios" ("do not embody civilizers or any culture whatsoever. . . . You embody your privileges") and are "¡Racistas, esto es lo que son ustedes, racistas y explotadores!" ("Racists, this is what you are, racists and exploiters!"; 232). He criticizes their need to resemble Europe. He acts more or less the same way with the young girls under his supervision. He shows no respect for the way they were raised, believes the upper class is useless, and expects the teenagers to replicate the outlook of their parents unless they assume his beliefs. He stresses that the girls need to *descastarse*, or shed the class into which they were born and the social privilege that comes with it: "Hay que vivir, descastarse, hí-bri-do, des-cas-vi-bri-do vivir" ("You have to live, shrug off your class, become hybrid, and live without privileges"; 253). For Teufel, becoming Mexican is a two-step process: the young scouts must reject their *casta* and accept the hybrid nature of their identity if they are to truly live. Naturally, this resonates with Mariana.

Teufel often tells the girls who attend his seminars that their way of life is not good enough, since it does not have a higher purpose beyond serving themselves: "Por Dios estudien algo útil, sean enfermeras, laboratistas, maestras, costureras, boticarias, algo útil, qué sé yo, algo que hace falta. ¿Por qué estudian lo que va a instalarlas en su estatuto de niñas bien? . . . ¿Cuándo van a servir a los demás? ¿Cuándo van a perderse en los demás?" ("For God's sake, study something useful, become nurses, laboratory technicians, teachers, seamstresses, pharmacists, I don't know, something useful, something that is needed. Why do you study what will confirm you in your status as well-to-do girls? . . . When are you going to serve others? When are you going to lose yourselves in others?"; 126). The priest wants them to realize how fortunate they are to live in a country such as Mexico, and tells the girls they were born to change the world.[11] He wants them to "tomar parte, pertenecer, expresarse, dar" ("join in, belong, express themselves, give"), but what strikes a chord with Mariana is his call to be Mexican: "Ustedes viven en un país determinado, denle algo a ese país, carajo. Sean mexicanas, carajo" ("You live in a specific country: give something to this country, damn it. Be Mexican, damn it"; 155). Teufel's speech affects Mariana profoundly, especially when he calls on the girls to become more Mexican, a process she has yet to complete. His objective is to get to know every member of the scout organization, and in a private meeting with Mariana, Teufel questions her sense of identity and points out her own contradictions; at this point in her evolution, she has assimilated aspects of Magda's Mexico, but still clings to her privileged social status. He tells her that being, in her own words, "de buena familia" ("from a good family") and "educada" ("educated") does not mean that she is better than "la otra gente . . . la de afuera" ("those other people . . . those on the streets"; 144–5).

Mariana is especially troubled by their conversation about servants, for she has internalized her family's belief that servants cannot achieve anything better in life. Of course, this view conflicts with the love and respect she feels for Magda:

> —Ustedes ¿tienen sirvientes?
>
> —Sí, padre.
>
> —Y ¿comen en la mesa? . . .
>
> —¡Ay no, padre!

—Ah, ya veo, ¿por qué no comen en la mesa con ustedes?...

—Porque son sirvientes. No tienen modales.... Son criados.

—¿Qué significa eso?

—Son distintos. A ellos tampoco les gustaría comer en la mesa con nosotros.

—Y usted ¿está de acuerdo en que los sirvientes coman en la cocina?

(Como un relámpago, Magda atraviesa frente a mis ojos, pero Magda es Magda.)

—No sé padre, nunca me he puesto a pensar en ello.



Do you have servants?

Yes, Father.

And do they eat with you at the table?...

Oh no, Father!

Ah, I see, why do they not eat at the table with you?...

Because they are servants. They have no manners.... They are paid help.

What does that mean?

> They are different. And they don't want to eat at the table with us.
>
> And you, do you agree that the servants should eat in the kitchen?
>
> (Like lightning, Magda flashes before my eyes, but Magda is Magda.)
>
> I do not know Father, I have never thought about it. (144–5)

At this point in her identity formation, Mariana has still not accepted all of her Mexican identity. She remains attached to some family traditions and to her status as part of the wealthier class. Although she perceives Magda as different from other maids—"Como un relámpago, Magda atraviesa frente a mis ojos, *pero Magda es Magda*" ("Like lightning, Magda flashes before my eyes, *but Magda is Magda*"; my emphasis)—she still perceives herself as a *niña bien* who could not work in a factory. Although she sees herself as Mexican and has added many Mexican elements to her world view, she is not as Mexican as Teufel, with his ostensibly Marxist beliefs, would want her to be. However, Teufel's understanding of Mexicanness is somewhat skewed by his perception of himself. Indeed, during a short stay with Mariana's family, he enjoys being served by the maids and by Luz, who grants him his every wish. Although Teufel calls into question Mariana's beliefs about identity, he is deeply hypocritical. When asked what he considers his first language, he states that although he learned Spanish first—a result of being born in Mexico—he considers French his mother tongue for it is "el de [su] gente," or that of his people (233). If language and nationality are closely related, and nationality is something one chooses, then, like Luz, Teufel considers himself more French than Mexican.

While the two main authority figures in Mariana's life reject Mexico and identify themselves with France, her grandmother loves her country and tries to convey—even to pass on—this love to her granddaughter, who is eager to learn. An adult Mariana remembers how her Mexican grandmother loved her country right up to her final days, and how she told her that she was next in line to embrace it:

> Frente a sus ojos veía extenderse su país como la continuación de su falda, inspeccionaba los campos de trigo, se alegraba si descubría panales.... Ahora, desde hace tres meses, mi abuela ya no quiere regresar a los sitios donde estuvo aquerenciada.
>
> —Tú tenías el afán de que el país te entrara por los ojos, abue...
>
> —Sí—me responde—ahora te toca a ti memorizarlo.

> Before her eyes she saw her country extend out beyond the skirt at her feet, she inspected wheat fields, was happy if she found honeycombs.... Now, for the past three months, my grandmother does not want to return to the places where she was appreciated...
>
> "You were eager to draw the country in through your eyes, Grandma..."
>
> "Yes," she tells me, "now it is your turn to memorize it." (177–9)

Mariana's relationship with her grandmother helps her to accept all the contradictions within her identity, and to finally see herself as Mexican, and therefore hybrid by nature. It is the mission that her grandmother gives her. In commenting that Mariana is actively looking for an identity with which she could be at peace, María Elena de Valdés claims that "the salient truth that emerges is that her own identity is dominated by her apprenticeship in being able to look at herself as an other; specifically, as the other of the persons who share in her life" (128). This discovery of "myself as an other" is a painful coming of age experience that marks Mariana's transition into adulthood. With Madga and her grandmother, she eventually accepts the hybridity of her identity.

By the end of her teenage years, Mariana has become a complex, multi-faceted being, still somewhat torn between her double sense of belonging, or as Serge Gruzinski puts it, "between contradictory spaces and loyalties" (*Mestizo Mind* 188). Even if she is more certain than ever of where she belongs, Mariana still oscillates between three identities—the maternal one, the one that her mother wishes for her, and the one she wants to embody. Her sense of doubt returns as soon as she remembers her mother's wishes, yet the presence of Mexican people soothes her:

> No sé qué será de mí. Mamá piensa enviarme a Francia, para cambiar de aire; que no me case joven y con un mexicano como Sofía. "Verás los bailes en París, qué maravilla. . . . Te vamos a poner en un barco, verás, o en un avión, verás, te vamos a subir a la punta de la Torre Eiffel; tendrás París a tus pies, te vamos a poner sombrero y guantes y bajarás por el Sena en un bateau mouche, verás te vamos a . . ."
>
> En la Avenida San Juan de Letrán, arriba del Cinelandia, tomo clases de taquimecanografía. En los días en que el recuerdo de Teufel me atosiga, camino entre la gente hacia la Alameda. Me siento junto a los chinos que platican en un semicírculo parecido al Hemiciclo a Juárez; allí también los sordomudos se comunican dibujando pájaros en el aire; me hace bien su silencio, luego escojo una banca junto a la estatua "Malgré tout" y miro cómo los hombres al pasar, le acarician las nalgas. Las mujeres, no. Me gusta sentarme al sol en medio de la gente, esa gente, en mi ciudad, en el centro de mi país, en el ombligo del mundo.

> I don't know what will become of me. *Mamá* wants to send me to France, to change scenes; so that I don't marry young and a Mexican, like Sofia. "You will see the dances in Paris, what a wonder. . . . We are going to put you on a boat, we'll see, or on an airplane, we'll see, we will take you to the

top of the Eiffel Tower; you will have Paris at your feet, we are going to put a hat and gloves on you and you will sail down the Seine in a *bateau-mouche*, we'll see, we will . . ."

On the Avenida San Juan de Letrán, above Cinelandia, I take shorthand typing classes. On days when the memory of Teufel haunts me, I walk among the crowd toward the Alameda. I sit next to the Chinese people who talk in a semicircle similar to the Hemicycle to Juárez; there are also the deaf and the mute who communicate by drawing birds in the air; their silence is good for me, then I choose a bench next to the *Malgré tout* statue and watch how the men caress her buttocks as they walk by. Women, no. I like to sit in the sun in the middle of the people, these people, in my city, in the centre of my country, in the navel of the world. (Poniatowska, La *"Flor de Lis"* 260–1)

Even with her doubts, Mariana now belongs to *her* city, *her* country. She names them as such, making them her own. For Mariana, to love is to morph into the loved one; as such she eventually melds into Mexico, becoming a part of it. Ultimately, she is able to shift from one figurative space to another, and to find herself in the middle.

Consequently, at the end of the novel, an adult Mariana, confident of the people to whom she belongs, states: "Mi país es esta banca de piedra desde la cual miro el mediodía, mi país es esta lentitud al sol . . . mi país es el tamal que ahora mismo voy a ir a traer a la calle de Huichapan número 17, a la "Flor de Lis" ("My country is this stone bench from which I take in the midday, my country is this slow midday sun . . . my country is the *tamal* that I am about to pick up at number 17 Huichapan Street, the 'Flor de Lis' "; 261). The title, *La "Flor de Lis,"* already alludes to the allegory of transculturation that is the novel: it refers in part to the noble French heritage of Mariana's family, while also paying homage to Mexican popular culture, sharing a name with a popular *tamalería* in Mexico City. In this title, two cultures and sensibilities converge, and the protagonist must face both at every step of her development. The title is not only indicative of the autobiographical nature of the narrative, but also of the idea of transculturation inherent within it; as the French symbolism evolves, it effectively becomes Mexican, and thus takes on a new meaning. It allegorizes transculturation since it represents the idea of cultures coalescing, and creates a bridge between cultures that allows them to meet and interact. In the process, social groups never fully discard their own cultural background; Mariana never entirely forgets her European heritage, but instead adjusts her perspective and reshapes her identity within a new, hybrid culture. In my reading, the selection of the *Flor de Lis* is especially significant: Mariana accepts and appropriates the Mexican aspects of this French symbol, thereby giving it new meaning. However, she chooses, interprets, and adjusts the past in a way that is useful to her in order to affirm her Mexican identity, as well as her right to adopt it and to speak of it. The Mariana who reaches the *tamalería* has embraced and feels part of a Mexico conceived in transcultural terms. Mariana has evolved, from a cosmopolitan identity inherited from her mother, to a transcultural one generated slowly through her interactions with the nation's multiple roots. She succeeds in negotiating a path between the Eurocentric and nationalist extremes, and from then on feels at home at the *Flor de Lis*.

## Conclusion

Mariana's transformation, read allegorically, represents the evolution of a discourse on cultural identity in Mexico. In resolving her identity crisis, in accepting her hydridity, and in admitting the role her mother played in the development of her identity, Mariana personifies Mexico's renewal. As a result of the Mexican Revolution, the country has undergone a cultural decolonization and has accepted its culture as born of the blending of various traditions and customs. Poniatowska's novel not only represents the rejection of the poorly conceived Eurocentric cosmopolitanism of the time, but is also a clear example of the displacement or substitution of cosmopolitanism by more politically expedient identity metaphors, in this case, transculturation.

La *"Flor de Lis"* is also reflective of the fact that cosmopolitanism has always played second fiddle to concepts such as miscegenation and transculturation in Latin America. In post-revolutionary Mexico, there was no place for cosmopolitanism; it was perceived as out of place in a country that was attempting to cater to the needs of the time. The contingencies of history—too much foreign influence, the rejection of Indigenous culture during the Porfiriato—forced the country to adopt *hibridismo* or transculturation as a driving force. In post-revolutionary Mexico, the only way to be Mexican—even for a worldly person—was by embracing this cultural hybridity, being less concerned with cosmopolitan values, and rejecting nationalist nativism.

While *La "Flor de Lis"* represents the rejection of cosmopolitanism and the adoption of cultural hybridity, Mario Vargas Llosa's *El Paraíso en la otra esquina* and *El sueño del celta* plot protagonists who embody cosmopolitan ideals through the acceptance of cultural diversity. This is a stark contrast; indeed, it is their discovery of cultural hybridity that turns them into cosmopolitans.

# 2

# Cosmopolitanism and Nationalism in the Global Era in the Fictions of Mario Vargas Llosa

> *Celui qui voit dans tout être humain son semblable, qui souffre de ses peines et jouit de ses joies, celui-là doit écrire ses mémoires, lorsqu'il s'est trouvé en situation de recueillir des observations, et ces mémoires feront connaître les hommes sans acception de rangs, tels que l'époque et le pays les présentent.*
>
> *Anyone who sees in every human being their counterpart—suffering their pains and celebrating their joys—this person must write their memoirs once they have found themselves in a position to gather observations, and these memoirs will make others known, regardless of rank, just as they were in their time and country.*
>
> —Flora Tristan, *Pérégrinations d'une paria*

Mario Vargas Llosa is one of the most prolific Latin American authors of the past six decades, the last living member of the Boom, and one of many Latin American writers to have led a very active cosmopolitan public life. He is also a very polarized, and polarizing, intellectual. In December 2010, Vargas Llosa entered the literary pantheon when he was awarded the Nobel Prize for Literature "for his cartography of structures of power and his trenchant images of the individual's resistance, revolt, and defeat" (Nobel Foundation). In his acceptance speech, the Peruvian brought up the importance reading has had in his life from an early age. "La lectura convertía el sueño en vida y la vida en sueño y ponía al alcance del pedacito de hombre que era yo el universo de la literatura" (Discurso Nobel 1)

("Reading changed dreams into life and life into dreams and placed the universe of literature within reach of the boy I once was"[1]), he recalled, and all the characters he encountered in his readings "hablaban un lenguaje universal" (4) ("spoke a universal language"). Perhaps unconsciously, this idea of *universality* never left him, and it is, to this day, one of the main features of his body of work. Although he does not state it clearly in the Nobel speech, he implies that writing serves as some sort of catharsis, a way to rectify past and current mistakes; it "embellece lo feo" (1) ("beautifies ugliness"). Vargas Llosa is adamant: "Seríamos peores de lo que somos sin los buenos libros que leímos, más conformistas, menos inquietos e insumisos y el espiritú crítico, motor del progreso, ni siquiera existiría. Igual que escribir, leer es protestar contra las insuficiencias de la vida" (2) ("We would be worse than we are without the good books we have read, more conformist, not as restless, more submissive, and the critical spirit, the engine of progress, would not even exist. Like writing, reading is a protest against the insufficiencies of life").[2] As a matter of fact, most of his characters—and namely, the three I study in this chapter, the fictionalized Flora Tristán and Paul Gauguin in *El Paraíso en la otra esquina* (2003), and Roger Casement in *El sueño del celta* (2010)—are strong leaders who do protest against *las insuficiencias de la vida* by drawing attention to new ideas in an attempt to change the world, to make it a better place for their fellow human beings.[3] In the same way Vargas Llosa believes in trying to make the world a better place through literature.

One of the recurring utopian visions in Vargas Llosa's books—though less studied than the role of nationalism in his work—is precisely cosmopolitanism. Often, in his novels, much like in his non-fiction, he represents it as a counterpoint to nationalism; both are often used by Vargas Llosa's characters as tools by which to protest against *las insuficiencias de la vida*. These utopian concepts are multi-faceted driving forces of humanity: after all, "lo más humano es tratar de alcanzar lo imposible" ("the most human reaction is to try to achieve the impossible"; Vargas Llosa qtd. in Camín). Vargas Llosa's interest in cosmopolitanism has evolved according to his experiences as an engaged writer and public intellectual over several decades, from the 1950s until the present. From the cosmopolitan literary experimentation of the 1960s to his current tackling of global issues, the Peruvian's writings reflect the evolution of Spanish American literature writ large; his own intellectual evolution also runs parallel to the evolution of the discourse about cosmopolitanism in Latin America.

The chapter is divided into two sections: a historical and theoretical framework, followed by the literary analysis of two novels. In the first, I map Vargas Llosa's personal and literary evolution toward cosmopolitanism, and later in his career toward a liberal, rooted cosmopolitanism. I then focus on how his political positions became intertwined with his literature. I also discuss how his latest fictions reconceptualize both the historical and the Latin American historical novel. The second section is dedicated to the literary analysis of *El Paraíso en la otra esquina* and *El sueño del celta*, two historical novels that advocate in favour of liberal rooted cosmopolitanism, and in so doing, reflect his own political leanings. In the current world order of rising nationalisms, individualism, and exclusionary political projects, these two narratives focus on the role individuals play in the making of history, and they encourage readers to draw lessons from the lives of strong-minded individuals and develop empathy with their fellow human beings through contact with difference. As Vargas Llosa himself said, "la literatura es fuego" ("literature is fire"): it sparks the changes we ought to see in the world.

## A Literary Evolution Defined by Tensions

Born on 28 March 1936, in Arequipa, Peru, Vargas Llosa now holds Peruvian and Spanish citizenship, and is socially and politically active in both countries. He spent his childhood between Peru and Bolivia; in 1958, he moved to Spain, only to relocate to Paris, then considered the epicentre of the world of letters, two years later. He has been crossing the Atlantic back and forth since then. In 1990, he ran for president of the Republic of Peru, losing to Alberto Fujimori (1990–2000). Even after he defeated the author, Fujimori became one of the most vocal opponents of his writings and intellectualism, equally criticizing his supposed lack of Peruvianness and his liberalism. This is but an example of the rather tumultuous relationship Vargas Llosa has maintained with his birth country. In fact, Vargas Llosa has always been a bit removed from his native land: he is part of an elite that lived abroad for many years, and as a result he wrote most of his novels in Europe. As a cosmopolitan, he has always made a point of thinking beyond the local aspects of his community, yet his fiction incessantly revisits Peru, where he has also participated in highly local endeavours. He embodies Reyes's formulation, being highly universal, while still remaining deeply national. In Vargas Llosa's own words, "¡Qué extraordinario privilegio el de un país que no tiene una identidad porque las tiene todas!" ("Discurso Nobel" 6) ("What an extraordinary privilege for a country not to have an identity because it has all of them!"). For the author, it is not only possible, but necessary, to look further than the bounds of nationality.

Vargas Llosa's openness to other cultures expanded over the years: while his early works were usually set in Peru, they contained literary cosmopolitan features, in that he was clearly influenced by such writers as William Faulkner and James Joyce (American and Irish, respectively). The author's fictionalized settings then grew to encompass Latin America; and while they still showed many of the same features they also broached more universal topics. Finally, his recent works are permeated with cosmopolitanism and involve much broader settings—namely, through the exploration of literary characters and the problems generated by their cosmopolitan attitudes and values. This transition from a national to an international framework began with *La guerra del fin del mundo* (*The War of the End of the World*; 1981), which takes place in Brazil, and built up to *El sueño del celta* (2010). However, most of these international and cosmopolitan novels still involve Peru to varying degrees.

Vargas Llosa's interest in cosmopolitanism is an important feature of his entire body of work, as is his aversion to all forms of absolutism and extremism. Nationalism is one such extreme against which he has advocated the most. Throughout his career, in fiction, literary manifestos, essays, and newspaper articles, he has warned his readers against its dangers. Vargas Llosa believes "that nationalists should be intellectually and politically challenged, all of them, head on, without apology, and not in the name of a different type of nationalism . . . but on behalf of democratic culture and freedom" (*Wellsprings* 94). With this type of political positioning, he joins a long tradition of public intellectuals in Latin America, where novelists, especially those of his generation, have also had a significant political voice.

## Politics and Utopia

Vargas Llosa's political voice is as strong in his essays as it is in his works of fiction. At the time of its publication in 2003, *El Paraíso en la otra esquina* was considered one of his most cosmopolitan novels. Two narrative strands run concurrently through the narrative, that of social activist Flora Tristán, and that of her grandson, the painter Paul Gauguin; both characters choose to be citizens of the world in a period marked by the rise of nationalism and the creation of modern nation-states. They are thus defined by their global trajectories, from France to Peru in Tristán's case, and from Peru to France to French Polynesia in Gauguin's. Both are utopian visionaries who fail to bring their visions to life. *El sueño del celta*, for its part, presents the story of the nationalist drift of one of the greatest cosmopolitan figures of the early twentieth century, Sir Roger Casement. Unlike most of Vargas Llosa's narratives, which show the protagonist's shift from a local to a universal outlook, this last novel explores the transformation of one of the first global human rights champions into a fervent nationalist, if only for a short period of time. The novels, albeit in different ways, show that utopias—be they social or national ones—are bound to fail, with their proponents defeated by their own ideals. As Vargas Llosa has himself emphasized, "the search for Utopia . . . is liberating when pursued as an artistic vision, but leads to bloodshed, disaster and tragedy when it becomes a political project" ("Confessions of an Old Fashioned Liberal"). Although the three characters cannot be compared to Antonio Conselheiro in *La guerra del fin del mundo* (1981) in terms of deadly fanaticism, they do show an obstinacy that borders on religious fanaticism, and thus embody Vargas Llosa's criticism of extremes. Consequently, the outcome that meets each character is proportionate to the depth of their extremism. My reading shows that both novels also advance the notion of rooted cosmopolitanism as the best articulation of a universal consciousness and engagement.

A lot of attention has been given to the role of utopia in Vargas Llosa's works, whether in the form of nationalism or deadly fanaticism. In *Vargas Llosa among the Postmodernists* (1994), Keith M. Booker maintains that the author had, to date, shown "an opposition to fanaticism of any kind, a thoroughgoing skepticism about Utopian and apocalyptic visions of history . . . and a similar skepticism toward absolutes of all kinds" (183).

Vargas Llosa's later novels proved that this was not just a phase. However, in "Vargas Llosa's Leading Ladies," Lynn Walford claims that he does not display an outright contempt for utopian projects, "but [rather] a deep and troubled ambivalence toward them" (71). She cites as proof the fact that, unlike Conselheiro, whom Vargas Llosa calls "a wretched failure" (76), Flora Tristán—and I may add Roger Casement—"does not fade into oblivion" (77); indeed, they are shown respect by the author. Walford sees in Tristán's portrayal "the possibility—if not the promise—of redemption [which suggests] perhaps, that Vargas Llosa is adding yet another, more hopeful, dimension to his vision" (78). The same can be said of Roger Casement, who is offered a possibility of redemption by the narrative voice in the novel's epilogue. Taking this into account, I argue that Vargas Llosa has advocated, perhaps unconsciously, for rooted cosmopolitanism since his early novels, and, taking into consideration his well-known political positions, for liberal rooted cosmopolitanism.

Vargas Llosa's political positioning is one of the main reasons that led to the tumultuous relationship he has had with Peru since he moved to Spain in the 1970s. These tensions were exemplified again when he became the sixth Latin American author to win the Nobel Prize for Literature.[4] Even if it is a great honour for any nation to have one of its citizens receive the Nobel Prize in any discipline, the Nobel Foundation was harshly criticized by many Peruvians for awarding such a prestigious prize to an author they deemed insufficiently Peruvian. He nevertheless dedicated his Nobel to his home country and later stated that "El Perú soy yo aunque a algunos no les guste, Fujimori no me quería reconocer como peruano, lo que yo escribo es el Perú también" ("I am Peru even if some do not like it, Fujimori did not want to recognize me as Peruvian, what I write is Peru too"; "El Perú soy yo"). On multiple occasions, he has reiterated his view that, while Spain and France allowed him to become a writer, his Peruvian experience remains the primary material from which he draws inspiration.[5]

In his Nobel acceptance speech, Vargas Llosa addressed the issue of citizenship, as well as his contentious relationship with his birth country. He claimed that living abroad not only made him a citizen of the world, but also a better Peruvian: echoing other Boom authors, he said that "lo que más agradezco a Francia [es] el descubrimiento de América Latina"

("Discurso Nobel" 4) ("But perhaps I am most grateful to France for the discovery of Latin America"). In Europe, he discovered that his nation "era parte de una vasta comunidad a la que hermanaban la historia, la geografía, la problemática social y política, una cierta manera de ser y la sabrosa lengua en que hablaba y escribía" (4) ("was part of a vast community united by history, geography, social and political problems, a certain mode of being, and the delicious language it spoke and wrote"), thus first developing a continental understanding of the region. Abroad, he also read writers who were revolutionizing literature and speaking "un lenguaje universal" (4) ("a universal language")—here he mentions Borges, Paz, Cortázar, García Márquez, Fuentes, Cabrera Infante, Rulfo, Onetti, Carpentier, Edwards, and Donoso. Through these writers stereotypes about Latin America were broken. Vargas Llosa described feeling at home wherever he went, and admits that travel and living abroad have brought him to great discoveries, to the extent that he came to embody the very idea of cosmopolitanism, being open to other cultures while also embracing his own. In the speech, Vargas Llosa pointed out that becoming a global citizen was never a conscious goal, and that it has never meant forgetting his home country. On the contrary, being at a distance from Peru has given him the critical perspective necessary to better tackle issues affecting his country:

> Creo que vivir tanto tiempo fuera del país donde nací ha fortalecido más bien aquellos vínculos, añadiéndoles una perspectiva más lúcida, y la nostalgia, que sabe diferenciar lo adjetivo y lo sustancial y mantiene reverberando los recuerdos. El amor al país en que uno nació no puede ser obligatorio, sino, al igual que cualquier otro amor, un movimiento espontáneo del corazón, como el que une a los amantes, a padres e hijos, a los amigos entre sí.

> I believe instead that living for so long outside the country where I was born has strengthened those connections, adding a more lucid perspective to them, and a nostalgia that can differentiate the adjectival from the substantive and keep memories reverberating. Love of the country where one was

born cannot be obligatory, but like any other love must be a spontaneous act of the heart, like the one that unites lovers, parents and children, and friends. (5)

Peru, then, is a part of him, whether his detractors believe he embodies the country well enough or not. His life and his work are shaped both by Peru and by his time abroad.

## The Way to (Liberal) Rooted Cosmopolitanism

One of Vargas Llosa's first novels to gain international fame—*La tía Julia y el escribidor* (*Aunt Julia and the Scriptwriter*), a work of autofiction published in 1977—delves into the tensions between the cosmopolitan and nationalist tendencies of the Latin American writer. In the novel, Vargas Llosa articulates, through his literary alter ego Varguitas, the type of author he aspires to become—namely, one who evolves in a more sophisticated and worldly literary system than the one he knows in Latin America. *La tía Julia y el escribidor* indicates a very conscious understanding of world literature, as well as a clearly articulated goal of living in Europe. This hints at the fact that while he did not plan to be a world citizen, Vargas Llosa always thought of literature in worldly terms, and wanted to be part of that cosmopolitan community.

The novel recounts the story of Mario (alternatively referred to as Marito or Varguitas), a twenty-something law student, radio newswriter, and short-story writer in the making, as he falls in love with his aunt by marriage, *la tía* Julia. The novel is divided into twenty-two chapters: the odd-numbered ones concentrate on Marito's life, while the even-numbered ones are soap opera scripts written by Pedro Camacho, *el escribidor*. Varguitas dreams of going to Paris, the cosmopolitan space par excellence, and of living in the world of letters. He hopes that distancing himself from his native land will open up new horizons, as well as allow him to develop a new perspective. The young Varguitas moves to Europe and makes a name for himself, while Camacho remains in Peru and goes mad, a consequence of being trapped in his national setting.

Once famous, the accomplished cosmopolitan narrator switches his name from Marito or Varguitas to Vargas Llosa. Looking back on his years in Latin America, he states that "el problema era que todo lo que escribía se refería al Perú. Eso me creaba, cada vez más, un problema de inseguridad, por el desgaste de la perspectiva (tenía la manía de la ficción *realista*)" (*La tía Julia y el escribidor* 473) ("The problem was that everything I wrote had to do with life in Peru. As time and distance began to blur my perspective, I felt more and more insecure about my writing [at the time I was obsessed with the idea that fiction should be 'realistic' "]; *Aunt Julia and the Scriptwriter* 359[6]). This *manía*, or obsession, was a characteristic of Vargas Llosa's early fiction, which explored Peruvian issues. However, in overcoming this obsession, the Peruvian author set the tone for the ever-expanding cosmopolitan concerns that would come to mark his oeuvre. Indeed, even if "el Perú [le] ha parecido siempre un país de gentes tristes" (473) ("Peru had always seemed to me a country of sad people"; 359), Varguitas makes a point of being able to go home at least once a year: "Para esa época, tenía un trato con una revista de Lima, a la que yo enviaba artículos y ella me pagaba con pasajes que me permitían volver todos los años al Perú por algunas semanas. Estos viajes, gracias a los cuales veía a la familia y a los amigos, eran para mí muy importantes" (472) ("In those days I had an arrangement with a magazine in Lima: I sent it articles and in return received a plane ticket that allowed me to come back to Peru every year for a few weeks. These trips, thanks to which I saw my family and friends, were very important to me"; 359). His creativity is tied to Peru, but only Europe allows him to live off his writings—the best of both worlds. As Varguitas explains,

> Ese mes que pasábamos en el Perú, cada año, generalmente en el invierno (julio o agosto) me permitía zambullirme en el ambiente, los paisajes, los seres sobre los cuales había estado tratando de escribir los once meses anteriores. Me era enormemente útil (no sé si en los hechos, pero sin la menor duda psicológicamente), una inyección de energía, volver a oír hablar peruano, escuchar a mi alrededor esos giros, vocablos, entonaciones que me reinstalaban en un medio al que me sentía visceralmente próximo, pero del que, de todos modos, me había alejado, del que cada año perdía innovaciones, resonancias, claves" (473).

> That month that Patricia and I spent in Peru each year, usually in winter (July or August), enabled me to steep myself in the atmosphere, the landscapes, the lives of the people that I had been trying to write about in the previous eleven months. It was tremendously useful to me (I don't know if it was true in purely material terms, but certainly it was true psychologically), a kind of "energy injection," to hear Peruvian spoken again, to hear all round me those turns of phrase, expressions, intonations that put me back in the midst of a milieu I felt viscerally close to but had nonetheless moved far away from, thus missing out each year on the innovations, losing overtones, resonances, keys. (360)

Herein also lies a defining tension in Vargas Llosa's body of work, present from early on: both Europe and Peru are absolutely necessary for him to produce strong narratives. This conception of literature triggered his embrace of political cosmopolitanism, both thematically and philosophically.

When the young Varguitas, who had always longed for and idealized Paris, arrives at the centre of the world republic of letters with the stated objective of fulfilling his destiny of becoming a writer, he also, ironically, learns about his cultural roots. His aesthetic cosmopolitanism evolves into a broader vision now encompassing world politics. This tension, which has been present from the very beginning—at least in literary terms—is, as we shall see, now more broadly defined as a main feature of Vargas Llosa's current writing. He discovered his true identity—wordly yet national—while abroad, and it expanded to a full embrace of the notion of global citizenship.

### Liberal Cosmopolitanism

Vargas Llosa's novels are set in a wide range of places, and as mentioned earlier, he has not hesitated to make cosmopolitanism a central theme of his later fiction. He overtly acknowledges and discusses the challenges of this position in many essays and newspaper pieces, as is to be expected of one of the most politically engaged and active Latin American authors of his generation; indeed, running for president was a logical step in his social involvement.

The impact of Vargas Llosa's political views on his corpus is so strong that, according to literary scholar Efraín Kristal, his work can be divided into three major cycles: 1) the pro-Cuban phase; 2) the refutation of Cuba's politics; and 3) the embrace of open capitalism and free markets. This third phase coincides with his most cosmopolitan works, written as the borders of nation-states were becoming porous and the very notion of the state deemed archaic. Although Kristal's three-part division appears logical enough, it only takes into consideration the novels published before 2012.[7]

While Kristal uses the term "capitalism" to refer to the third phase, Vargas Llosa discusses, in various interviews, his adherence to liberalism as opposed to neo-liberalism. In fact, both supporters and detractors have described his cosmopolitanism as liberal. Vargas Llosa himself is very open about his political views, and has linked his conversion to this approach to his second reading of French thinker Albert Camus—who was very critical of all sorts of revolutions—as he was drifting away from the Latin American Left in the 1970s.[8]

While classical liberalism espouses liberty and equality, two tenets of human dignity, neo-liberalism, articulated in the 1950s as the Cold War began, emphasized economic policy over other aspects of the nineteenth-century philosophy, and "argued that inequality was a positive value—in reality necessary" (Anderson qtd. in De Castro and Birns 51) for the world to develop properly. Although he has been branded as a neo-liberal both by the adherents and detractors of that label, Vargas Llosa does not meet the definition in the strictest sense of the term, for he has always advocated in favour of equality. In my view, his intellectual trajectory shows that he reoriented his political affiliations and intellectual philosophy after the so-called Padilla Affair in 1971, in which Cuban poet Heberto Padilla was imprisoned for criticizing the government.

Vargas Llosa does not disavow his past allegiances, but he is very critical of the young man he once was. In his George Lengvari Sr. Lecture, delivered in 2013 and entitled *My Intellectual Itinerary: From Marxism to Liberalism*, he recalls his teenage and young adult years as a series of discoveries and disappointments that led to his espousal of liberalism.[9] He recounts how the military dictatorships that plagued most of Latin America during the 1950s and '60s, and the social inequalities that arose from years of poor government, pushed him "toward radicalism, toward extremism" (39). In the speech he is extremely self-aware, admitting that because of the historical and social circumstances in which he came of age, it could not have been otherwise. He uses the expressions "enormous enthusiasm" (39) to describe his first steps into Marxism, says that he "became completely infatuated" (39), even calling himself "very Stalinist" (41). He shared, it seems, the same blindness to the dangers of extremisms and absolutism he now blames some of his characters for; in retrospect, he appears to forgive his younger self for having fallen into "this romantic underground way" (41), a characteristic attribute of collectivist ideologies. It soon became clear, however, that he was not suited to communist circles, since they constrained his creativity: "So I couldn't remain with the communists much longer. They were really extremely dogmatic and I felt imprisoned in something that I couldn't share 100%" (42). This rejection of dogmatic beliefs, in line with his much-admired Camus, is still at the forefront of Vargas Llosa's philosophy.

The Cuban Revolution of 1959 marked a turning point for young intellectuals in Latin America: while most of them rejected communism, they still believed in socialism, only to be disappointed some years later when the dictatorial tendencies of the Castro regime became apparent. Once again, Vargas Llosa expresses his regrets at having been fooled by his own enthusiasm (15). A trip to the Soviet Union in 1966 was "the most terrible political disappointment that I have had in my life" and the Padilla Affair marked his break with collectivist ideologies; he even says that the years spent reading about Marxism were wasted (17). His disillusion with socialism brought him to the works of Isaiah Berlin and Karl Popper, two liberal thinkers who shaped his thinking from then on.

Vargas Llosa's 2005 Irving Kristol Lecture, entitled "Confessions of an Old Fashioned Liberal," expresses his liberal tendencies in an even more open fashion. In it, he directly addresses his long-standing political affiliations, as well as the various problems that arose out of his outspokenness about such philosophical positions. He begins by thanking the American Enterprise Institute for Public Policy Research for allowing him to be seen "as a unified being, the man who writes and thinks," rather than simply a writer or essayist, the usual dichotomy proposed by scholars who admire his fictions but despise his political positions. He laments that the term "liberal" has become a dirty word, especially in Latin America, one used "to exorcize or discredit" him, a variation of the criticism about his lack of national allegiance.

Vargas Llosa understands liberalism as a philosophy, not an ideology, with numerous ramifications, and argues that there are as many liberalisms as there are liberals. He defines himself as a liberal in the strictest sense of the term: "a lover of liberty, a person who rises up against oppression," one for whom "the free market is the best mechanism in existence for producing riches and, if well complemented with other institutions and uses of democratic culture, launches the material progress of a nation to the spectacular heights with which we are familiar." At first glance, this could fit the standard definition of neo-liberalism. However, as does his *maître à penser* Isaiah Berlin, Vargas Llosa advocates in favour of the free market because it brings economic progress, as long as this progress does not harm society. In fact, if inequalities are created, individual freedom is affected, since not everyone has access to the same opportunities; this goes against his vision ("La corrección política es enemiga de la libertad"). Individual liberties, as well as the free movement of people and goods, are two key elements of Vargas Llosa's liberalism. The liberal he "aspire[s] to be considers freedom a core value"; in that he concords with most liberals.

Even if Vargas Llosa calls himself a liberal, I propose that his positioning is also based on cosmopolitanism, inasmuch as it echoes the very premise of Appiah's conceptualization of contemporary cosmopolitanism. Indeed, Vargas Llosa expresses his liberalism as a commitment to others deeply rooted in tolerance and understanding: "Basically, [liberalism] is tolerance and respect for others, and especially for those who think differently from ourselves, who practice other customs and worship another god or who are non-believers. By agreeing to live with those who are different, human beings took the most extraordinary step on the road to civilization" ("Confessions of an Old Fashioned Liberal"). He went further in his George Lengvari Sr. Lecture when he said that "This kind of openness is, I think, the essential virtue of liberalism, and that is the reason why liberalism is the roots of civilization" ("My Intellectual Itinerary" 50). This resonates with Appiah's conceptualization of two major strands of cosmopolitanism, as well as his understanding that a cosmopolitan is someone who is willing to be open to difference. Vargas Llosa maintains that "We should coexist in diversity" (51). His liberalism coexists with globalization. In his Irving Kristol Lecture, Vargas Llosa says that he believes that "the inter-dependence of nations in a world in which borders, once solid and inexpugnable, have become porous and increasingly faint" is unavoidable ("Confessions of an Old Fashioned Liberal"). The disappearance of borders is the premise of global governance as proposed by liberal cosmopolitanism. He concludes with a sharp articulation of his position as a liberal cosmopolitan: "We dream, as novelists tend to do: a world stripped of fanatics, terrorists and dictators, a world of different cultures, races, creeds and traditions, co-existing in peace thanks to the culture of freedom, in which borders have become bridges that men and women can cross in pursuit of their goals with no other obstacle than their supreme free will." What Vargas Llosa expresses here as a dream is close to the actual definition of liberal cosmopolitanism, which, along with uniting the world into one single entity, "wishes to overcome absolute states' rights through the development of a global order governing the internal as well as the external behaviour of states" through the growth of transnational organizations (Gowan 2). The step from liberalism to liberal cosmopolitanism was a logical one. Vargas Llosa argues that people should be as free as things to move around—no frontiers for people—which is a very cosmopolitan attitude.

## Characters Making History

History is another lens through which to view Vargas Llosa's works. In the article "Mario Vargas Llosa et le démon de l'histoire—Entre histoire et narration" (Mario Vargas Llosa and the Demon of History—Between History and Narration), Christian Giudicelli argues that, although it has been thoroughly studied, setting is not everything in Vargas Llosa's oeuvre.[10] He argues that history should be used to assess the novelist's evolution, claiming that "Quarante années d'écriture soulignent une sorte de constance, le retour régulier de l'Histoire et une tendance marquée à transformer l'historique en narratif" ("Forty years of writing reveal a constant of sorts: the perpetual reappearance of History and a marked tendency to transform the historic into narrative"; 189). This *tendance marquée* ("marked tendency") is a feature not only of Vargas Llosa's works, but more broadly of Latin American authors of his generation. The fact that Vargas Llosa has written many historical novels is unsurprising, considering that it is a literary genre that has been, and still is, particularly dominant in Latin America. However, his historical novels do not fit neatly into either Georg Lukács's definition of the classical historical novel or Seymour Menton's assessment of its postmodern evolution in Latin America.

In *The Historical Novel* (1955), Lukács defines the genre as pedagogical in nature, in that it makes the reader reflect on a historical past and seeks a certain degree of accuracy: it "has to *demonstrate* by *artistic* means that historical circumstances and characters existed in precisely such-and-such a way" (43). The best way to tell a story in an authentic manner is to do it through a secondary character that did not partake in the historical events being recounted, and to avoid romanticizing these characters (42). Marginalized secondary characters are then the vessel of the narration; they see history happen before their eyes, but are not part of it—they only witness it. In Lukács's understanding, historical novels are humanist by nature, since they teach and educate readers about different historical contexts.

In *Latin America's New Historical Novel* (1993), Menton rearticulated Lukács's theories of the classical historical novel to elaborate a view that would be specific to the contemporary production of Latin America.[11] According to Menton, the publication of Alejo Carpentier's *El reino de este mundo* (*The Kingdom of this World*) in 1949 marked the emergence of this new historical novel. Its main characteristics include "the subordination . . . of the mimetic recreation of a given historical period to the illustration of . . . philosophical ideas." According to Menton, "these ideas are a) the impossibility of ascertaining the true nature of reality or history; b) the cyclical nature of history; and c) the unpredictability of history." This includes "the conscious distortion of history through omissions, exaggerations, and anachronisms" and "the utilization of famous historical characters as protagonists" (22–3).[12] This new articulation, then, differs from Lukács's since the historical context is distorted to fit the needs of the author—not everything is perfectly accurate, as in Lukács's formulation—and the protagonists are actual historical characters, not bystanders who watch as history is being made. Nevertheless, most of the characters do not actively try to change the course of history.

For Giudicelli, two major cycles can be observed in Vargas Llosa's body of work, and contrary to what Kristal claims, they are not delineated politically. "Avec le recul des ans," he maintains, "on peut constater que sa production romanesque oscille entre deux pôles principaux, le roman dans l'histoire immédiate ou le roman à la recherche de l'histoire en tant que flot événementiel connu et constitué" ("looking back over the years, we can see that his literary production oscillates between two main poles, the novel set within immediate history, or the novel in search of history as a known and constituted stream"; "Mario Vargas Llosa et le démon de l'histoire" 190). On the one hand, works such as *Historia de Mayta* (*The Real Life of Alejandro Mayta*; 1984) or *Lituma en los Andes* (*Death in the Andes*; 1993) "s'enracin[ent] dans le présent de leur énonciation" ("are rooted in the present of their enunciation"; 190); although not necessarily historical novels in the strictest sense of the definition, it could be argued that they make good use of the historical materials available to the author. On the other, *La guerra del fin del mundo* (1981) or *La fiesta del Chivo* (*The Feast of the Goat*; 2000) reflect on the historical past, using it as a means to improve the historical narrative, since, as Vargas Llosa has explained, "la literatura cuenta la historia que la historia que escriben los historiadores no sabe ni puede contar" ("Literature recounts the history that the history written by the historians would not know how, or be able, to write"; *La verdad de las mentiras* 14, "The Truth of Lies" 326). Literature, then, is a means to counter *las insuficiencias de la historia* ("the insufficiencies of history"). Historical fictions are not less true than historiography; they only present a different version of the past.

Now that the political and ideological underpinnings of Mario Vargas Llosa's oeuvre have been established, we can explore how this understanding applies to specific novels. Both *El Paraíso en la otra esquina* and *El sueño del celta* are set in the historical past; they also present cosmopolitan characters with ties to Peru who become aware of the depth of their cosmopolitan vision while in the country. Although the narratives are set in the past, the ideas explored are contemporary; the remoteness of history and the proximity of contemporary ideas are intertwined. This also reveals an interest on the part of the author in retelling the past to engage with the present through the perspective of past lives and trajectories. The wave of globalization at the end of the twentieth century triggered novels about internationalism, nationalism, and cosmopolitanism; yet, these novels never propose a solution to the problems they highlight. *El Paraíso en la otra esquina* and *El sueño del celta* also present their characters at a point in their lives when all hope is lost, implying that the utopia of cosmopolitanism is hard to achieve in reality. As long as the characters are striving to embody the philosophical implications of the concept without also understanding its inherent limitations, they are bound to fail. Both novels present their characters as death is closing in on them: "cette dernière étape d'une vie à chaque fois consacrée à un enjeu qui la dépasse est présentée comme une *course à la mort*" ("this final act of a life devoted to a greater cause is presented every time as *a race toward death*"; Lefort 67), meaning that the three protagonists—Flora Tristán, Paul Gauguin, and Roger Casement—are trying to cheat death to attain their goals.

The two novels I analyze in this chapter are also, to date, two of Vargas Llosa's more explicit explorations of cosmopolitanism; it is no coincidence, then, that both are historical novels. It would appear that this is his chosen genre for portraying extremism, and to address philosophical ideas—in this case the cosmopolitan question and its intricacies. Indeed, these novels openly grapple with global concerns and depict characters who are actively trying to undo either the patriarchy or the colonial legacy. They also concentrate on travelling, and how travel can awaken a passion for one's fellow human beings and broaden one's horizons. Venturing outside a known culture and historical circumstances leads to envisioning other possibilities, expanding horizons, and embracing a desire to change how we engage with our culture and the wider world. In Vargas Llosa's narratives, cosmopolitanism is acquired abroad but realized at home. Interestingly, this mirrors his own trajectory, as portrayed in *La tía Julia y el escribidor*.

## Cosmopolitanism and Internationalism in *El Paraíso en la otra esquina*

*El Paraíso en la otra esquina* presents cosmopolitanism as a grounded utopia; it is fuelled by dreams of change, but nevertheless bound to disappoint. The novel spans the nineteenth century, ranging from France to French Polynesia, and tells the story of two historical figures that left a mark in their respective spheres: the social activist Flora Tristan, who worked toward a proletarian remapping of the world order, and her grandson, the painter Paul Gauguin, who, paradoxically, needed to escape European decadence in order to create European art.[13] In a narration reminiscent of Plutarch's *Parallel Lives*, *El Paraíso en la otra esquina* interweaves the destinies of these two characters, draws parallels between them, and highlights certain paradoxes. Born into wealth, Tristán's life turns into a nightmare when her father dies when she is a young child, leaving her and her mother penniless and forced to fend for themselves. At a young age, Tristán must therefore start to work. Eventually, she marries her boss, André Chazal, a man who shows little respect for his wife and children. Outraged by this treatment, and most of all by the fact that it is not punishable by law, she abandons her husband and two daughters to travel to Peru in search of her ancestors. Her ultimate goal is to secure an allowance for herself and her daughters—although she does not tell her family in Peru, for that might hurt her chances. Rejected by her Peruvian family, she returns to France, and motivated by all the hardships she has faced, turns to social activism. In fact, it is her Peruvian experience that cements her social commitment, and awakens her to the possibility of social activism and proletarian internationalism.

One of Flora Tristán's daughters is the mother of Paul Gauguin, the son who, in spite of a flourishing career as a stockbroker, turns to art. Like his grandmother, Gauguin also has strong ties to Peru; at an early age, his family migrates to the country from France to escape social unrest. Years later, upon returning to France, he would refer to this period of his life as the first time he felt like a "savage," a primitive state he believed he needed in order to paint. It is at the moment when Gauguin is dedicated to his true passion—painting—that he experiences the greatest changes: to fulfill his drive to create groundbreaking art, he travels to several parts of Europe, including the southern French city of Arles, where he lives with his friend, the painter Vincent Van Gogh; he finally settles in Polynesia, where he produces most of his paintings. Both Flora and her grandson Paul are passionate beings who fight for their ideals, but while Flora's main opponents are patriarchal society and the general apathy of workers, Paul enjoys a life full of love and passion in his search for pure art.

The novel is divided into twenty-two chapters; the odd-numbered ones are dedicated to Flora Tristán, while the even-numbered ones concentrate on Paul Gauguin. This symmetrical structure allows for the parallel evolution of both characters, and for Gauguin to refer to his grandmother's work and compare it to his own. Tristán's story starts in Auxerre, France, in 1844, Gauguin's in Mataiea, French Polynesia, in 1892; both their lives are recounted through various flashbacks and memories. An omniscient narrator recounts the story, but the narration is frequently altered by the interruptions of a second-person narrator. Interpretations vary as to what purpose these breaks serve: the ambivalent use of *tú* could either be the internal voices of the characters talking to themselves, or a highly informal way for the narrative voice to address the characters. Either way, it fosters intimacy, and some insight into Tristán's and Gauguin's thinking processes, as well as the narrator's positioning vis-à-vis either of them; the reader gets to see their minds at work.[14] During these short moments, the reader gains insight into the characters' thoughts. In this way, that narrative voice is part of an ongoing dialogue with Tristán and Gauguin: it questions their choice of actions or expresses outright disapproval; it is sometimes a voice of reason, but also an empathetic and often consoling one.

Current articulations of cosmopolitanism emphasize that any cosmopolitan individual belongs first and foremost to a nation. Cosmopolitanism, then, is a dual stance between one's nation and one's desire to reach out to the world. Isaac Sanzana Inzunza describes two kinds of cosmopolitanism: a formal, universalist one and an imagined one. He holds that there is a significant discrepancy between this first type, which is grounded in philosophy, and possible cosmopolitanism, which he describes as "aleatorio, propio a las culturas, esto es, interculturalista" ("accidental, pertaining to cultures, in other words, intercultural"). In sum, the latter form might be termed concrete cosmopolitanism: "La metáfora adecuada para representar este tipo de cosmopolitismo, sería la del 'viaje' (en el sentido clásico y estricto). . . . El viaje que proponemos es aquel que siempre implica cambios, transfiguraciones, encuentros y aprendizajes" ("The most appropriate metaphor to represent this type of cosmopolitanism would be that of travel [in the classic and strict sense]. . . . The travel that we propose is one that always implies change, transfiguration, encounters and learning"; 2). By contrast, the first type of cosmopolitanism—formal and universalist—is closely related to utopia, and hence can only exist in the realm of ideas. However, concrete cosmopolitanism, constructed by travels and encounters, is within reach of individuals with an open mind. While Tristán's and Gauguin's cosmopolitan stances are widely acknowledged, few scholars have explored the complexities of the characters' quests around the globe.

Tristán's and Gauguin's search for a utopian location and their cosmopolitan outlook, as well as their contributions to a revolution in, respectively, socialist politics and modern art, have been widely noted, although not systematically studied. For instance, in "Cosmopolitismo y hospitalidad en *El Paraíso en la otra esquina*, de Mario Vargas Llosa" ("Cosmopolitanism and Hospitality in Mario Vargas Llosa's *The Way to Paradise*"), Ricardo Gutiérrez Mouat states that the characters, as portrayed in the novel, are cosmopolitan individuals who have travelled and explored the world, and are a source of change in their milieu. Nevertheless, he posits that their differences lie in the type of cosmopolitanism they display: Tristán embodies what he calls *cosmopolitismo de la igualdad* ("a cosmopolitanism of equality") while her narrative counterpart, Gauguin, thrives on *cosmopolitismo de la diferencia* ("a cosmopolitanism of difference"). They share not only certain cosmopolitan traits, but also a longing for utopia that culminates in their demise. While the social militant is pursuing a utopian ideal, concretely rooted in a form of cosmopolitan socialism, the painter is looking for a lost paradise, the search for which leads him to the edge of colonialism and nationalism, stances he once despised. However, in my view, it is Tristán's engagement with other cultures that underscores, to use Gutiérrez Mouat's proposition, her *cosmopolitismo de la igualdad*. But unlike Gutiérrez Mouat, I contend that she also exhibits *cosmopolitismo de la diferencia*. During her travels to Peru, she becomes cosmopolitan through acknowledging difference, and also through interacting with such difference, be it with strong female military figures such as the Mariscala, her own extended family, or Peruvians in general. Only then, after this close contact with difference, does she embrace cosmopolitanism. In this, Tristán undergoes a major transformation: from a young, rather self-centred woman, to a strong promoter of equality between cultures, genders, and classes. Gauguin, by this measure, is not cosmopolitan at all.

The quest for a perfect place arises from the outset with the very title of the novel. The title "viene de un juego de niños que existe prácticamente en todas partes del mundo, aunque con pequeñas variantes. Los niños buscan un lugar que es imposible de encontrar, es como un espejismo que desaparece cuando uno se va a acercar a él" ("comes from a child's game that exists practically everywhere in the world, although with small variations. Children search for a place that is impossible to find, it is like a mirage that disappears whenever one begins to approach it"; Vargas Llosa qtd. in Camín). Vargas Llosa's explanation highlights that this search for paradise is universal but doomed, as he acknowledges that paradise can never be found where one seeks it. Ultimately, the title implies that there is no way that such a perfect place can be reached, since it is bound to recede as the seeker approaches. From the outset, *el juego del paraíso* appears as the leitmotif for both characters.

Flora remembers playing the game as a child in Vaugirard, France, in the mansion where she was born, and later witnessing it in Arequipa as an adult:

> Cuando regresaba al albergue por las callecitas curvas y adoquinadas de Auxerre, vio . . . a un grupo de niñas que jugaban . . . al Paraíso, ese juego que, según tu madre, habías jugado en los jardines de Vaugirard con amiguitas de la vecindad. . . . ¿Te acordabas, Florita? «¿Es aquí el Paraíso?» «No, señorita, en la otra esquina.» . . . Recordó la impresión de aquel día en Arequipa, el año 1833, cerca de la iglesia de la Merced, cuando, de pronto, se encontró con un grupo de niños y niñas que correteaban en el zaguán de una casa profunda. «¿Es aquí el Paraíso?» «En la otra esquina, mi señor.» Ese juego que creías francés resultó también peruano. Bueno, qué tenía de raro, ¿no era una aspiración universal llegar al Paraíso? (Vargas Llosa, *Paraíso* 18–19)

> As she was returning to the inn along the winding cobbled streets of Auxerre, she saw . . . a group of girls playing . . . the game called Paradise, which, according to your mother, you used to play in the gardens of Vaugirard with other

little girls from the neighborhood. . . . Did you remember, Florita? "Is this the way to Paradise?" "No, miss, try the next corner." . . . She remembered the surprise she felt one day in Arequipa in 1883, near the church of La Merced, when all of a sudden she came upon a group of boys and girls running around the courtyard of a big house. "Is this the way to Paradise?" "Try the next corner, sir." The game you thought was French turned out to be Peruvian too. And why not? Didn't everyone dream of reaching Paradise? (*The Way to Paradise* 11)[15]

Paul, two generations later, also remembers the game, to which he is exposed on various occasions during his life, among others in Arequipa, as a child, and shortly before his death, in the Marquesas Islands:

Pero inmediatamente adivinó qué juego era ése, qué preguntaba la niña «de castigo» saltando de una a otra compañerita del círculo y cómo era rechazada siempre con el mismo estribillo:

—¿Es aquí el Paraíso?

—No, señorita, aquí no. Vaya y pregunte en la otra esquina.

. . . Por segunda vez en el día, sus ojos se llenaron de lágrimas. . . . ¿Por qué te enternecía descubrir que estas niñas marquesanas jugaban al juego del Paraíso, ellas también? Porque, viéndolas, la memoria te devolvió . . . tu propia imagen . . . correteando también, como niño «de castigo», en el centro de un círculo de primitas y primitos y niños . . . preguntando en tu español limeño, «¿Es aquí el Paraíso?», «No, en la otra esquina, señor, pregunte allá.» (466–7)

But he immediately guessed what game it was, and what the girl in the middle asked as she skipped from one child to the other in the circle, and was always rebuffed with the same refrain.

"Is this the way to Paradise?"

"No, miss, go and ask on the next corner."

. . . For the second time that day, his eyes filled with tears. . . . Why did it move you to discover that these Marquesan girls played the game called Paradise, too? Because seeing them, a picture had formed in your memory . . . of yourself . . . also running back and forth in the center of a circle of cousins and children . . . asking in your Limeñan Spanish, "Is this the way to Paradise?" "No, try the next corner, sir; ask there." (435–6)

Ultimately, the universality of the game—"no era una aspiración universal llegar al Paraíso?" (19) ("Didn't everyone dream of reaching Paradise?"; 11)—poses the leitmotif of the novel as the universal search for the unattainable, and the ensuing engagement with cultures around the world to find it. This quest for the impossible is reminiscent of Thomas More's *Utopia* (1516), in which he describes a remote yet paradisiacal island on which a perfect society—that is, an alternative to the one he knew—has come to exist. Naturally, this non-place embodies an intrinsic ambivalence: it is utopian because it is longed for, but as soon as it can be grasped its perfection is bound to fade. Utopia, or *el Paraíso*, then, is an aspiration for a better life, which cannot be achieved.

As mentioned earlier, utopia and cosmopolitanism appear to be accessible by travel; it is, then, of the utmost importance to understand the evolution of the novel's protagonists. Through a double narration that alternates from one dreamer to the other, *El Paraíso en la otra esquina* presents two characters who are polar opposites yet who are defined by their trajectories around the globe. They share similar experiences with regards to their travels, which have shaped them into who they are. Accordingly, they have an interest in the foreign: "Por lo menos en eso coincidías con las locuras internacionalistas de la abuela Flora, Koke. Dónde se nacía era un accidente; la verdadera patria uno la elegía, con su cuerpo y su alma" (151). ("In that respect you shared your grandmother Flora's internationalist manias, Koké. A person's birthplace was an accident; his true homeland he chose himself, body and spirit"; 135).[16] Even if they express it and live it in radically different manners, their trajectories are intrinsically cosmopolitan.

In Varga Llosa's novel, Tristán's character undergoes a transformative experience that leads her from Eurocentrism to cosmopolitanism. However good they turn out to be, at first her actions are not those of a true cosmopolitan individual, but rather the result of her direct contact with other cultures. Indeed, when she travels to Arequipa in 1833–34 to meet with her grandfather, Don Pío de Tristán, she does so because her life in France has become a nightmare. Separated from her husband, and alone with her children, she has no permanent place to live and is forced to tell everyone she meets that she is a widow for fear that she will be forced to send the children back to their father. In 1829, she meets Captain Zacharie Chabrié, who later helps her contact her Peruvian family. That same year, she sends a letter to Don Pío de Tristán y Moscoco, her paternal uncle, asking him for financial assistance. He grants her a monthly allowance but refuses categorically to give her the inheritance she deems to be hers, since there is no document proving that she is the legitimate daughter of Don Mariano de Tristán. Furious, she then starts planning her journey to Peru, during which she hopes to convince her family of her birthright. She idealizes the voyage to her father's land, hoping that her grandfather will recognize her as a true Tristán and grant the inheritance. She longs for

> [el] encuentro [con sus] parientes paternos, con la esperanza de que, además de recibir[la] con los brazos abiertos y dar[le] un nuevo hogar, [le] entregaran el quinto de la herencia de [su] padre. Así se resolverían todos [sus] problemas económicos, saldría de la pobreza, podría educar a [sus] hijos y tener una existencia tranquila, a salvo de necesidades y de riesgos, sin temor de caer en las garras de André Chazal. (176)

> the meeting with [her] father's family, [she] hoped that not only would they welcome [her] with open arms and give [her] a new home, they would turn over to [her] a fifth part of [her] father's fortune. Then all [her] money problems would be solved, [she] would no longer be poor, [she] could educate [her] children and lead a peaceful life free of want and risk, and never again fear falling into the clutches of André Chazal. (158)

Accordingly, her trip to Latin America is motivated by her critical financial situation. To convince her family to fund her travels, she even omits key information about herself—namely, her marital situation and the very existence of her three young children. She rightfully fears that her plans would be doomed before she even leaves France. During her stay in the land of her father, she visits orphanages and convents, and becomes aware of other people's poverty and dire situations. She is also inspired to change the social order, and specifically the status of women, by Doña Francisca Zubiaga de Gamarra, also known as La Mariscala (the Lady Marshal), the wife of President Augustín Gamarra, "un personaje cuya aureola de aventura y leyenda [la] fascinó desde que [oyó] hablar de ella por primera vez" (273) (a woman who "possessed an aura of adventure and legend that had fascinated you ever since you first heard talk of her"; 249). La Mariscala becomes her role model, the kind she never had in France. Her short stay in Lima exposes Tristán to more of the world than she would have thought possible, and awakens her to new realities:

> Curiosa ciudad esta capital del Perú, que, pese a tener sólo unos ochenta mil pobladores, no podía ser más cosmopolita. Por sus callecitas cortadas por acequias donde los vecinos echaban las basuras y vaciaban sus bacinicas, se paseaban marineros de barcos anclados en el Callao procedentes de medio mundo, ingleses, norteamericanos, holandeses, franceses, alemanes, asiáticos, de modo que, cada vez que salía a visitar los innumerables conventos e iglesias coloniales, o a dar vueltas a la Plaza Mayor, costumbre sa-

> grada de los elegantes, Flora oía a su alrededor más idiomas que en los bulevares de París. (318)

> An odd city this Peruvian capital. Though its population was only eighty thousand, it could not have been more cosmopolitan. Along its little streets, intersected by channels into which residents tossed their refuse and emptied their chamberpots, there passed sailors from ships anchored in the harbor of Callao, hailing from all over the world—English, Americans, Dutch, French, Germans, Orientals—so that when Flora went outside to visit the countless colonial monasteries, and churches, or walk around the Plaza Mayor, a sacred pastime of the well-dressed, she heard more languages than she had on the boulevards of Paris. (291–2)

At that point in her life Tristán understands Lima as a cosmopolitan city, and even a global one, because it is a crossroads where cultures meet and interact. In this sense, she has yet to fully add all the social layers to her cosmopolitan commitment. She develops a cosmopolitan outlook in Peru—the European becomes cosmopolitan in Latin America, thus embodying the true spirit of unprejudiced discovery and opening. In fact, Peru's capital is her first cosmopolitan school.[17]

This scene is reminiscent of modern globalization, further reinforcing my contention that Vargas Llosa's rearticulation of the historical novel is triggered by discussions about globalization, world government, and nationalist backlashes. Here, the reader can infer that Lima is used as a metaphor for the current world order. Lima is not only cosmopolitan; it is also a vision of liberal Peru in the nineteenth century—a period of openness to commerce and foreign influence.[18]

In Peru, Tristán discovers otherness and equality, and it is her engagement with other cultures that leads her to develop both her *cosmopolitismo de la igualdad* and her *cosmopolitismo de la diferencia*. Later, she further develops her cosmopolitan sensibilities in England, where she works as a housemaid, but where she also visits brothels and factories as an observer. Her journey to London teaches her about the similarities in working conditions across Europe, or even the world, and that the abuse by the rich has to be stopped: "Flora se dedicó a estudiarlo todo . . . para mostrar al mundo cómo, detrás de esa fachada de prosperidad, lujo y poderío, anidaban la más abyecta explotación, las peores iniquidades, y una humanidad doliente padecía villanías y abusos a fin de hacer posible la vertiginosa riqueza de un puñado de aristócratas y propietarios" (401) ("spent studying everything . . . to show the world that, behind the facade of prosperity, luxury, and power, there lurked the most abject exploitation, the worst evils, and a suffering humanity enduring cruelty and abuse in order to make possible the dizzying wealth of a handful of aristocrats and industrialists"; 373). Even if she detests her experience in England, and particularly London, she is aware that her vision of universal charity was born out of her various stays on that side of the English Channel:

> tenías que reconocer que, sin ese país, sin los trabajadores ingleses, escoceses e irlandeses, probablemente nunca hubieras llegado a darte cuenta de que la única manera de emancipar a la mujer y conseguir para ella la igualdad con el hombre, era hermanando su lucha a la de los obreros, las otras víctimas, los otros explotados, la inmensa mayoría de la humanidad. (402)

> you had to admit that without it and its English, Scottish, and Irish workers, you would probably never have come to realize that the only way to achieve emancipation for women and win them equal rights was by linking their struggle to that of the workers, society's other victims, the downtrodden, the earth's immense majority. (374)

She reluctantly admits that her experience abroad, be it working for the Spence family or investigating and documenting the factory workers' precarious living conditions, opened her eyes and expanded her field of action. Consequently, her universalist project is informed by difference, since it seeks to create conditions of equality in different cultures. In fact, there can be no true universal utopia without proper appreciation of the various cultures involved in its creation. Tristán will therefore promote her dreams of gender and economic equality only after becoming a true cosmopolitan.

The views that Vargas Llosa's Flora Tristán holds on cosmopolitanism are partially rooted in the Stoics' teachings. As a young woman she declares that "nuestra patria debe ser el universo" (352) ("the universe should be our nation"; 325), thus rejecting the idea of limiting herself to changing only her nation and displaying a vision that encompasses all human beings. In opposition to most thinkers of her time, whom she engages in heated debates (both real and imaginary), Tristán acknowledges that all human beings are created equal, regardless of culture or gender. Her *Union ouvrière* (*The Workers' Union*), an essay in which she advocates for the liberation of women and the working class, is an inclusive project that leaves no one behind. However, even if she dreams of a global workers' revolution, she must start, in true cosmopolitan spirit, within her own country: France.

From the outset, the novel emphasizes the French activist's rejection of her contemporary universe. She is portrayed as a resolute woman who has but one objective in mind: to change France, if not the world. She is not daunted by the prospect of failure; her one goal is to build a new world order, and as such she believes that it is time for concrete actions. She is single-minded, driving herself to the point of exhaustion: "Abrió los ojos a las cuatro de la madrugada y pensó: «Hoy comienzas a cambiar el mundo, Florita». No la abrumaba la perspectiva de poner en marcha la maquinaria que al cabo de algunos años transformaría a la humanidad, desapareciendo la injusticia. Se sentía tranquila, con fuerzas para enfrentar los obstáculos que le saldrían al paso" (11) ("She opened her eyes at four in the morning and thought, Today you begin to change the world, Florita. Undaunted by the prospect of setting in motion the machinery that in a matter of years would transform humanity and eliminate injustice, she felt calm, strong enough to face the obstacles ahead of her"; 3). Through her travels in Latin America and Europe, she becomes aware of the growing injustice plaguing the world. Her unwavering resolution, fuelled by her personal utopia, knows no limit. For Madame-la-Colère, as the narrator alternatively calls her, political commitment is more important than anything else in her life; in Vargas Llosa's own conceptualization, the "obsesión matemática de todas las utopías delata lo que quieren suprimir: la irracionalidad, lo instintivo, todo aquello que conspira contra la lógica y la razón" ("mathematical obsession of all utopias betrays what they want to suppress: irrationality, instinct, everything that conspires against logic and reason"; *Verdad de las mentiras* 136). Tristán embodies this *obsesión matemática*: for instance, she rejects the painter Jules Laure's declaration of love, and she deems it necessary to leave her female lover, Olympia. In Flora's opinion, close-knit human relationships, in forming a bond between two individuals, are deeply egotistical. They cannot, therefore, be more important than her ideal of justice and social change: "Le dijo, de manera categórica, que no insistiera: su misión, su lucha, eran incompatibles con una pasión amorosa. Ella, para dedicarse en cuerpo y alma a cambiar la sociedad, había renunciado a la vida sentimental" (*Paraíso* 367) ("She told him categorically that he must not insist: her mission, her struggle, were incompatible with passionate love. In order to devote herself entirely to reforming society, she had renounced affairs of the heart"; 338–9). This echoes Vargas Llosa himself, who in one essay mentions that "En la mayoría de las utopías . . . el sexo se reprime y sirve sólo para la reproducción. . . . Los utopistas suelen ser puritanos que proponen el ascetismo pues ven en el placer individual una fuente de infelicidad social" ("In most utopias . . . sex is repressed and serves only for reproduction. . . . Utopians are usually puritans who propose asceticism because they see in individual pleasure a source of social unhappiness"; *Verdad de las mentiras* 133). On her path to universal freedom, Tristán, then, puts her own desires on the back burner; her collectivist ideas are more important than she is. Even after finding love with Olympia Maleszewska, an artist who understands her and with whom she could have had a meaningful, albeit secret, relationship, she deems that the fate of women and workers is more important than her own happiness: "Y esta relación [with the workers] no tendría el sesgo excluyente y egoísta que tuvieron tus amores con Olympia—por eso los cortaste, renunciando a la única experiencia sexual placentera de tu vida, Florita—; por el contrario, se sustentaría en el amor compartido por la justicia y la acción social" (*Paraíso* 130) ("And your relationship . . . would not have the exclusivist and egotistic slant that your affair with Olympia had had [which is why you ended it, giving up the only pleasurable sexual experience of your life, Florita]; on the contrary, it would be sustained by a shared love for justice and social action";

116). In her mind, the love between two individuals is egotistical and lacks the collective dimension required to change the world; sacrificing love for revolution, then, is proof of altruism.

In denying (repressing?) the basic human need for meaningful relationships, she paves the way for her grandson, who ends up following the same path. "Both protagonists have suffered the traumatic experience of being expelled from a childhood paradise," claims Sabine Köllman; "in Flora's case through her father's death when she was five years old, in Paul's through his mother remarrying and sending him off to boarding school. But neither of them had any scruples about abandoning their own families in order to pursue their projects, thus perpetuating a cycle of traumatic life experiences" (246). History, in other words, repeats itself.

Indeed, Gauguin's search for paradise is ruthless and leaves no place for anyone else. He is willing to abandon almost anyone with whom he has been involved for the sake of his art, be it his wife and children or his friends. While his grandmother is shown to understand human relationships as an impediment to grand social change, the artist perceives them as a waste of time, even considering them detrimental to his artistic production: "En 1888 ya habías llegado a la conclusión de que el amor, a la manera occidental, era un estorbo, que, para un artista, el amor debía tener el exclusivo contenido físico y sensual que tenía para los primitivos, no afectar los sentimientos, el alma" (Vargas Llosa, *Paraíso* 290) ("By 1888 you had come to the conclusion that Western-style love was a hindrance; that love, for artists, should be exclusively physical and sensual, as it was for primitive peoples, that it should not involve the emotions or the soul"; 265). After leaving for Polynesia a second time, Gauguin is fully aware that he and his wife, Mette Gad, will never be together again, nor will he ever be reunited with his children. This seems to be of little importance to him since his stay in French Polynesia allows him to produce great art. Like his grandmother, Gauguin seeks cosmopolitanism without taking his inner circle into consideration. However, whereas Tristán openly works on a universalist project, one that could improve workers' lives, Gauguin is looking for utopia through an individual project. This is, ultimately, incompatible with cosmopolitanism.

Gauguin's stance is in complete opposition to the very definitions of utopia and cosmopolitanism, two projects that seek to transcend egocentrism. Hence, Gauguin's vision of paradise breaks from most theoretical visions that had been formulated previously: it implies neither a collective experience nor redemption. In his rejection of the world, he shares the views of the Greek Cynics, who claimed that organized civilization was man's main problem, and that a return to a natural state—Gauguin's primitive state—would provide the solution. The Cynics' views on cosmopolitanism are of primary importance to understanding Gauguin's character. His utopian quest is undermined by the sheer selfishness of his actions; the negation of others, including family, undercuts the very notion of a collective paradise.

Louisa Shea explains, in *The Cynic Enlightenment*, that the Cynics were "fiercely opposed to any form of theoretical abstraction or institutional organization and famous for defying all codes of decency" (ix). Their main target "was the parochialism of civic and national attachments" (16). By living at the margins of society, they sought to purge themselves from the *polis* itself, but also of social ties of any sort; Shea describes their cosmopolitanism as "the refusal to pay homage to a transient, man-made system of laws; the refusal to contribute to society through work or political office; the refusal to abide by the laws and customs of the polis; the refusal to respect religious rituals, as well as local traditions" (76–7). Just as the Cynics aimed to remove themselves from society in order to criticize it with a fresh perspective, so does Gauguin, fleeing to Polynesia, in order to remove himself from European society, which he considers to be "corrompida por el becerro de oro" (Vargas Llosa, *Paraíso* 245) ("corrupt[ed] by the golden calf"; 222). Later on, he freely admits that Europe's contamination of Oceania is despicable, and has transformed his quest into a failure: "la sustitución de la cultura primitiva por la europea ya había herido de muerte los centros vitales de aquella civilización superior, de la que apenas quedaban miserables restos. Por eso, debía partir" (209) ("the displacement of primitive culture by European ways had already dealt a death blow to the vital core of the island's higher civilization, of which just a few miserable shreds remained. That was why he had to leave"; 190).

Yet, wherever Gauguin goes, he is always dissatisfied with what he finds, for he is looking for a perfect culture in exclusivist terms, a culture untouched by other cultures, which contradicts the very premise of cosmopolitanism. His many travels—to Denmark, Martinique, Panama, and the Marquesas Islands, incidentally covering a greater span than his grandmother—never lead him to develop a truly cosmopolitan outlook on life; he prefers instead a personal, even egotistical, search for a primitive state as the basis for his artistic vision. This journey cannot be cosmopolitan, for it begins with a denial of his own European culture. He looks for the perfect society that would correspond to his impossibly high ideals of perfection,[19] which he has been seeking for a long time:

> Él buscaba eso desde que se sacudió la costra burguesa en la que estaba atrapado desde la infancia, y llevaba un cuarto de siglo siguiendo el rastro de ese mundo paradisíaco, sin encontrarlo. Lo había buscado en la Bretaña tradicionalista y católica, orgullosa de su fe y sus costumbres, pero ya la habían mancillado los turistas pintores y el modernismo occidental. Tampoco lo encontró en Panamá, ni en la Martinica, ni aquí, en Tahití. . . . Apenas reuniera algo de dinero tomaría un barquito a las Marquesas. (209)

> He had been seeking all this since he broke free of the bourgeois shell binding him since childhood, and he had spent a fruitless quarter of a century on the trail of that earthly paradise. He had looked for it in tradition-bound, Catholic Brittany, proud of its faith and customs, but there it was already sullied by tourist painters and Western modernism. Nor had he found it in Panama, Martinique, or here in Tahiti. . . . As soon as he got some money together, he would buy a ticket for the Marquesas. (189–90)

However, by definition, utopia can only be a project, a symbolic place that exists solely in thought and the imagination. It cannot, under any circumstances, become reality. As Allemand emphasizes, "l'utopie, on ne peut pas la vivre (il y a contradiction dans les termes); on peut seulement l'imaginer" ("we cannot experience utopia [there is a contradiction in the terms], we can only imagine it"; 8). Moreover, Ernst Bloch stresses, in *L'esprit de l'utopie* (*The Spirit of Utopia*), how crucial it is to differentiate between the ideal—the utopia—and the idealization—the realization of such a utopia. Therefore, the problem in Gauguin's quest is simply to think that utopia is bound by place, that it has a specific locality upon which he will eventually stumble. His quest, then, becomes an attempt to travel to this very locality, which can only disappoint him once he reaches it.

One of Gauguin's major flaws is that he shows little to no respect for the different places where he is seeking paradise, or to his fellow human beings in general, making his quest, in Appiah's terms, hardly cosmopolitan. For instance, even if he knows how contagious syphilis is—Doctor Lagrange, although uncomfortable, does not shy away from reminding him: "Usted sabe, también, que ésta es una enfermedad muy contagiosa.... Sobre todo, si se tienen relaciones sexuales. En ese caso, la transmisión del mal es inevitable" (Vargas Llosa, *Paraíso* 168) ("You know, too, that this is a very serious illness. . . . Especially if one has sexual intercourse. In that case, the transmission of the malady is inevitable"; 152)—he keeps having sexual intercourse with his many wives and girlfriends, thus spreading the disease. Not only does he reject Europe, he effectively spurns Tahiti's culture as well through his destructive and reprehensible behaviour.

Another example of his lack of respect appears when, while in Papeete, he leads a quasi-revolution against what he considers to be a Chinese invasion of the island. Most people, including his inner circle, disagree with the revolution Gauguin tries to stage: "Cuando Paul convocó . . . un mitin del Partido Católico contra «la invasión de los chinos», muchas personas, entre ellas su amigo y vecino de Punaauia, el ex soldado Pierre Levergos y hasta Pau'ura, su mujer, concluyeron que el pintor excéntrico y escandaloso se había acabado de loquear" (279) ("When Paul called a meeting . . . against 'the Chinese invasion,' many people, among them the ex-soldier Pierre Levergos, his Punaauia friend and neighbor, and even Pau'ura, his wife, concluded that the eccentric, scandal-rousing painter had finally lost his mind"; 254). What Gauguin fails to see is that the so-called Chinese invaders moved to Polynesia a long time before he arrived. He has no right to criticize their presence on the island, and being a foreigner with no official ties to Polynesia whatsoever, he is an intruder himself. He is unable to admit that the culture of the island has been shaped for over a century by the presence of the Chinese. His aversion to another people and their culture constitutes a denial of cosmopolitan ideals. It renders him narrow-minded and distances him from his ideal, which is to be open to the possibilities offered by encounters with other cultures. He reverts to colonial stances about what he deems to be an inferior people, often referring to them as "savages," which for him has the pejorative connotation that "primitive" lacks. In fact, while Gauguin is arguably in search of the primitive, he often confronts the savage, thus oscillating between an artistic utopia and a colonial ideology. While his grandmother had *locuras internacionalistas* ("internationalist manias") that encompassed the whole of humanity and thrived on cosmopolitanism, both *de la igualdad* ("of equality") and *de la diferencia* ("of difference"), Gauguin *se loquea* ("loses his mind") through racism and colonialism.

Examining the characters' commitments to others shows *El Paraíso en la otra esquina*'s particular exploration of utopia, as well as the complexity of Flora Tristán's and Paul Gauguin's ideological positions as depicted in the novel. While Tristán eventually develops a truly cosmopolitan attitude, especially after her time in Peru and England, her grandson never ceases to perceive travelling as a means to escape a civilization he rejects. Consequently, he never actually sets out to live up to the contemporary ideal of simultaneously acknowledging one's nation as well as the world. Tristán and Gauguin both dedicate their whole existence to their quest for paradise: the French activist seeks to change France with her social utopias, hoping and expecting to be successful during her lifetime, while the post-Impressionist painter, for his part, keeps seeking better inspiration for his art.

Flora dies before she can spread her revolutionary gospel and witness the revolution into which she had put so much faith: "Si las cosas no habían salido mejor no había sido por falta de esfuerzo, de convicción, de heroísmo, de idealismo. Si no habían salido mejor era porque en esta vida las cosas nunca salían tan bien como en los sueños. Lástima, Florita" (459) ("If you hadn't had more success, it wasn't for lack of effort, conviction, heroism, or idealism. It was because things never succeed as well in this life as they do in dreams. A pity, Florita"; 429). This last intervention by the narrative voice highlights the relationship between utopia and *sueños*, hinting at the fact that Tristán's project was doomed to failure from the beginning. Her ill-fated *Tour de France*, in which she wishes to promote her ideals and form unions, is the ultimate proof of her dedication to her collectivist project. She dies on 14 November 1844, in the house of fellow activists in Bordeaux. She is forty-one years old. Gauguin, for his part, never seems to be able to find his paradise, even after having travelled to so many countries: "¡El juego del Paraíso! Todavía no encontrabas ese escurridizo lugar, Koke. ¿Existía? ¿Era un fuego fatuo, un espejismo?" (467) ("The game of Paradise! You had yet to find that slippery place, Koké. Was it an illusion, a mirage?"; 436). He dies without having found it.

Both Tristán and Gauguin have travelled and explored the world, which makes their trajectories cosmopolitan, but not in the sense outlined by the literary critic Gutiérrez Mouat. According to this scholar, their main difference lies in the distinct type of cosmopolitanism they display, which, I contend, is a conceptually problematic stance for Gutiérrez Mouat to take. He holds that "Flora proclama un *cosmopolitismo de la igualdad* mientras que su descendiente y contraparte narrativo aboga por un *cosmopolitismo de la diferencia*" ("Flora proclaims a cosmopolitanism of equality while her descendent and narrative counterpart defends a cosmopolitanism of difference"; 399). In this theorizing, Flora is reduced to fighting for equality for men and women, the rich and the poor, while Paul is rooted in the Cynic tradition and seeks exoticism as a counterpoint to European civilization—which is not a cosmopolitan stance at all. For Gutiérrez Mouat, Gauguin's notion of paradise is an engagement with difference. This quest for difference is problematic, since the painter ends up transmitting venereal diseases, defending French colonization, and rejecting not only his own culture, but also the very Europe his grandmother died trying to change. In sum, on the one hand, contact and engagement with actual cultures compel Tristán to evolve, to become cosmopolitan, and eventually to include all cultures in her utopian dream. She is a cosmopolitan with a well-defined political utopia in mind. On the other hand, engagement with the concrete cultures of Oceania only pushes Gauguin to disappointment, since the concrete always leads him to abstraction, and then to the need to keep seeking its realization, ultimately in vain. Vargas Llosa's Gauguin is really a non-cosmopolitan with an artistic utopia, the tentative achievement of which spurs him to flirt with nationalism toward the end of his life, bringing doom.

Both in Tristán's and Gauguin's existence, cosmopolitanism is closely related to utopia. Since utopia is by nature elsewhere, rooted in another culture that has something to teach its seeker, it shows an engagement with other cultures and is a way of reaching out to the world. The major difference between the two concepts lies in the fact that while cosmopolitanism thrives through concrete cultures, utopia is about imagined cultures and societies. Tristán always has a positive attitude toward different cultures—she learns to love Peru, ultimately even considering it superior to France when it comes to the freedom of women, who, under the guise of a *saya y manto*—veil and mantle covering the face but for one eye—are free to roam the streets of the capital without being bothered (Vargas Llosa, *Paraíso* 319; Pratt 164). In that sense, she is a cosmopolitan who moves from the abstraction of utopia to a more concrete cosmopolitanism in her search for gender and social equality. She partially abandons the abstraction of thoughts and acts in order to improve the world. Yet, she is incapable of half measures: she is not balanced, and that causes her demise. Gauguin, by contrast, lingers in the realm of utopia and is always disappointed with concrete cultures, which never turn out to meet his expectations. Tristán's utopian and collectivist quest is the true cause of her downfall, and, according to Vargas Llosa, this is but the logical outcome of such projects: "La utopía representa una inconsciente nostalgia de esclavitud, de regreso a ese estado de total entrega y sumisión, de falta de responsabilidad, que para muchos es también una forma de felicidad y que encarna la sociedad primitiva, la colectividad ancestral, mágica, anterior al nacimiento del individuo" ("Utopia represents an unconscious nostalgia for slavery, back to that state of total surrender and submission, of lack of responsibility, which for many is also a form of happiness and which embodies primitive society, the ancient, magical collectivity prior to the birth of the individual"; *Verdad de las mentiras* 136). By putting her faith in the collectivity, she undermines her individuality, which, in Vargas Llosa's liberal thinking, can only bring doom. Yet, Gauguin's utopia, although rooted in art, is also destined to fail, for he goes to the extremes of individualism, and shows anti-cosmopolitan behaviour.

In being fuelled by utopian ideals, both Tristán and Gauguin embody Vargas Llosa's aversion to all types of extremism. However, the narrative voice is kinder toward the French social activist: she is eager to change the world, and her utopian extremism stems from her good intentions. Gauguin does not receive such a redeeming treatment from the narrator, for, in the final stage of his life, he turns to nationalism, a stance the author despises as the worst form of extremism. Utopia can be realized in art, but as soon as Gauguin leaves his artistic realm and tries to realize his utopia concretely, he fails. Politics is, as we shall see in our exploration of Roger Casement, also a space in which utopian ideals are bound to fail.

## The Fate of the Cosmopolitan Patriot in *El sueño del celta*

The characters of Antonio Conselheiro in *La Guerra del fin del mundo* and Paul Gauguin both embody, in unequivocal terms, Vargas Llosa's aversion to nationalism. He has held this position since he severed his ties with the Castro regime, and leftist ideologies generally, in 1971 after the Padilla Affair, seeing in nationalism a rejection of the foreign cultural influence he deems necessary for artistic creation, and for human development more broadly.

Although Vargas Llosa's position on nationalism appears rather unambiguous, I argue that *El sueño del celta* (2010) explores the complex nuances of the nationalist position in a manner that marks an innovation in the novelist's body of work. Still, it remains a harsh criticism of extreme ideologies. Unlike most of Vargas Llosa's narratives, which show the protagonist's shift from a local to a universal outlook, this novel explores how one of the first global human rights champions flirts with fervent nationalism, albeit only for a short period of time, before retracting his statements.

Most articles published on *El sueño del celta* read the novel as a criticism of colonialism, post-colonialism, and nationalism (Weldt-Basson; Kanev), a reading with which I agree. As indicated by Helene Carol Weldt-Basson in "*El sueño del celta*: Postcolonial Vargas Llosa," the novel can be read through the lens of post-colonial theory. She highlights the ambivalence present in every aspect of Casement's personality and actions. The protagonist is the epitome of post-colonial contradiction, "portrayed as both a saint and sinner, as both colonizer and colonized" (232). Casement oscillates between denouncing the atrocities committed against the Black and Indigenous populations of developing countries and stereotyping and fetishizing them for his own sexual gratification. However, the text has not been read through the lens of Vargas Llosa's cosmopolitan liberalism and recurrent focus on individual liberty, and little attention has been given to how the narrative voice redeems the character of Roger Casement. Indeed, it is interesting to note that while Vargas Llosa's Casement rejects nationalism at the end of his life, the real-life Casement stayed true to his beliefs until the very end. He is quoted as having said, shortly before his death, "Surely [the nationalist Irish cause] is the most glorious cause in history" (Dudgeon 2). As I already mentioned, Walford argues that Vargas Llosa is ambivalent toward utopian projects (76); I add as proof that unlike the wretched failure that is Conselheiro, not only does Roger Casement "not fade into oblivion" (77), but he is also shown a certain respect by the author, and in the epilogue is offered the possibility of redemption by the narrative voice.

"Cada uno de nosotros es, sucesivamente, no *uno*, sino *muchos*. Y estas personalidades sucesivas, que emergen las unas de las otras, suelen ofrecer entre sí los más raros y asombrosos contrastes" (Vargas Llosa, *El sueño del celta* 90) ("Each one of us is, successively, not *one* but *many*. And these successive personalities that emerge one from the other tend to present the strangest, most astonishing contrasts among themselves"; *The Dream of the Celt*[20]). And so begins *El sueño del celta*, the novel announcing even before the narrative starts that its focus will be the evolution of the character, the multiple facets of Casement's personality, and his stepwise growth. *El sueño del celta* is, in Köllman's conception of Vargas Llosa's body of work, the last—to date—in his series of "grand design novels" (223), or, as they were called during the Boom, *novelas totales*.

This historical novel lays out the nationalist drift of Irishman Roger Casement, a cosmopolitan hero turned nationalist anti-hero. A consul for the British Foreign Office during the first decades of the twentieth century, Casement became acquainted with the Irish nationalist movement later in his life, after he attempted to put an end to colonialism in various regions of the world.[21] According to Kristal, "in Vargas Llosa's novel, Casement is transformed into a man who embraces a number of utopias and fantasies, and who reinvents himself several times as each of the dreams he embraces comes undone: the imperial dream [of civilizing Africa], the dream that human rights activism can change society, the dream of Irish nationalism, and the dream of the afterlife" ("From Utopia to Reconciliation" 143). The novel opens in 1903 in the Belgian Congo, and ends in 1916 in

Pentonville Prison, a British jail where Casement hopes to be pardoned by the king following his conviction for high treason. After a successful career in the diplomatic corps, Casement had given up his position to devote himself to the Irish cause. In 1915, Casement had formed an alliance with the Germans, then enemies of the British Empire, in a failed attempt to free Ireland during the doomed Easter Rising of 1916.

I maintain that *El sueño del celta* presents a character who makes a tragic mistake, albeit one that is somewhat justified by historical circumstances. The Irish cause that Casement embraces implicates him in a type of nationalism that traps him and makes him stray from the universalist premises that had characterized his work in Africa and Latin America. The protagonist is then forced to coexist with extreme nationalism—betraying his own principles—and becomes a tragic figure who dies without having been understood either by his compatriots or by his British enemies. In my reading of the novel, Casement embodies Vargas Llosa's ideas about the dangers of nationalism, but also the intricacies of the cosmopolitan position—namely, that engagement with other cultures can awaken a passion for one's own, as well as give space to and coexist with patriotism. The novel also portrays the cosmopolitan Casement's patriotic commitment as fraught with the dangers of nationalism. Vargas Llosa makes a distinction here between nationalism and patriotism, the latter being a stance he can reconcile with cosmopolitanism. As he himself explained in his Nobel speech,

> No hay que confundir el nacionalismo de orejeras y su rechazo del "otro," siempre semilla de violencia, con el patriotismo, sentimiento sano y generoso, de amor a la tierra donde uno vio la luz, donde vivieron sus ancestros y se forjaron los primeros sueños, paisaje familiar de geografías, seres queridos y ocurrencias que se convierten en hitos de la memoria y escudos contra la soledad. La patria no son las banderas ni los himnos, ni los discursos apodícticos sobre los héroes emblemáticos, sino un puñado de lugares y personas que pueblan nuestros recuerdos y los tiñen de melancolía, la sensación cálida de que, no importa donde estemos, existe un hogar al que podemos volver. (8)

> We should not confuse a blinkered nationalism and its rejection of the "other," always the seed of violence, with patriotism, a salutary, generous feeling of love for the land where we were born, where our ancestors lived, where our first dreams were forged, a familiar landscape of geographies, loved ones, and events that are transformed into signposts of memory and defenses against solitude. Homeland is not flags, anthems, or apodictic speeches about emblematic heroes, but a handful of places and people that populate our memories and tinge them with melancholy, the warm sensation that no matter where we are, there is a home for us to return to. (8)

Patriotism, then, can be reconciled with one's cosmopolitan commitment, as the attachment to one's home is a crucial aspect of rooted cosmopolitanism.

Casement fits neatly within the conceptualization of the tragic hero as defined in Aristotle's *Poetics*. First, the Irishman is noble in nature (not from birth, mind you, but he does have a title). He also shows nobility of character throughout the novel, and he is, to use Aristotle's formulation, "highly renowned and prosperous," his magnum opus being his works in the Belgian Congo and the Putumayo region of Peru. Second, he commits an error of judgment (*hamartia*), and thus proves that he is a man "who is eminently good and just, whose misfortune is brought about not by vice or depravity, but by some error or frailty"—namely, the alliance with the Germans in an attempt to free the Irish people. Third, his reversal of fortune (*peripeteia*) is of his own making, something he readily acknowledges (*anagnorisis*). Finally, he invokes a sentiment of pity when he falls from grace, be it in his falling out of love after a partner's betrayal or more broadly the homophobic slander that tarnishes his good name when he is arrested and jailed. Casement, like any other human being, makes mistakes, and his "change of fortune [is] from good to bad," another characteristic of the tragic hero. However, his major flaw is not his extreme hubris, but his longing for love, and, as highlighted by Kristal, his incapacity to set his mind on only one goal. The construction of Casement as a tragic hero seems to be an indication of the textual intention to redeem him. This idea of redemption is apparent in the portrayal of Casement, whom the narrator describes as a candid idealist. Unlike *El Paraíso en la otra esquina*'s Paul Gauguin, who also turns to nationalism, Casement is depicted as a sympathetic person who is caught up in historical circumstances. Although he embraces a dangerous ideology, Casement appears to have a chance at redemption, for he made a tragic mistake and must pay the price. As a matter of fact, the epilogue stands apart from the rest of the narration, as the implicit author is not only aware that Casement was rehabilitated by the United Kingdom in 1965, but also advocates for a balanced understanding of his trajectory. This narrative intervention points to the textual sympathy that I have identified.

*El sueño del celta* closely follows Roger Casement's life and recounts his many travels. Like most Vargas Llosa novels, it has a relatively dense structure, which reflects precisely the literary form of the *novela total* (grand design novel). It is divided into three major sections—"El Congo," "La Amazonía," and "Irlanda"—and fifteen chapters, which chronologically follow the protagonist's career. Each part represents his state of mind as he discovers either cosmopolitanism or nationalism. "El Congo" takes place both in Great Britain and the Belgian Congo, consists of seven chapters, and introduces a Roger Casement who can still be described as naive when it comes to his work in Africa, as he realizes only later the extent of the horrors perpetrated there by Leopold II. The second part, "La Amazonía," plays out in Ireland, Brazil, and Peru, consists of five chapters, and highlights Casement's slow awakening to nationalism. Finally, "Irlanda" takes place in Norway, the United States, and Germany, consists of three chapters, and reveals Casement's dedication to the Irish cause. Oddly enough, not much of it actually occurs in Ireland, although the country remains the sole focus of his thoughts. The novel's three parts, then, correspond to the character's three progressive states of mind: first, Casement internalizes the colonizer's perspective and seeks to spread civilization to less fortunate souls; he then becomes disillusioned with colonialism, embraces a more cosmopolitan outlook, and becomes an Irish patriot rediscovering his roots and asserting Irish culture; and finally, he turns to nationalism, seeing it as the only way for Ireland to earn respect. In every stage of Casement's development, his single-mindedness is his defining characteristic; in a way, he is fanatical every step of the way. Each trip he makes brings him one step closer to what he believes to be his true self.

The novel's narration alternates between past and present. In the odd-numbered chapters, the reader is privy to Casement's last weeks in prison, with a clear focus on his state of mind and newfound religious convictions. In the even-numbered chapters, the major events that shaped his life, and that ultimately led to his being jailed, are recalled in great detail, indeed in an almost didactic tone. Most of the narration is delivered through a third-person omniscient narrator, but the passages in which Casement recalls his life while he is waiting for royal clemency are told through his own perspective. In most instances, the narrator appears to be sympathetic to Casement's situation.

Casement is depicted as an Irish intellectual who from an early age develops a keen interest in various cultures.[22] "El Congo" concentrates on his childhood, adolescence, and young adulthood, a period that is synonymous with his discovery of the world. The first phase of Casement's life is one of awakening to other cultures from a Eurocentric or British-centric perspective, during which he endorses the colonizer's perspective and sees himself as superior to colonials. This interest in travel and cultures different from his own appears to come from his father, who served in the Light Dragoons, a cavalry regiment in the British army: "Lo que de veras le interesaba en ese tiempo [his childhood] eran las historias que, cuando estaba de buen ánimo, le contaba el capitán Casement a él y a sus hermanos. Historias de la India y Afganistán, sobre todo sus batallas contra los afganos y los sijs" (Vargas Llosa, *Sueño* 19) ("What really interested him at this time were the stories Captain Casement, when he was in a good humor, recounted to him and his brothers and sister. Stories about India and Afghanistan, especially his battles with Afghans and Sikhs"; 8). As a child, Roger is fascinated by the descriptions of these foreign lands, these "remotas fronteras del Imperio" (19) ("remote frontiers of the Empire"; 8), that somehow belong to the same kingdom he lives in: "Aquellos nombres y paisajes exóticos, aquellos viajes cruzando selvas y montañas que escondían tesoros, fieras, alimañas, pueblos antiquísimos de extrañas costumbres, dioses bárbaros, disparaban su imaginación" (19) ("Those exotic names and landscapes, those travels crossing forests and mountains that concealed treasures, wild beasts, predatory animals, ancient peoples with strange customs and savage gods, fired his imagination"; 8). At such a young age, these Others against whom his father must fight to maintain order intrigue Casement. His father's memories and tales are surrounded by an oriental aura, which only adds to the fascination they provoke in the child. This fascination with foreignness is reminiscent of the West's attitude toward the East during the eighteenth and nineteenth centuries as expressed by Edward Said in *Orientalism*, and of Bhabha's theory of ambivalence toward the colonial subject as outlined in *The Location of Culture*. This black and white understanding of the world already sets up a binary distinction in young Casement's mind.

Although his father was part of the army, Roger is not interested in military feats: "no eran los hechos de armas lo que más encandilaba la imaginación del pequeño Roger, sino los viajes" (19–20) ("it wasn't feats of arms that most dazzled the young Roger's imagination, it was the journeys"; 8). He hopes to be able to visit these faraway countries someday. When both his parents die—his mother in 1873 and his father three years later (22)—Roger moves in with relatives. His "tío Edward Bannister, que había corrido mucho mundo y hacía viajes de negocios en África" (24) ("uncle Edward Bannister, who had traveled much of the world and made business trips to Africa"; 11), is a perfect match for the adolescent, for he encourages Roger's hopes of seeing more of the world. Casement's dream of travelling is fuelled by his readings of the explorers David Livingstone and Henry Morton Stanley (24–5); he, too, aspires to discover Africa.

In 1883, at nineteen years of age, Casement embarks on a ship sailing to West Africa as a purser for a shipping company, the Elder Dempster of Liverpool, making three trips that very year. He becomes familiar with the life of a sailor, and catches a glimpse of the terrible conditions of the African populations that will eventually allow him to develop the humanistic spirit that leads him to overtly criticize the colonial system some twenty years after he first sets foot on the continent. However, at first, he believes and internalizes the Elder Dempster's values, and makes its publications his own sacred texts, to the extent that he is sometimes the object of ridicule at the hands of his colleagues: "Su pasión por África y su empeño en hacer méritos en la compañía lo llevaban a leerse con cuidado, llenándolos de anotaciones, los folletos y las publicaciones que circulaban por las oficinas relacionadas con el comercio marítimo entre el Imperio británico y el África Occidental. Luego, repetía convencido las ideas que impregnaban esos textos" (26) ("His passion for Africa and his commitment to doing well in the company led him to read carefully, and fill with notes, the pamphlets and publications dealing with maritime trade between the British Empire and West Africa that made the rounds of the offices. Then he would repeat with conviction the ideas that permeated those texts"; 13). Casement is imbued with the sense of entitlement that was characteristic of colonial power in this period, and he feels, in Rudyard Kipling's famous expression, the "white man's burden" to bring civilization to those less fortunate:

> Llevar al África los productos europeos e importar las materias primas que el suelo africano producía, era, más que una operación mercantil, una empresa a favor del progreso de pueblos detenidos en la prehistoria, sumidos en el canibalismo y la trata de esclavos. El comercio llevaba allá la religión, la moral, la ley, los valores de la Europa moderna, culta, libre y democrática, un progreso que acabaría por transformar a los desdichados de las tribus en hombres y mujeres de nuestro tiempo. En esta empresa, el Imperio británico estaba a la vanguardia de Europa y había que sentirse orgullosos de ser parte de él y del trabajo que cumplían en la Elder Dempster Line. (26)

> Bringing European products to Africa and importing the raw materials that African soil produced was, more than a commercial operation, an enterprise in favor of the progress of peoples caught in prehistory, sunk in cannibalism and the slave trade. Commerce brought religion, morality, law, the values of a modern, educated, free, and democratic Europe, progress that would eventually transform tribal unfortunates into men and women of our time. In this enterprise, the British Empire was at the vanguard of Europe, and one had to feel proud of being part of it and the work accomplished at the Elder Dempster Line. (13)

In his twenties, Casement is convinced of the inherent good of his work—work that must be done to help the Africans overcome their backwardness. His certainties are so strong that, as he resigns from his job with the Elder Dempster and is about to leave for Africa for good, his uncle, in a thinly veiled allusion to the dangers of fanaticism, remarks that Roger is "como esos cruzados que en la Edad Media partían al Oriente a liberar Jerusalén" (27) ("like those crusaders in the Middle Ages who left for the East to liberate Jerusalem"; 14). The image of crusaders, although hinted at only subtly in the beginning of the novel, becomes more important as the narrative progresses, and ultimately the vision the crusaders have of themselves triggers the Easter Rising.

In 1884, "en un arranque de idealismo y sueño aventurero, [Casement] decidió . . . dejar Europa y venir al África a trabajar para, mediante el comercio, el cristianismo y las instituciones sociales y políticas de Occidente, emancipar a los africanos del atraso, la enfermedad y la ignorancia" (35) ("in an outburst of idealism and a dream of adventure, [Casement decided] to leave Europe and come to Africa to work, by means of commerce, for Christianity, western social and political institutions, and the emancipation of Africans from backwardness, disease, and ignorance"; 22). Casement is blinded by his chance to work with Stanley, his childhood hero, and believes that the work he and his team are accomplishing is "la punta de lanza del progreso en este mundo donde apenas asomaba la Edad de Piedra que Europa había dejado atrás hacía muchos siglos" (38) ("the tip of the lance of progress in this world where the Stone Age that Europe had left behind many centuries earlier was only just beginning to be visible"; 24). Casement is convinced of "las intenciones benévolas de los europeos" ("the benevolent intentions of the Europeans") who come to Africa: "vendrían a ayudarlos a mejorar sus condiciones de vida, librarlos de plagas como la mortífera enfermedad del sueño, educarlos y abrirles los ojos sobre las verdades de este mundo y el otro, gracias a lo cual sus hijos y nietos alcanzarían una vida decente, justa y libre" (39) ("they would come to help them improve their living conditions, rid them of deadly plagues such as sleeping sickness, educate them, and open their eyes to the truths of this world and the next, thanks to which their children and grandchildren would attain a life that was decent, just, and free"; 25). He does not need much time to shed his illusions, and this disappointment brings about a new phase in his intellectual and professional development, that of criticizing colonialism and awakening to a more cosmopolitan outlook.

This awakening happens as a result of conversations with journalist and explorer Stanley. Casement becomes aware of the many injustices faced by the native African populations, the main one being that they are signing away all power over their own affairs: not only do they not understand the various contracts they are forced to sign—they are written in French, in a legal language that even the expedition leaders do not understand, and translations in African languages are not provided (41)—but they are also enslaving themselves by agreeing to such terms. Stanley is well aware of this, but maintains that it is for their own good: they ought to be civilized, he argues, to learn that "un cristiano no debe comerse al prójimo" ("a Christian should not eat his neighbor") and stop speaking in "esos dialectos de monos" (43) (those monkey dialects"; 28). Casement is outraged and cannot agree to be involved in such a scheme—a first step in the development of his cosmopolitan outlook and his becoming a defender of human rights.

Casement's certainty about the various atrocities committed by Europeans becomes stronger when he reaches the Congo, controlled at the time by King Leopold II of Belgium, where he works for several companies and where he meets Anglo-Polish novelist Joseph Conrad, the author of *Heart of Darkness* (1899).[23] In 1903, the Foreign Office charges him with investigating the alleged abuses perpetrated under the rule of Leopold II. He denounces the hardships suffered by the local population at the hands of settlers and entrepreneurs. He is utterly disillusioned and even comes to regret having worked for the Belgian monarch:

> Todo el resto de su vida, Roger lamentó . . . haber dedicado sus primeros ocho años en Africa a trabajar, como peón en una partida de ajedrez, en la construcción del Estado Independiente del Congo, invirtiendo en ello su tiempo, su salud, sus esfuerzos, su idealismo y creyendo que, de este modo, obraba por un designio filantrópico. (49)
>
> For the rest of his life, Roger lamented . . . dedicating his first eight years in Africa to working, like a pawn in a game

of chess, on the building of the Congo Free State, investing his time, health, effort, and idealism, and believing that in this way he was contributing to a philanthropic plan. (33)

The resulting Casement Report, released in 1904, details the atrocities carried out in the name of "civilization" and monetary gains, causes a great scandal, and confirms the universalist pretensions of the protagonist, who has now become a vocal opponent to colonialism. His stay in the Congo also makes him reassess his origins. In a letter to his cousin Gertrude, he admits that his time in Africa has allowed him not only to discover his own country, but also his true self: "te parecerá otro síntoma de locura pero este viaje a las profundidades de Congo me ha servido para descubrir a mi propio país. Para entender su situación, su destino, su realidad. También he encontrado mi verdadero yo: el incorregible irlandés. . . . Tengo la impresión de haber mudado de piel . . . de mentalidad y acaso hasta del alma" (109) ("it may seem like another symptom of madness to you, but this journey into the depths of the Congo has been useful in helping me discover my own country, and understand her situation, her destiny, her reality. . . . I've also found my true self: the incorregible Irishman. . . . I have the impression that . . . I've shed the skin of my mind and perhaps my soul"; 80).[24] Travelling to the Congo allows him, then, to become another man, *uno de los muchos hombres* of the epigraph, although it must be noted that the protagonist refers to his own discovery of Ireland as *locura* (madness), much like Gauguin refers to his grandmother's *locuras internacionalistas*.

Casement ponders the state of Ireland to draw parallels between the two countries of which he has most experience, and he notices a sad similarity that will shape his thinking from then on:[25]

> ¿No era también Irlanda una colonia, como el Congo? Aunque él se hubiera empeñado tantos años en no aceptar esa verdad que su padre y tantos irlandeses del Ulster, como él, rechazaban con ciega indignación. ¿Por qué lo que estaba mal para el Congo estaría bien para Irlanda? ¿No habían invadido los ingleses a Eire? ¿No la habían incorporado al Imperio mediante la fuerza, sin consultar a los invadidos y ocupados, tal como los belgas a los congoleses? Con el tiem-

> po, aquella violencia se había mitigado, pero Irlanda seguía siendo una colonia, cuya soberanía desapareció por obra de un vecino más fuerte. Era una realidad que muchos irlandeses se negaban a ver. (110)

> Wasn't Ireland a colony too, like the Congo? Though for so many years he had insisted on not accepting a truth that his father and so many Ulster Irishmen like him rejected with blind indignation. Why would what was bad for the Congo be good for Ireland? Hadn't the English invaded Ireland? Hadn't they incorporated it into the Empire by force, not consulting those who had been invaded and occupied, just as the Belgians did with the Congolese? Over time the violence had eased, but Ireland was still a colony whose sovereignty disappeared because of a stronger neighbor. It was a reality that many Irish refused to see. (80–1)

Like many Irishmen and -women, this was a reality that had escaped him until then, and its recognition has a deep impact on Casement. Although convinced of what he discovered in the Congo, it is an epiphany that he dares to share only with his closest friends:

> A la segunda o tercera vez que estuvieron solos, Roger abrió su corazón a su flamante amiga, como lo habría hecho un creyente a su confesor. A ella, irlandesa de familia protestante como él, se atrevió a decirle lo que no había dicho a nadie todavía: allá, en el Congo, conviviendo con la injusticia y la violencia, había descubierto la gran mentira que era el colonialismo y había empezado a sentirse un "irlandés," es decir, ciudadano de un país ocupado y explotado por un Imperio que había desangrado y desalmado a Irlanda. Se avergonzaba de tantas cosas que había dicho y creído, repitiendo las enseñanzas paternas. Y hacía propósito de enmienda. Ahora que, gracias al Congo, había descubierto a Irlanda, quería ser un irlandés de verdad, conocer su

país, apropiarse de su tradición, de su historia y su cultura. (119–20)

The second or third time they were alone, Roger opened his heart to his new friend, as a believer would have done with his confessor. He dared tell her, like him from an Irish Protestant family, what he hadn't told anyone yet: there in the Congo, living with injustice and violence, he had discovered the great lie of colonialism and begun to feel "Irish," that is, a citizen of a country occupied and exploited by the Empire that had bled and weakened Ireland. He was ashamed of so many things he had said and believed, repeating his father's teachings. And he vowed to make amends. Now that he had discovered Ireland, thanks to the Congo, he wanted to be a real Irishman, know his country, take possession of her tradition, history, and culture. (88)

After his stay in the Congo, Casement is happy to return to the United Kingdom—first to England, then to Ireland—to recover both his physical and mental strength, and here he becomes "un irlandés de verdad" (120) ("a real Irishman"; 88). Having discovered his Irishness, he is particularly pleased to go back to Magherintemple House, "la casa familiar de su infancia y adolescencia" (121) ("the family home of his childhood and adolescence"; 89). He immerses himself in Irish culture, discovers its mythology, and attempts to learn the language—to no avail—but also becomes acquainted with members of the Gaelic League, an organization that promotes "el irlandés y la cultura de Irlanda" (122) ("Irish and the culture of Ireland"; 90). Under a pseudonym, he even starts writing politically oriented newspaper columns defending Irish culture. Since he is still working for the Foreign Office, he does not criticize Great Britain too openly.

Casement's immersion in Irish culture is for him the first step toward the reappropriation of his Irish past, but it is also his undoing, for it marks the beginnings of his patriotic fervour, which eventually sets him off on a nationalist trajectory. According to Vargas Llosa, in *Wellsprings*, the published draft of a lecture he gave at Harvard University, reclaiming the past is a natural behaviour for nationalist movements: "the victim nation may be forced to feign 'acculturation' for a time; but underneath, it continues to resist, preserving its essence, remaining true to its origins, holding its soul intact, awaiting the hour when its sovereignty and liberty will be redeemed" (76). This form of ethnic nationalism, based on myths, customs, and traditions, is pernicious. Vargas Llosa also disagrees with Casement's view on the necessity of the preservation of Irish culture at all costs: "Nationalism's defenders start with a false assumption: that the culture of a country is, like the natural riches and raw materials harbored in its soil, something that should be protected from the voracious avarice of imperialism, and kept stable, intact, unadulterated, and undefiled" (98). The Irish culture, although obviously worth preserving, cannot be defined in absolute and fixed terms—a culture *de verdad*—and can only be enriched by the coexistence with foreign cultural elements. This idea of purity is reminiscent of Paul Gauguin in *El Paraíso en la otra esquina*, who also sees cultures as artefacts worth preserving as they are, and for whom contacts between cultures are equivalent to a loss of *primitivity*.

This view of cultures as subject to change and enrichment by interaction is the basis of current theorizations of cosmopolitanism, a cosmopolitanism that is understood as a conversation between cultures, based on mutual respect. Casement, a rooted cosmopolitan, gives credence to other cultural practices, and he accepts their specificity, aware that cultural enrichment only happens through difference. As a cosmopolitan patriot, Casement is willing to accept such differences between people, for he feels a moral obligation toward all of them, whatever their birthplace. Like Flora Tristán, he embraces both a *cosmopolitismo de la igualdad* and a *cosmopolitismo de la diferencia*. Moreover, he reaches a cosmopolitan outlook through his acceptance of differences. However, his path is in some ways the opposite of the canonical one. Unlike most cosmopolitans who take an interest first in the local, then in the global aspects of their lives, Casement first takes a keen interest in foreign peoples, then in his own. His various stays in Ireland are milestones in the definition of his world view. For Casement,

> Aquellos meses significaron el redescubrimiento de su país, la inmersión en una Irlanda que sólo había conocido por conversaciones, fantasías y lecturas, muy distinta de aquella

> en que había vivido de niño con sus padres, o de adolescente con sus tíos abuelos y demás parientes paternos, una Irlanda que no era cola y sombra del Imperio británico, que luchaba por recobrar su lengua, sus tradiciones y costumbres. (Vargas Llosa, *Sueño* 143)

> Those months meant the rediscovery of his country, his immersion in an Ireland he had known about only in conversations, fantasies, and readings, very different from the one where he had lived as a child with his parents, or as an adolescent with his great aunt and great uncle and the rest of the paternal family, an Ireland that was not the tail and shadow of the British Empire, that fought to recover its language, traditions, and customs. (108–9)

Being in Ireland brings him to a better understanding of his origins, but also makes him more aware of the everyday struggles the Irish face. Around this time, some friends and acquaintances start telling him jokingly that he "[ha] vuelto un patriota irlandés" (143) ("[he has] become an Irish patriot"; 109). Casement, rather, thinks that "[está] recuperando el tiempo perdido" (143) ("[he is] making up for lost time"; 109). "All nationalist doctrine is based on an act of faith," claims Vargas Llosa, "not on a rational, empirical conception of history and society. Nationalism is a *collectivist* act of faith that imbues a mythical entity—the nation—with a fictive coherence, homogeneity, and unity preserved over time, untouched by historical change" (*Wellsprings* 75). In *El sueño del celta*, the protagonist's behaviour falls under the idea of the recovery of a past—the mythical Irish past—that he idealizes and wants to make his own, a sort of paradise lost that he wants to recover. Still, according to Vargas Llosa, such melancholy, a "longing for what did not exist" (81), is a useful tool in imagining the nation:

> The fact that this nation was never a tangible reality is no obstacle for people who, blessed with the terrible, formidable instrument that is the imagination, manage to fabricate it. This is why fiction exists: to populate the emptiness of

life with phantoms that human beings require in order to make sense of their own cowardice, generosity, fear, pain or stupidity. The ghosts that fiction inserts into reality can be benign, innocuous, or malignant. Nationalism's specter falls into this last group. (81)

This desire to recover a past that is beyond reach is similar to Paul Gauguin's lost primitive state. And much like Tristán and Gauguin, the search for this lost paradise triggers Casement's demise.

From this time on, Casement makes a point of correcting his interlocutors about his origins. He often repeats: "No soy inglés sino irlandés" (297) ("I'm not English, I'm Irish"; 222). He wants Ireland to become a proper state, but he remains a pacifist and believes that Irish institutions can replace most British ones, if only they are given the chance:

> Había que ir creando, junto a las instituciones coloniales, una infraestructura irlandesa (colegios, empresas, bancos, industrias) que poco a poco fuera sustituyendo a la impuesta por Inglaterra. De este modo los irlandeses irían tomando conciencia de su propio destino. Había que boicotear los productos británicos, rehusar el pago de impuestos, reemplazar los deportes ingleses como el cricket y el fútbol por deportes nacionales y también la literatura y el teatro. De este modo, de manera pacífica, Irlanda iría desgajándose de la sujeción colonial. (144)

> It was necessary to create, along with colonial institutions, an Irish infrastructure (schools, businesses, banks, industries) that gradually would replace the one imposed by Britain. In this way the Irish would become conscious of their own destiny. It was necessary to boycott Irish products, refuse to pay taxes, replace British sports such as cricket and soccer with national sports, and literature and theater as well. In this way, peacefully, Ireland would break free of colonial subjugation. (109–10)

The objective for Ireland is to become an independent country by creating new Irish foundations. However strong his feelings for his native land may be, the protagonist can still reconcile his cosmopolitan openness and his willingness to denounce the poor living and working conditions of the oppressed peoples around the world with his love for Ireland. His cosmopolitanism and nationalism are not irreconcilable; they are, in fact, complementary. This complementarity embodies the contemporary conceptualization of cosmopolitanism, rooted in locality yet open to the world. This is Casement's vision: every person he encounters, whether in Africa, Latin America, or Europe, is someone toward whom he has a moral responsibility. In the first years of his nationalist drift, Casement appears to be a moderate nationalist—in fact, more a patriot than a nationalist, as defined by Vargas Llosa—who sees the situation in Ireland through the prism of human rights. The colonialism that Casement observes abroad leads him to nationalism. His awareness of the atrocities committed in foreign lands and his commitment to the cause of colonized peoples allows him to identify colonialism at home, in his own culture. Ultimately, he adopts the Irish nationalist cause because of his openness and empathy toward others, and his cosmopolitan vision. However, he understands nationalism in a way that does not contradict his cosmopolitan engagement. Indeed, Casement never disavows the work he has performed during his service for the British Foreign Office. Even if he does not share many affinities with the United Kingdom, and does not want it to rule Ireland, after leaving the consular services he remains happy with his work as a foreign service officer. Casement perceives as quite ironic the fact that the United Kingdom, a country that denounces colonial atrocities, itself has colonies that it oppresses. Embracing other cultures leads Casement to accept his own, which had been somewhat sidelined during his career in the British Foreign Service.

Indeed, his concern for Ireland coexists with his interest in other cultures and histories. His second mandate as a diplomat changes his pacifist perception of things. In 1906, the Foreign Office sends Casement to Peru to investigate abuses in the Putumayo, a district on the border between Peru and Colombia. During his stay, he concludes that the employers who exploit rubber treat the Indigenous populations in the same way that the English have treated the Irish for centuries: while the *indios* are made to forget their traditions, "A [the Irish] se les hacía creer que Irlanda era un bárbaro país sin pasado digno de memoria, ascendido a la civilización por el ocupante, educado y modernizado por el Imperio que lo despojó de su tradición, su lengua y su soberanía" (135) ("The Irish were still made to believe that Ireland was a savage country with no past worth remembering, raised to civilization by the occupier, educated and modernized by the Empire, which stripped it of its tradition, language, and sovereignty"; 102). The protagonist cannot handle the idea of his people being inhumanely treated, and is aware that "Los irlandeses somos como los huitotos y los boras, los andoques y los muinanes del Putumayo. Colonizados, explotados y condenados a serlo siempre si seguimos confiando en las leyes, las instituciones y los Gobiernos de Inglaterra, para alcanzar la libertad. Nunca nos la darán" (239) ("We Irish are like the Huitotos, the Boras, the Andoques and the Muinanes of Putumayo. Colonized, exploited, and condemned to be that way forever if we continue trusting in British laws, institutions, and governments to attain our freedom. They will never give it to us"; 186). He becomes convinced that Ireland will only free itself through an armed rising: Why, he asks, would "el Imperio que [les] coloniza" give the Irish their freedom "si no siente una presión irresistible que lo obligue a hacerlo? Esa presión sólo puede venir de las armas" (239) ("the Empire that colonized do that unless it felt an irresistible pressure that obliged it to do so? That pressure can only come from weapons"; 186). Casement returns to Europe in 1911 with only one idea in mind: to free Ireland.

The Blue Book, Casement's accounts of the atrocities perpetrated in Latin America, comes out in July 1912 and "produ[ce] una conmoción" (324) ("produces an upheaval"; 254), first in Europe, then in the United States. Even before its publication, Casement quits the diplomatic service to focus on the Irish cause and to "ocuparse de otros indígenas, los de Irlanda. También ellos necesitaban librarse de las 'arañas' que los explotaban, aunque con armas más refinadas e hipócritas que las de los caucheros peruanos, colombianos y brasileños" (378) ("concern himself with other natives, the ones from Ireland. They, too, needed to free themselves from the Aranas exploiting them, though with weapons more refined and hypocritical than those of the Peruvian, Colombian, and Brazilian rubber barons"; 297. Arana/Araña is both a character's last name and the Spanish word for "spider," thus establishing a negative parallel between the exploitative entrepreneur and the insect). When his commitment as a cosmopolitan patriot turns into political engagement, it assumes the form of nationalism, and his interest in liberating Ireland turns obsessive: "Una idea volvía una y otra vez a su conciencia, una idea que en los días, semanas y meses siguientes retornaría obsesivamente y empezaría a modelar su conducta: 'No debemos permitir que la colonización llegue a castrar el espíritu de los irlandeses como ha castrado el de los indígenas de la Amazonía. Hay que actuar ahora, de una vez, antes de que sea tarde y nos volvamos autómatas'" (247) ("An idea came to mind over and over again, an idea that in the coming days, weeks, and months would return obsessively and begin to shape his conduct: *We should not permit colonization to castrate the spirit of the Irish as it has castrated the spirit of the Amazonian Indians. We must act now, once and for all, before it is too late and we turn into automatons*"; 192; emphasis in trans.). Casement fears that the Irish will turn into puppets and lose their desire to fight for the freedom of their homeland. Gradually, he loses most of the friendships he had made during his stays in Africa and Latin America, "Pero pese a todo ello, no había cambiado de manera de pensar. No, no se había equivocado" (197) ("But in spite of everything, he hadn't changed his way of thinking. No, he had not been wrong"; 151). He shows the same single-mindedness and obstinacy that had been his trademark during his period with the Elder Dempster, and later as a human rights activist in the Congo and Peru. His best friend Herbert, whom he met in the Congo, "desconfiaba de todos los nacionalismos. Era uno de los pocos europeos cultos y sensibles en tierra africana" (183) ("mistrusted all nationalisms. He was one of the few educated, sensitive Europeans on African soil"; 141). Through many conversations, he reminds Casement that "el patriotismo es el último refugio de las canallas" (184)—an obvious reference to English writer Samuel Johnson's famous phrase, "Patriotism is the last refuge of the scoundrel"—and overtly laughs at his friend's conversion to nationalism, exhorting him to "volver a la realidad y salir de ese 'sueño del celta' en el que se había encastillado" (268) ("return to reality and leave 'the dream of the Celt' into which he had retreated"; 210). For Herbert, it simply cannot be: Casement's openness to the world and desire to save the oppressed populations of Africa and Latin America are irreconcilable with the idea of nationalism, and he is *encastillado*, enwalled—too stubborn to realize it. Herbert ends up burning his bridges with Casement:

> Herbert Ward nunca tomó muy en serio la progresiva conversión de Roger a la ideología nacionalista. Solía burlarse de él, a la manera cariñosa que le era propia, alertándolo contra el patriotismo de oropel—banderas, himnos, uniformes—que, le decía, representaba siempre, a la corta o a la larga, un retroceso hacia el provincialismo, el espíritu de campanario y la distorsión de los valores universales. Sin embargo, ese ciudadano del mundo, como Herbert gustaba llamarse, ante la violencia desmesurada de la guerra mundial había reaccionado refugiándose también en el patriotismo como tantos millones de europeos. (345)

> Herbert Ward never took very seriously the progressive conversion of Roger to the nationalist ideology. He tended to mock him, in the affectionate manner typical of him, warning him against tinsel patriotism—flags, anthems, uniforms—which, he would say, always represented, sooner or later, a regression to provincialism, mean-spiritedness, and the distortion of universal values. And yet, this citizen of the world, as Herbert liked to call himself, when faced with the inordinate violence of the world war, had reacted like so many Europeans and had also taken refuge in patriotism. (270–1)

Some of Casement's friends liken his turn to nationalism to a religious conversion; they call him "extremista" ("extremist" 383) and "intolerante" ("intolerant" 388), tell him that he has become "un revolucionario radical" ("a radical revolutionary" 399), and ultimately they abandon him. They do not understand his desire to sacrifice his knighthood and forsake all the work he has done to save the oppressed peoples of Africa and Latin America. But as far as Casement is concerned, these friends are unable to universalize the conditions of oppression in which the Irish live.

In Vargas Llosa's words, the fact that Casement sees the Irish as being oppressed would be an example of "victimization—it serves up a long list of historical grievances to demonstrate the ways in which colonizing powers have tried to destroy or contaminate the victim nation" (*Wellsprings* 76). Casement's allies and friends do not share this victim-centric view of history, and they warn him that this will feed the revolutionary potential in Ireland. This outlook once again mirrors Vargas Llosa's criticism of nationalism:

> the truth is that in the conception of humankind, society, and history endorsed by the ideology of nationalism, there is a seed of violence that inevitably germinates whenever nationalists try to meet the demands of their own postulates, especially the main one: to rebuild what Benedict Anderson calls the "imagined community," an illusory nation that is culturally, socially, and linguistically integrated and whose human offspring gain their identity from membership in this collective. (79–80)

However, there is a tragic dimension to Casement's view: by his very own universal concern, he advocates a moderate nationalism that is impossible in these historical circumstances. He wants to free Ireland, and is willing to die doing so, but he does not profess an exclusionary nationalism, nor does he possess the momentum of other extremist patriots with whom he ends up working. At first, he thinks that the process of national liberation has to be sought through dialogue, not necessarily bloody conflict. He agrees, for example, with the idea of home rule—that is, self-government on the part of the Irish—but within the United Kingdom of Great Britain and Ireland. He seems to agree with the criticism some of his friends voice against extreme patriotism and nationalism; it may be that he thinks he is able to overcome the problems of extreme nationalism:

> El patriotismo cegaba la lucidez. Alice había hecho esta afirmación en un reñido debate, en una de esas veladas en su casa de Grosvenor Road que Roger recordaba siempre con tanta nostalgia. ¿Qué había dicho exactamente la historia-

> dora? «No debemos dejar que el patriotismo nos arrebate la lucidez, la razón, la inteligencia.» Algo así. Pero, entonces, recordó el picotazo irónico que había lanzado George Bernard Shaw a todos los nacionalistas irlandeses presentes: «Son cosas irreconciliables, Alice. No se engañe: el patriotismo es una religión, está reñido con la lucidez. Es puro oscurantismo, un acto de fe». Lo dijo con esa ironía burlona que ponía siempre incómodos a sus interlocutores, porque todos intuían que, debajo de lo que el dramaturgo decía de manera bonachona, había siempre una intención demoledora. «Acto de fe», en boca de ese escéptico e incrédulo, quería decir «superstición, superchería» o cosas peores todavía. (Vargas Llosa, *Sueño* 197)

> Patriotism blinded lucidity. Alice had affirmed this in a hard-fought debate during one of the evening get-togethers at her house on Grosvenor Road that Roger always recalled with so much nostalgia. What had the historian said exactly? "We should not allow patriotism to do violence to our lucidity, our reason, our intelligence." Something like that. But then he remembered the ironic dart thrown by George Bernard Shaw at all the Irish nationalists present: "They're irreconcilable, Alice. Make no mistake: patriotism is a religion, the enemy of lucidity. It is pure obscurantism, an act of faith." He said this with the mocking irony that always made the people he spoke to uncomfortable, because everyone intuited that beneath what the dramatist said in a general way there was always a destructive intention. "Act of faith" in the mouth of this skeptic and unbeliever meant "superstition, fraud," or even worse. (152)

Casement's interlocutors often use the word "patriotism" as a synonym for "nationalism." However, as we have seen, Vargas Llosa makes a distinction between these two concepts in *Wellsprings*, and it seems that Casement's rediscovery and promotion of Irish roots, his love for Ireland, is not pernicious per se. Problems arise when patriotism becomes nationalism, tied to the realm and excesses of politics; it can then lead down a treacherous path. Nationalist politics invariably tend to become exclusionary, and therefore asphyxiating.

Eventually, Casement comes to terms with the fact that the United Kingdom is unlikely to agree to Irish autonomy: "Ésta no era la solución para Irlanda. Lo era la independencia, pura y simplemente, y ella no sería jamás concedida por las buenas" (*Sueño* 397) ("This was not the solution for Ireland. Independence was, pure and simple, and that would never be granted willingly"; 313). He does not reject the idea of the Irish Brigade, a military outfit that would help Irish forces against the British Empire. In 1914, Casement sails to Germany via Norway, in the hope of setting in motion a mutually beneficial plan on which the Irish and German leaders had previously agreed: if Germany agreed to sell guns to the Irish rebels and provide military leaders, they, in return, would stage a revolt against England, diverting troops and attention from the continental war effort. Once in Germany, when Casement tries to convince the Irish war prisoners to enroll in the brigade, his proposal is met with little interest. Most soldiers call him "traidor," "vendido," or "cucaracha" (185) ("*traitor, sold, cockroach*"; 142; emphasis in trans.), which shows that even if they are Irish-born, their allegiance lies with Great Britain, something that is a cause of great disappointment to Casement.

Over time, he becomes acquainted with more extreme forms of nationalism and for reasons of political expediency he seems to embrace these views, although he does so with a degree of ambivalence. While some nationalists believe that "De la inmolación de los hijos de Eire nacería ese país libre, sin colonizadores ni explotadores, donde reinarían la ley, el cristianismo y la justicia" (416) ("From the immolation of the children of Ireland a free country would be born without colonizers or exploiters, where law, Christianity, and justice would reign"; 327–8), he is worried by "la obsesión de [unos colegas] de concebir a los patriotas irlandeses como la versión contemporánea de los mártires primitivos: 'Así como la sangre de los mártires fue la semilla del cristianismo, la de los patriotas será la semilla de nuestra libertad,' escribió [Patrick Pearse, a colleague] en un ensayo. Una bella frase, pensaba Roger. Pero ¿no había en ella algo ominoso?" (391) ("Pearse's obsession with conceiving of Irish patriots as the contemporary version of the early martyrs:

'Just as the blood of the martyrs was the seed of Christianity, that of the patriots will be the seed of our liberty,' he wrote in an essay. A beautiful phrase, Roger thought. But wasn't there something ominous in it?"; 307–8). Casement is confused by such passion, such "celo ardiente, [tanta] glorificación de la sangre y la guerra" (420) ("burning zeal, the same glorification of blood and war"; 330). He sees that his colleagues are bordering on fanaticism, and, while, as a patriot, he wants to free Ireland, he is still not willing to sacrifice lives to do so, and indeed never will be.

However, an impulsive Casement lends credence, out of empathy and loneliness, to everything that the revolutionaries say:

> A Roger, el romanticismo un tanto enloquecido de Joseph Plunkett y Patrick Pearse lo había asustado a veces, en Irlanda. Pero estas semanas, en Berlín, oyendo al joven poeta y revolucionario [Plunkett], en esos días agradables en que la primavera llenaba de flores los jardines y los árboles de los parques recobraban su verdor, Roger se sintió conmovido y ansioso de creer todo lo que el recién venido le decía. (416–17)

> The somewhat mad romanticism of Joseph Plunkett and Patrick Pearse had frightened Roger at times in Ireland. But during these weeks in Berlin, listening to the young poet and revolutionary on pleasant days when spring filled the gardens with flowers and trees in the parks were recovering their green, Roger felt touched, longing to believe everything the newcomer was telling him. (328)

Isolated from the rest of his group in Berlin, Casement ends up believing in "materializar el sueño místico," and in "el martirio de los santos" (351) ("giving material form to his life's mystic dream" and "the martyrdom of the saints"; 275). He listens to revolutionary poet Joseph Plunkett as he speaks "con la seriedad de quien se sabe poseedor de una verdad irrefutable" (420) ("with the gravity of someone who knows he possesses an irrefutable truth"; 330–1). Casement is blinded by his desire to save Ireland; Plunkett is a diehard nationalist who knows too well that the planned uprising is bound to fail and cost many supporters their lives, yet he is convinced of the necessity of such a sacrifice: the immolation of combatants is a new martyrdom, similar to that of the first Christians fed to the lions. For Vargas Llosa, the comparison between religion and nationalism is an obvious one: "like churches, nationalist groups do not engage in true dialogue: they sanctify and excommunicate. Nationalism feeds on instinct and passion, not intelligence; its strengths lie not in ideas but in beliefs and myths. For this reason it is closer to literature and religion" (*Wellsprings* 82). This echoes Benedict Anderson who, in *Imagined Communities*, argues that "national imaginings [have] a strong affinity with religious imaginings" (10), and who traces the rise of nationalism in the eighteenth century to a certain erosion of religious beliefs (12). Plunkett is a prime example of sanctification and excommunication, since he is both absolutist and categorical. There is no room for conversation or middle ground.

One of the priests with whom Casement works in Germany, Father Crotty, believes that, while this desire for martyrdom is aligned with the profound Catholicism of Ireland, it is also dangerous:

> La nuestra es una religión sobre todo para los que sufren. Los humillados, los hambrientos, los vencidos. Esa fe ha impedido que nos desintegráramos como país pese a la fuerza que nos aplastaba. En nuestra religión es central el martirio. Sacrificarse, inmolarse. ¿No lo hizo Cristo? Se encarnó y se sometió a las más atroces crueldades. (Vargas Llosa, *Sueño* 436–7)

> Ours is a religion above all for those who suffer. The humiliated, the hungry, the defeated. That faith has prevented us from disintegrating as a country in spite of the force crushing us. In our religion martyrdom is central. To sacrifice oneself, immolate oneself. Didn't Christ do that? He became flesh and subjected himself to the most awful cruelty. (344)

Father Crotty also balances the nationalist discourse and echoes something Casement had already heard back in Peru—namely, that martyrs, or people who see themselves as potential martyrs, are dangerous:

Este muchacho es alguien fuera de lo común, sin duda. Por su inteligencia y por su entrega a una causa. Su cristianismo es el de esos cristianos que morían en los circos romanos devorados por las fieras. Pero, también, el de los cruzados que reconquistaron Jerusalén matando a todos los impíos judíos y musulmanes que encontraron, incluidas mujeres y niños. El mismo celo ardiente, la misma glorificación de la sangre y la guerra. (419–20)

This boy is out of the ordinary, no doubt about it. Because of his intelligence and devotion to a cause. His Christianity is that of the Christians who died in Roman circuses, devoured by wild beasts. But also of the Crusaders who reconquered Jerusalem by killing all the ungodly Jews and Muslims they encountered, including women and children. The same burning zeal, the same glorification of blood and war. (330)

Casement eventually realizes that the priest is right. There is no nuance in Plunkett's approach to nationalism: for him the end justifies the means. This scares the priest, who tries to convince Casement: "Te confieso, Roger, que personas así, aunque sean ellas las que hacen la Historia, a mí me dan más miedo que admiración" (419–20) ("I confess, Roger, that people like him, even though they may be the ones who make history, fill me with more fear than admiration"; 330). Here Father Crotty echoes Vargas Llosa's concerns with nationalism, for he believes that it dehumanizes men and turns them into irrational beings. Aware that the arms he has sought will get to Ireland in time, Casement returns to the island in a hurry, and is intercepted and arrested by the British army.

In one of his last conversations with his confessor Father Carey, in the Pentonville Prison, Casement recognizes his shortcomings and now admits that his hatred toward England was pointless:

—Si me ejecutan, ¿podrá mi cuerpo ser llevado a Irlanda y enterrado allá?

Sintió que el capellán dudaba y lo miró. Father Carey había palidecido algo. Lo vio negar con la cabeza, incómodo.

—No, Roger. Si ocurre aquello, será usted enterrado en el cementerio de la prisión.

—En tierra enemiga—susurró Casement, tratando de hacer una broma que no resultó—. En un país que he llegado a odiar tanto como lo quise y admiré de joven.

—Odiar no sirve de nada—suspiró el padre Carey—. La política de Inglaterra puede ser mala. Pero hay muchos ingleses decentes y respetables.

—Lo sé muy bien, padre. Me lo digo siempre que me lleno de odio contra este país. Es más fuerte que yo. Tal vez me ocurre porque de muchacho creí ciegamente en el Imperio, en que Inglaterra estaba civilizando al mundo. Usted se hubiera reído si me hubiera conocido entonces. (133)

"If I'm executed, can my body be taken to Ireland and buried there?"

He sensed the chaplain hesitating and looked at him. Father Carey had paled slightly. He saw his discomfort as he shook his head.

"No, Roger. If that happens, you'll be buried in the prison cemetery."

"In enemy territory," Roger murmured, trying to make a joke that failed. "In a country I've come to hate as much as I loved and admired it as a young man."

"Hate doesn't serve any purpose," Father Carey said with a sigh. "The policies of England may be bad. But there are many decent, respectable English people."

"I know that all very well, Father. I tell myself that whenever I fill with hatred towards this country. It's stronger than I am. Perhaps it happens because as a boy I believed blindly in the Empire and that England was civilizing the world. You would have laughed if you had known me then." (100–1)

Casement has come full circle and has lived through all of his contradictions. In the last conversation he has with his friend Alice Stopford Green in the Pentonville Prison, she reminds him of his cosmopolitan oscillation:

A mí y a ellos nos pasaba algo parecido contigo, Roger. Envidiábamos tus viajes, tus aventuras, que hubieras vivido tantas vidas distintas en aquellos lugares. Se lo oí decir alguna vez a Yeats [the Irish poet]: «Roger Casement es el irlandés más universal que he conocido. Un verdadero ciudadano del mundo.» Creo que nunca te lo conté. (358–9)

Something similar happened to me and them with you, Roger. We envied your travels, your adventures, your having lived so many different lives in those places. I once heard Yeats say, "Roger Casement is the most universal Irishman I've known. A real citizen of the world." I don't think I ever told you that. (281)

Travel is a defining characteristic of Casement as a character, and a determining factor in his cosmopolitan trajectory. Even on the eve of his execution, he inevitably continues to embody the tension between cosmopolitanism and nationalism. Historical circumstances do not allow him to resolve it. According to Kristal, "Vargas Llosa's Casement slowly abandons all of his commitments and convictions: the dedication with which he had served Great Britain as a diplomat, the passion with which he had defended human rights in Africa and the Amazon, his adherence to Germany during the Great War, and his dedication to the cause of Irish independence" ("From Utopia to Reconciliation" 145). His indecisiveness and oscillation are the cause of his demise.

Vargas Llosa's position on nationalism is clear and well documented: it is a fatal ideology that has to be avoided at all costs; it destroys everything—and everyone—it touches. *El sueño del celta* can be seen as a cautionary tale about these well-known dangers. Most of Vargas Llosa's writings do not allow for the possibility of cosmopolitan patriotism, since all types of nationalism are rejected as evil. In the novel, however, Casement is treated in a more nuanced way than most of Vargas Llosa's nationalist characters, precisely because he is a cosmopolitan patriot. However harsh its author's criticism of this ideology, *El sueño del celta* portrays Roger Casement in a positive light and redeems the historical character, for he is a tragic hero whose patriotic fervour fatally leads, in convoluted historical circumstances and in the turmoil of political expediency, to extreme nationalist politics. Vargas Llosa's Casement never ceases to oscillate between the two apparent ends of the spectrum linking nationalism and cosmopolitanism. In spite of the author's rejection of nationalism, the novel interprets the historical character through the prism of a nuanced reflection on the intricacies of the nationalist position, which essentially advocates for the sympathetic portrayal of Casement as a cosmopolitan patriot.

## Conclusion

My reading of *El Paraíso en la otra esquina* and *El sueño del celta* is predicated on the following proposition: they are, to date, Mario Vargas Llosa's two most cosmopolitan novels, in terms of ideas and conceptual articulation.[26] Furthermore, while they plot political cosmopolitanism and advocate for rooted cosmopolitanism, they do not shy away from using counter-examples to argue in favour of this position. Indeed, neither Flora Tristán nor Paul Gauguin is a rooted cosmopolitan: it is precisely the fact that they deny one aspect of rooted cosmopolitanism that causes their demise. Tristán is not rooted in her milieu, and does not see the purpose of being so; her goals are global. In turning to nationalism, Gauguin ends up being so rooted that he denies the importance of intercultural contact in the preservation of cultures. Roger Casement does not fare much better: his temporary rejection of rooted cosmopolitanism amidst the historical turmoil of the fight for Irish independence brings him to nationalism, causing his death. However, it is precisely because he was, at heart, a rooted cosmopolitan that he is given a chance at redemption.

The three protagonists have in common their extensive travels and their interest in other cultures, and it is the contact with these other cultures that marks the beginning of their intellectual, artistic, and political journeys. This alters them in a radical way, and triggers their reflection about the world, but also about the very role cultural diversity plays in the life of individuals. Yet while Flora Tristán and—except for a brief and fatal moment—Roger Casement thrive on cultural diversity, Paul Gauguin rejects it as a dangerous force. The three characters are also openly dissatisfied with their environments, and, through an extra-national encounter with cultural diversity, come to embrace their roles in changing the world order. It is this contact with cultural diversity that leads them to develop a cosmopolitan position, however problematic it might turn out to be.

Flora Tristán closely resembles Roger Casement. Both discover their ideological affiliations in Latin America: Tristán in Lima, Casement in the Putumayo. The contact with different cultures is beneficial for both of them, and cements their respective philosophical positions. While Lima's cultural diversity allows Tristán to discover cosmopolitanism, Casement's stay in Peru allows him to move from the cosmopolitan outlook he had developed in Africa to a more nation-centred one. This brings him to universalize the sufferings of Indigenous peoples, to argue that the Irish are in fact a member of that larger group, exploited and stranded in their subalternity. While Peru opens Tristán up to new possibilities, it reinforces Casement's feelings that his nation needs his help. But Peru, and Latin America more broadly, mark a turning point in both of their lives. Their stay in Peru is also the first step in their undoing.

Both Tristán and Casement are ruled by their feelings, by the experiences they share with those they want to help. In her case, it is workers and women to whom she dedicates most of her time; in his, it is the Indigenous populations of Africa and Latin America. Both devote their life to helping people they perceive as their equal but who are subalternized by exploitative capitalism, colonialism, or patriarchy. The pattern that Casement follows is the reverse of Tristán's: she universalizes her own condition, she goes from the specific to the universal (one woman, all women); Casement, for his part, goes from the universal to the specific (Indigenous populations in the Belgian Congo and the Putumayo, the Irish). For Tristán and Casement, the discovery of cosmopolitanism leads to the development of some sort of messianic spirit; they both see their work as their mission in life. In each case, the narrative comments on their respective *locura*—internationalism and nationalism, respectively. Such fanaticism does bring about their demise, but the narrator also redeems both characters: indeed, the narrative voice appears sympathetic to their suffering, and is never judgmental. The same cannot be said of Gauguin, of whom the narrative voice is highly critical, for his extremism—in the form of colonialism—is permeated with racism and the rejection of other cultures. Although Gauguin and Casement share the same nationalist political preferences, their treatment could not be more different.

Paul Gauguin and Roger Casement both turn to nationalism, at first glance for the very same reason: the preservation of cultures as *pure* artefacts. Gauguin, in his search for an artistic utopia, cannot bring himself to admit that it is the plurality of cultural backgrounds that makes the Marquesas the very Paradise he was seeking. He rejects the cultural exchanges he encounters—namely, Chinese cultural elements—as some sort of perversion of what he understands to be *pure* Marquesas culture, without grasping that cultures are porous and can only be enriched by coming into contact with others. Casement, for his part, wants to recover a mythical Irish culture that has been destroyed by the English colonizers, but ironically, it is his contact with a plurality of cultures that enables him to detect the importance of his own. Gauguin's rejection of other cultures leads him to colonialism, the worst form of nationalism, a stance rendered despicable by the novel's narrative voice. Casement, for his part, turns to nationalism precisely as a rejection of colonialism, and even then, he remains first and foremost a convinced patriot tragically caught up in the nationalist movement. Gauguin, on the contrary, becomes a radical and exclusionary French colonial nationalist.

In a narration reminiscent of Plutarch's *Parallel Lives*, *El Paraíso en la otra esquina* intertwines the destinies of Flora Tristán and Paul Gauguin, drawing parallels between grandmother and grandson, and highlighting the resulting paradoxes. In addition to allowing Gauguin to refer to his grandmother, this structure also reinforces my contention that the narrator acts as a voice of reason and tries to extract lessons from the protagonists' behaviour. In a few instances, when Gauguin is about to make the same type of mistakes Tristán once did, the narrator highlights how grandmother and grandson, although extremely different in their philosophical leanings, are cut from the same cloth. The narrative voice does not stop Gauguin from making mistakes; it only comments on the similarities shared by grandmother and grandson. They are both stubborn and will not stop short of their goals, even if it kills them. This contrapuntal structure demonstrates that liberalism is at play: Plutarch's objective was to study the way individuals affect the course of history, which is, in modern terms, a liberal view of history.

As in Plutarch's text, which presents, by way of conclusion, four unpaired lives, *El sueño del celta* only explores the life of Roger Casement. However, a close reading allows me to argue that the novel is nevertheless about parallel lives, albeit in a broader sense. The epigraph is already a clear indication of the textual intention to present *muchos hombres*—in this case, three different men. Casement's evolution, from a young and naive colonizer to a cosmopolitan patriot, and in the end to a full-fledged nationalist—albeit for a short period of time—runs parallel to the evolution of the Indigenous populations he encounters. Whereas Tristán and Gauguin are clearly parallel lives, Casement's counterpoint is the Indigenous populations he meets at every stage of his life, and the individual he becomes, with the beliefs and values that he develops as a consequence.

The cosmopolitan question has always permeated Vargas Llosa's body of work. Some of his recent novels embody the urgent need to address the cosmopolitan question in the context of debates about globalization. The plotting of characters in narrations reminiscent of *Parallel Lives* promotes a liberal view of history, but also the enunciation of the idea that lessons are to be extracted from the trajectories of exceptional individuals. It should not come as a surprise, then, that the Peruvian intellectual chose to address these themes in a series of historical novels, for they are usually a means of returning to the past so as to reflect on the present. For Vargas Llosa, literature is a space to inspire, to motivate individuals to change things. I have proposed that Vargas Llosa's historical novels fall within both Lukács's and Menton's articulations, yet also differ from both; they represent an evolution of the historical novel in which the characters take on a very active role. Through their awakening to a global consciousness, they tackle global concerns: while Flora Tristán confronts women's and workers' issues, Roger Casement fights colonialism. Vargas Llosa's novels are framed in historicity and are pedagogical in nature, and the extensive investigation the author undertakes before writing each of his novels indicates a detail-oriented mind that attempts to reproduce his characters' historical context in the most accurate way possible, as Lukács argues, while his protagonists are based on historical characters and discuss philosophical ideas, as Menton claims. Both *El Paraíso en la otra esquina* and *El sueño del celta* show the same attention to detail and make extensive use of the actual writings—be they personal journals or factual reports—of the historical figures they portray. Within these novels, moreover, Vargas Llosa goes one step further than Menton's theorization: the novels are *about* ideas—cosmopolitanism, nationalism, rooted cosmopolitanism; he focuses on real characters; and these characters are the main focus of the narrative. This is, I contend, a powerful example of Vargas Llosa's liberal positions: his novels are about individuals and the very active role they play in the making of history.

Another major difference is that the characters he portrays are not only witnesses to history, as in Lukács's theories, they register what is happening, and more importantly, criticize and overtly denounce the failings of their historical context in unambiguous terms. Flora Tristán writes a travel journal during her stay in Latin America, publishing it under the title *Pérégrinations d'une paria*, while Roger Casement releases the Casement Report and the Blue Book after his stays in the Congo and Peru—such accounts serve as indictments of the abuses they have witnessed, and the implicit author of Vargas Llosa's novels makes the narrators interact with those documents, or the documents are introduced and paraphrased in the novels. Unlike in many recent historical novels, where Latin America plays a central role, in Vargas Llosa's historical novels the continent plays what appears, at first sight, to be a minor role: only a section of each novel takes place on the continent. Yet, it is also a major one: it is the source of both Tristán's and Casement's awakening to cosmopolitanism, as well as the *Paraíso* that Gauguin longs to reproduce. Thus, unlike major contemporary historical novels, while Vargas Llosa's works are in dialogue with Latin America's history in an oblique manner, they are nonetheless deeply engaged in the debates and ideas that have shaped the continent.

The choice of the historical novel corresponds to the Peruvian author's literary intention and vision. I posit that Vargas Llosa's historical novels "exprime[nt] une vérité" ("express a truth"; qtd. in Michaud and Bensoussan 219)—namely, his own. About historical novels and truth, he has said that "cette vérité n'est pas celle des faits qui se sont réalisés objectivement, en dehors de nous-mêmes. Elle relève de la vérité intérieure de l'homme" ("this truth is not the truth of the facts that occurred objectively, outside of ourselves. It is part of the inner truth of man"; 219).[27] This truth, this different version of the historical past depicted in the two novels studied in this chapter, has to do with the philosophical perspective with which the author has chosen to frame each novel as a whole, but most specifically, the very characters he plots. This treatment of the past is especially clear in the case of Roger Casement: while Vargas Llosa's Casement recognizes the error of his ways and ultimately rejects extreme nationalism, the real-life Casement never disavowed his nationalist convictions, proclaiming them anew just minutes before his execution.

Both *El Paraíso en la otra esquina* and *El sueño del celta* are about collectivist ideologies—internationalism and nationalism—yet their literary treatment is framed through liberalism. Albeit in a different contrapuntal manner, both novels focus on the lives of individuals rather than on historical processes, once again warranting comparison with Plutarch's *Parallel Lives*. This intertext highlights the role of individuals, rather than collectivities, in the making of history, and consequently is conceptually framed in a liberal vision of societal processes. While for Marxism, individuals are subordinated to the processes of history and societal structures, liberalism emphasizes the very role of the individual in the making of history. This philosophical and historical intertextuality—Marxism, liberalism, and *Parallel Lives*—illuminate Vargas Llosa's political tendencies: through the plotting of individuals, their impressions of things, the way they struggle and shape history and society, as well as their production—philosophical, literary, and political in Tristán's case; artistic in Gauguin's; and political in Casement's—shine a light on the liberal beliefs of the author, for whom liberty is of the utmost importance. This literary form reflects Vargas Llosa's liberalism, the aesthetics reveal the political stance of their author, and ultimately, the focus is on individual liberty. In rejoicing in a collectivist project, both Tristán and Casement deny their individual freedom, which leads them to failure: indeed, for Vargas Llosa, "detrás de las utopías sociales yace la fascinación por la servidumbre, el terror primitivo, atávico, del hombre de la tribu—de la sociedad colectivista—a asumir aquella soberanía individual que nace del ejercicio pleno de la libertad" ("behind social utopias lies the fascination for servitude, the primitive, atavistic terror of the man of the tribe—of collectivist society— to assume the individual sovereignty that is born from the full exercise of freedom"; *Verdad de las mentiras* 136). The *tribu* to which both Tristán and Casement want to belong is problematic: for her, because in embracing the whole of humanity she denies the very basic human need for meaningful relationships; for him, because in supporting the Irish national cause, he shuts himself off from the rest of the world. Gauguin, for his part, does enjoy individual liberty, to the extent that he denies his fellow human beings their own, a stance as problematic as his grandmother's.

Vargas Llosa's rearticulation of the historical novel not only allows him to frame his subjects through his liberal positions, but also to discuss ideas and address contemporary issues. As a liberal public intellectual, he is engaged in polarizing debates about democracy and globalization. The Peruvian author plots in fiction the debates in which he is involved; he transposes into fiction the ideas found in these debates, as well as in his newspaper articles and essays, for, as he himself acknowledges, the majority of people are more likely to read and appreciate his fictions, since they are wrongly perceived as less politicized than his essays (Vargas Llosa, "Confessions of an Old Fashioned Liberal"). Both *El Paraíso en la otra esquina* and *El sueño del celta* deal with the dangers of extremism, and in so doing allude to the contemporary world. These fictional worlds invite readers to establish meaningful parallels between the historical past they depict and the present. The characters of Flora Tristán, Paul Gauguin, and Roger Casement all share the same cosmopolitan ethos, and their struggle resonates with current issues, even if they are opposed to each other on many fronts, from the way they understand sexuality to the articulation of their desire to save the world.

The character of Flora Tristán is a case in point: Vargas Llosa plots her to portray contemporary concepts, and to criticize the drift of liberal globalization. Tristán's trip to London to work with the Spence family, whom she despises, takes place during the period of liberal industrialization and early globalization, a situation that mirrors a later form of globalization and its shortcomings—namely, the power of the 1 per cent. Yet, the novel does not propose any solution, it merely makes clear that socialism is not the key to past or current problems. However, in Flora's case, the novel also makes a case for globalization: indeed, it is this nineteenth-century globalized Peru that turns her into a social activist, thus proving the author's point—namely, that "globalization must be welcomed because it notably expands the horizons of individual liberty" (Vargas Llosa, "Culture of Liberty" 69). Furthermore, it is worth clarifying that Vargas Llosa's liberalism does not amount to complacency vis-à-vis the current global order. On the contrary, both novels uphold the denunciations made by the characters of Flora Tristán and Roger Casement, vindicating them and suggesting that their struggles were justified in the past, and would be again today.

Vargas Llosa's current criticism of nationalist forces as killers of freedom is evident in his depiction of both Gauguin and Casement, and resonates with some interventions he has made on the topic of separatist movements, be they in Catalonia or in Scotland. Gauguin's adherence to nationalism is despicable, a return to the primitive state Vargas Llosa claims is removed from civilization; moreover, it is dangerous and has terrible consequences. Unlike Gaugin, Casement is at least partially redeemed through his balanced approach to both his homeland and the world, although he comes close to missing any redemption at all. For example, during his stay in Germany, the once open-minded Casement tries to impose his views on Irish soldiers serving in the British army who refuse to cede to his impassioned nationalist speech. "Seeking to impose a cultural identity on a people," claims Vargas Llosa, "is equivalent to locking them in a prison and denying them the most precious of liberties—that of choosing what, how, and who they want to be" (69). In trying to impose his will on the Irish soldiers, Casement denies them freedom of choice.

Moreover, the characters of Gauguin and Casement embody Vargas Llosa's criticism of nationalist views of cultural identity. Indeed, he claims that "If there is anything at odds with the universalist propensities of culture, it is the parochial, exclusionary, and confused vision that nationalist perspectives try to impose on cultural life. . . . Cultures must live freely, constantly jousting with different cultures" (70). This is both Gauguin's and Casement's mistake: by arguing that cultures must be preserved, they show an exclusionary vision that rejects the premise that cultures thrive when enriched by others. They conflate *preservation* and *purity*. Their flawed understanding reinforces Vargas Llosa's stance that "globalization does not suffocate local cultures but rather liberates them from the ideological conformity of nationalism" (69).

In conclusion, Vargas Llosa posits that in an era such as ours, rooted cosmopolitanism is the best way to tackle the issues facing the world. By discussing these ideas in historical novels, Vargas Llosa starts a conversation that is not only cosmopolitan in nature, but that also puts cosmopolitanism proper at the forefront, an evolution of his own literary production that mirrors that of Spanish American letters writ large. His rearticulation of the historical novel allows him to discuss philosophical ideas under the guise of historical fiction. Ultimately, both *El Paraíso en la otra esquina* and *El sueño del celta* are about current issues and the role of individuals in resolving them, sparking a reflection without providing answers.

In the next chapter, we will see how contemporary authors use the global novel to discuss these issues of global citizenship in the contemporary era. They, too, struggle to reconcile the nation and the world while exploring different avenues.

# 3

# Cosmopolitanism at the End of History in the Fictions of Jorge Volpi

> *Yo soy mexicano y seguramente escribo como mexicano, por más que lo que escriba no ocurra en México.*
>
> *(I am Mexican and surely I write as a Mexican, even if what I write does not unfold in Mexico.)*
>
> —Jorge Volpi

Mexican author Jorge Volpi is known for his complex, deterritorialized narrative worlds. He is, in his own words, "un latinoamericano que—rara cosa—no escribe sobre América Latina" ("a Latin American, who—rare as it may seem—does not write about Latin America; *Insomnio* 24), who even doubts that such a thing as Latin America actually exists. This perspective has led him to conceptualize literature in cosmopolitan and global terms, but he also has an acute understanding of his place in the ever-changing Latin American and Mexican canons.[1]

Born on 10 July 1968, in Mexico City, Volpi is a lawyer-turned-novelist known for his involvement in the Crack movement as well as his thought-provoking essays. In 1996, after practising law for a few years, he travelled to Salamanca, Spain, to complete his doctorate in Hispanic philology. In the prologue to *El insomnio de Bolívar* (*Bolívar's Insomnia*; 2009) he reminisces about this period in his life.[2] Much like some of his forefathers, Volpi asserts that he discovered his Latin American affiliations abroad; in his case, while studying in Spain, of all places. He recalls that he "acababa de cumplir 28 años y hasta entonces había vivido en México, donde jamás fui consciente de esta condición y donde nunca tuve la fortuna o la desgracia de toparme con alguien que se proclamase miembro de esta especie" ("I had just turned twenty-eight and until then I had lived in Mexico, where I had never been aware of this condition and where I never had the fortune or the misfortune of running into anyone who claimed to be a member of this species"; 17). Volpi claims that for him, like many Mexicans of his generation, "América Latina—término rimbombante, resbaladizo—era un hermoso fantasma, una herencia incómoda, una carga o una deuda imposible de calcular" ("Latin America—a grandiose, slippery term—was a beautiful ghost, an uncomfortable inheritance, a burden or a debt that was impossible to measure"; 18). This is perhaps one of the reasons why Latin America is given no more privilege of place than the other parts of the world Volpi writes about in the novels I analyze in this chapter. It is, after all, a *fantasma*, a ghost, something that escapes its very seeker.

These narratives are a case in point: both *El fin de la locura* and *No será la Tierra* articulate Mexico and Latin America in a global context by erasing major indicators of identity as they relate to the Spanish American novel, whether through their narrators, the events depicted, or their very settings. They also concentrate on events that marked and shaped the twentieth century around the globe. *El fin de la locura* (2003) starts on 10 November 1989, with the fall of the Berlin Wall, and chronicles the journey of Mexican psychoanalyst Aníbal Quevedo from the Paris of May 1968 to Mexico under President Carlos Salinas de Gortari (1988–94). Quevedo converses with fellow intellectuals Jacques Lacan, Louis Althusser, Michel Foucault, and Roland Barthes, and then travels to Fidel Castro's Cuba and Salvador Allende's Chile. The novel explores the figure of the intellectual in order to represent it as a global category of the twentieth century, one whose representation requires the articulation of a global conscience. The novel also concentrates on intellectual history, another departure from most Spanish American narratives. *No será la Tierra* (2006) starts with the Chernobyl nuclear disaster (1986) in Ukraine, and interweaves the fates of three women scattered around the world: Irina Gránina, a Russian biologist, Jennifer Moore, an American economist with a senior position at the International Monetary Fund, and Éva Halász, a Hungarian American computer genius. These three women must learn to live in a world influenced by the implosion of the Communist Bloc and the emergence of the anti-globalization movement. *No será la Tierra* is about the emergence of the so-called New World Order and the end-of-history discourse elaborated by Francis Fukuyama in the 1990s. In my reading, the novel uses the cosmopolitan aspirations of characters of different nationalities to probe modes of universal engagement, and it advances rooted cosmopolitanism as a desirable mode of community membership in the global era. In both these texts, Latin America is but a ghost seen below the surface of the narrative. The works nevertheless embody Volpi's contentions about the future of Latin America. For the author, the way forward is to "renuncia[r] de una vez por todas a estas convicciones patrióticas, a los himnos y banderas, a los odios y las exclusiones, a las caducas ideas de soberanía, para entrar en un mundo nuevo, en una era donde la pertenencia a un solo país no sea crucial, donde sea posible articular una ciudadanía—y una identidad—más amplia" ("renounce once and for all these patriotic convictions, hymns and flags, hatreds and exclusions, outdated ideas of sovereignty, to enter into a new world, an era where belonging to a single country is not crucial, where it is possible to articulate a broader citizenship and identity"), in which "la aplicación de soluciones primero *regionales* y luego *globales* sirva para mejorar las condiciones de vida" ("the application of *regional* solutions first and then *global* solutions serves to improve living conditions"; *Insomnio* 249–50; my emphasis) in both the national and global setting. Both of these narratives propose globality as an effective way of relating to our fellow human beings.

Although a lot of attention has been given to Jorge Volpi's narratives, the scholarship on his body of work lacks a nuanced analysis that does not pit cosmopolitanism against nationalism, but rather seeks to assess the national, regional, and continental influences in his cosmopolitan and universal works. While no one really questions that his extensive body of work shows a profound understanding of the Spanish American literary tradition, no one has yet done a complete analysis of the various influences in his works, nor assessed how Volpi positions himself as a Latin American author in the strictest sense. I challenge the notion that his work rejects the Latin American literary tradition. I contend that a close reading of his novels actually shows that his narratives, although not necessarily set in Latin America, can be read as metaphors for the events occurring across the continent. Even if Latin America has no pride of place in Volpi's literary universe, it is not erased; it is rather placed in conversation with the world.

This chapter is divided in two sections: a historical and theoretical framework, followed by the literary analysis of two novels. In the first section, I map Volpi's literary evolution over the past twenty years, from the early years of the Crack movement up to the present. This serves to highlight the fact that unlike Vargas Llosa, whose allegiance to cosmopolitanism evolved over time, Volpi's work has always showcased that philosophical position. I also discuss how his latest novels erase markers of the canonical Spanish American narrative, and as such, are global novels. The second section is dedicated to the literary analysis of *El fin de la locura* and *No será la tierra*, two historical novels that favour rooted cosmopolitanism and propose universal modes of engagement in an ever-globalized world. They challenge the readers to take a stand about the future of humanity—the first step in the development of a cosmopolitan consciousness.

## "Mi biblioteca es mi patria"

Volpi is part of a group of contemporary novelists who publish widely acclaimed narrative works while also being involved in critical debates about culture, literature, and politics. Much like the Boom authors, Volpi and his peers are more than writers: they are Latin American intellectuals whose voices can be heard across many platforms. In various literary manifestos, such as the "Manifiesto Crack" (1996), and essays, Volpi has tackled the topic of literary production and its reception in the domestic and international arenas. A recurring theme in his reflection is that of a literary tradition conceptualized in cosmopolitan terms, but he also has a profound understanding of the Mexican tradition.

### The Crack

The Crack emerged in 1996; its members describe it as a literary friendship, since it is both a group of novels and the very authors that aimed to renovate Mexican literature. Twenty-five years after the publication of the original manifesto, they are still active. In the 1996 "Manifiesto Crack," Ignacio Padilla explains that at the beginning of the 1990s, he and his fellow members did not identify with the work of contemporary Mexican and Latin American writers. The manifesto, then, was a way to articulate their literary vision, express new concerns, and open new possibilities for the Spanish American narrative, one removed from *realismo mágico* and discussions about an authentic identity.[3] In short, they appeared to be rejecting the previous fifty years of Latin American literary tradition. While the movement was generally well received, *The Critical Dictionary of Mexican Literature (1955–2010)* is not laudatory toward the objectives of the Crack: "the Crack novels form a heteroclitic band of uneven . . . tales that fly the banner of false cosmopolitanism. It's literature written by Latin Americans who decided to abandon—as if this in and of itself were novel or radical—old national themes and present themselves as contemporaries not of all men but of the superstars of world literature" (532). Much like their Boom forefathers, they were criticized for their worldwide sales and cosmopolitan outlook.

While they admired the literary experimentation of the Boom, they despised the work of the Post-Boom, for it was *easy* literature. Instead, they advocated for a return to more complex narratives. In the "Postmanifiesto del Crack, 1996–2016," Pedro Ángel Palou addressed this very issue, which he ties to universality: "El *Crack* apostó por esa globalidad de la novela desde las tradiciones locales. No buscó destruir al Boom, como se dijo, sino continuarlo. Hizo *Crack*, una fisura en la tradición" (see Volpi et al.) ("The Crack began with local traditions and bet on universality. It did not seek to destroy the Boom, as some have stated, but rather to continue it. There was a literal 'crack,' a fissure in the tradition"; 197–8[4]), a crack that is nevertheless part of that very tradition of global novels that discuss local themes. According to Alberto Castillo Pérez, in *El Crack y su manifiesto* (2006), "el título mismo, elegido para definirse, señala ya un afán de internacionalización, sino de anglofilia; *crack*, palabra que en inglés significa fisura o grieta y es también la onomatopeya de algo que se quiebra" ("the title itself, chosen to self-define, already indicates a desire for internationalization, if not for anglophilia; *crack*, a word that in English means fissure or rift and is also the onomatopoeia for something shattering"; 83). According to the scholar, there is a clear genealogical intent in the Crack, in that its members aimed at defining themselves as heirs of a novel they call *profound*, which signalled a break with the literature produced after the Boom. Much like the *novelas totales* of the 1960s, the Crack novels propose complex literary worlds, non-linear structures, and narrative polyphony. There does not seem to be a specific thematic legacy in the production of the Crack authors; their only concern is that the topics broached be substantial and worth developing. In this sense, it could be argued that the Crack had a more intellectual and elitist approach than McOndo, another literary manifesto that appeared in the mid-1990s. Nevertheless, the movements come together in their rejection of a restrictive vision of the continent, understood through magical realism only. They both reflect Latin America's reality as more globalized and decentralized than ever.

The members of the Crack consider that they "tienen el derecho—como todos los escritores del mundo—de escribir sobre cualquier tema que se les ocurra" and "de ubicar la acción de sus novelas en el lugar que se les ocurra" ("have the right—like all the writers in the world—to write about any topic they choose" and "to locate the action in their novels wherever they so choose"; Volpi, "Código" 183). Using international settings and global events in their narratives does not make them less Latin American than authors who choose to set theirs in a familiar environment; indeed, "la ubicación es subsidiaria de la forma y no al revés" ("setting is subordinate to form and not the reverse"; 184). Using global settings is a choice that allows them to write about any topic in a credible manner. However international it may be, the Crack is above all "un grupo mexicano" ("a Mexican group") that "se siente orgulloso de pertenecer a la rica tradición literaria latinoamericana," but which "detesta el nacionalismo entendido como marca excluyente" ("is proud to belong to the rich Latin American literary tradition, but which detests nationalism understood as an exclusionary trait"; 186). They see nationalism as an "invento del siglo diecinueve, orgullo impuesto en el veinte, atavismo que nos enfermó de amor a lo particular para alejarnos de lo universal que . . . nos empuja a decir 'mi cultura' en detrimento de 'la cultura.' . . . La nación en singular no existe" ("invention of the nineteenth century, a sense of pride imposed in the twentieth, an atavism that made us lovesick for the specific, moving us away from the universal that . . . propels us to say 'my culture' to the detriment of 'culture.' . . . The nation in the singular does not exist"; Palou, *Pequeño diccionario* 202). It is not surprising, then, that Volpi, much like Vargas Llosa, denounces all forms of nationalism and extreme ideologies, for "cualquier ideología es, de entrada, una forma excluyente de otras variedades de pensamiento" ("any ideology is, from the outset, a way of excluding other types of thought"; Volpi, "Yo soy una novela"), which goes against his very understanding of literature and fiction. This also sets the tone for the supranational narratives for which the members of the Crack are known.

## The End of National Narrative

Like his fellow authors of the Crack, Volpi transgresses the traditional values of Mexican society, and, as we have already seen, expresses an existential ambivalence when asked to define his identity. Wilfrido H. Corral claims, in *La prosa/cultura no ficticia según Leonardo Valencia y Jorge Volpi* (*Prose and non-fiction culture according to Leonardo Valencia and Jorge Volpi*), that "si hasta cierto punto Volpi parece argüir que todos podemos ser ciudadanos en la república de las letras, lo cual es cierto, por otro parece decir que primero hay que ser ciudadano del país donde uno ha nacido. Esta impresión se desprende de su invariable elección de autores mexicanos, y su constante mención de ellos como ejemplos a seguir" ("if to a certain extent Volpi seems to argue that we can all be citizens in the republic of letters, which is true, on the other hand he seems to say that one must first be a citizen of one's country of birth. This impression stems from his invariable choice of Mexican authors, and his constant mention of them as examples to follow"; 377). As such, Volpi is aware that his literary production is part of his national history, although he is very critical of that history. In this regard, he appears to relate to the cosmopolitan outlook of intellectuals such as Alfonso Reyes and Jorge Luis Borges, who stated that identity lies not in national stereotypes, but rather in a common sense of belonging and openness to others—in many ways, an articulation of rooted cosmopolitanism. Volpi has expressed this view of literature, literary tradition, and criticism in various short stories, essays, blog posts, and newspaper articles. In what follows, I analyze two representative texts to illustrate his vision of literature.

Volpi uses satire and parody in "El fin de la narrativa latinoamericana" ("The End of Latin American Narrative"; 2004) to examine the "purity" of the Latin American author's identity. It arguably mirrors Borges's "El escritor argentino y la tradición" ("The Argentine Writer and Tradition") and could be considered Volpi's own cosmopolitan manifesto. Volpi's examination led to some of the same contradictions, disagreements, and disputes within Mexican letters, not unlike when Borges ironically tried to resolve the essence of Argentinean identity in his time. These ties to his predecessors, in terms of both genre and form, reveal Volpi's understanding of the literary tradition in which he is evolving.

In the essay, which takes the form of a literary review, Volpi parodies the work of critic Ignatius Hieronymus Berry, a fictional professor at the University of North Dakota. The hybrid writing allows him to formulate a critical perspective, sarcastic in tone, on the pessimistic view allegedly held by scholars of the new generations of Latin American authors. The fictional Berry, with whom the Mexican disagrees, is a fierce critic of new Latin American novelists like Chilean Alberto Fuguet and Volpi himself. (Born in 1964, Fuguet is one of the founding members of the McOndo movement.) The scholar argues that the Boom was the golden age of the Latin American narrative, and that anything that came afterwards is of little critical interest: "como se sabe, a toda época de esplendor le sigue una de decadencia, y es justamente lo que ocurrió a partir de este momento" ("as we know, every age of splendour is followed by one of decadence, and that is exactly what happened from that moment on"; 33). He highlights the decadence of the new production, and how it strays from what he deems proper literature. Berry harshly criticizes the status of certain international authors, and explains that

> a partir de la década de los noventa, un grupo de escritores comenzó a revelarse torpemente contra su condición hispánica. Nacidos a partir de los sesenta, no experimentaron las convulsiones ideológicas de sus predecesores y tal vez por ello no se involucraron con los problemas esenciales de sus países. Su desarraigo fue tan notorio, que al leer sus obras hoy en día, resulta imposible reconocer sus nacionalidades.
>
> beginning in the 1990s, a group of writers started to awkwardly reveal themselves as rejecting their Hispanic condition. Born in the 1960s, they did not experience the same

> ideological upheavals as their predecessors and perhaps that is why they did not get involved in the essential problems of their countries. Their lack of roots was so obvious that in reading their works today, it is impossible to ascertain their nationalities. (35)

First, Berry comments that these authors rejected their *condición hispánica* ("Hispanic condition"), which could not be further from the truth. The novels of the younger generations are written in Spanish—even if all the authors speak English, and most of them French—which makes these novels part of the de facto Hispanic tradition. Second, he criticizes their supposed lack of national allegiance, which he bases on the premise that they are not using explicit identity markers. The scholar thus disregards the production of Mexican cosmopolitan authors such as Carlos Fuentes and Jorge Cuesta, among others, who are giants of Spanish American letters, but who also produced a corpus of deterritorialized narratives that do not openly discuss national identity. The fictional Berry firmly believes that the cosmopolitan and ahistorical outlook of this *grupo de escritores* toward Latin American literary tradition is wrong. He regrets their obstinacy and stubbornness in rejecting the legacy of such great writers as Jorge Luis Borges and Juan Rulfo, who achieved worldwide success without despising their country of origin or their national identity (33). This criticism echoes the one made by many actual literary critics, like Christopher Domínguez Michael, who deemed the works of the new generations insufficiently national. Berry further suggests that novelists born after the 1960s forgot true national concerns "con el propósito de integrar su obra al mercado internacional" ("in order to integrate their work into the international marketplace"; 35). In addition to their imputed commercial interests, Berry points out a flaw in their reasoning: while the younger generations condemn the idea of a light literature—as did their forefathers, from whom the younger generations want to distance themselves at all costs—they are complacent toward the global literary market, since they do not mind adapting their novels to the needs of the marketplace. Berry argues that they do not long to join the Latin American canon, or even the global one, which would ensure their longevity, and that they would rather succeed by selling books, a stance that the professor considers despicable. As we will see shortly, this criticism is also levelled at the global novel.

Berry's position is similar to that of Argentinean nationalists who criticized Borges in the 1950s, which prompted him to write "El escritor argentino y la tradición." He completely disqualifies the members of the new wave due to the absence of distinctive national traits in their work: he affirms that their abandonment of the homeland, as well as its literary tradition, is clear evidence of their disdain for their country and continent. He deplores the fact that globalization has blurred the boundaries between different national cultures in Latin America, and appears frustrated that, today, it would be completely impossible to distinguish a Mexican writer, such as Volpi (Crack), from a Chilean counterpart, such as Fuguet (McOndo). For him, 1996 marked the beginning of the "tarea de demolición, a través de dos sucesos paralelos" ("task of demolition, through two parallel events"; 36) that doomed Latin America literature—namely,

> la publicación de la antología *McOndo*, prologada por los chilenos Alberto Fuguet y Sergio Gómez—su título era ya una burda sátira del territorio imaginario de Márquez—y la provocadora presentación del Manifiesto del autodenominado "grupo del *crack*" en México. Ambos fenómenos inaugurales evidenciaban ya las disfunciones de ambas cofradías: su afán teatral, su vocación de dirigirse a los *mass media* y su común rechazo del realismo mágico eran pruebas suficientes de que sus ambiciones estaban más del lado de la publicidad y del mercado que de la verdadera literatura.

> the publication of the McOndo anthology, with its preface by Chileans Alberto Fuguet and Sergio Gómez—its title already a heavy-handed satire of the imaginary territory created by Márquez—and the provocative release of the Manifesto of the self-proclaimed "crack group" in Mexico. Both of these inaugural phenomena already displayed the dysfunctions within both fraternities: their theatrical eagerness, their vocation for addressing themselves to the mass

media and their shared rejection of magical realism were sufficient proof that their ambitions leaned more toward publicity and marketing than toward real literature. (36)

He calls them *dysfunctional*, which implies that, for Berry, as for many scholars before him, there is only one literary tradition in Latin America: the national one. He also considers magical realism the true Latin American genre. Moreover, this new group of writers "se encargó de eliminar para siempre la identidad de la narrativa hispánica" ("took upon itself the task of permanently eliminating the identity of Hispanic narrative"; 35), "comportándose públicamente como cualquier escritor occidental corriente" ("behaving publicly like any other normal Western writer"; 36). Accordingly, there is such as thing as a defined *Latin American literary identity*, which should always be evident in these writers' works. It would thus appear that the world literary tradition is available for all writers, save for Latin American ones. This satire aims to underscore the obvious contradictions in the points outlined by the professor, since he, as previously mentioned, gives much credit to Borges's input into the Latin American canon, but conveniently forgets that the Argentinean short-story writer was once criticized for having set aside national concerns, as well as over the question of identity definition.

The creation of the Berry character positions Volpi to comment upon—and satirize—the prevailing academic opinion and myopia regarding the new generation of writers. Well aware of previous literary traditions, Volpi maintains that literary critics of Berry's kind are mistaken, since "se olvidan de algo muy importante: desde el siglo XVI, los escritores de lo que hoy es América Latina siempre han creído pertenecer a Occidente" ("they forget something very important: since the sixteenth century, the writers of what is now Latin America have always believed that they belong to the West"; 38). There is no contradiction whatsoever in being both a Mexican and a Western author. Cosmopolitanism is not such a far-fetched stance for the new generations; it has always been part of the literature of the continent. Volpi dismisses the idea that literature should be defined "por los rasgos diferenciales del país que la produce" ("by the distinguishing features of the country that produces it"; 38), and adds that

> en América Latina han coexistido estos dos bandos irreconciliables: los "nacionalistas" y los "cosmopolitas." Sin embargo, no fue sino hasta los años treinta del siglo XX cuando el escritor mexicano Jorge Cuesta asentó el argumento definitivo en contra de los primeros: el nacionalismo—afirmó—es también, a fin de cuentas, una invención europea. Por desgracia, sus palabras no lograron terminar la discusión, la cual se ha prolongado con diversos ropajes hasta nuestra época.
>
> in Latin America these two irreconcilable sides have coexisted: the "nationalists" and the "cosmopolitans." However, it was not until the 1930s that Mexican writer Jorge Cuesta set out the definitive argument against the first group: nationalism, he claimed, is also, after all, a European invention. Unfortunately, his words did not succeed in putting an end to the discussion, which has continued in various disguises until our time. (38)

Cuesta made this affirmation about twenty years before Borges published his seminal essay, which highlights the evergreen nature of that discussion. Instead of lamenting the supposed demise of Latin American letters, the Mexican "prefiere preguntarse con cierto escepticismo qué significa, a fin de cuentas, ser latinoamericano al principio del siglo XXI" ("prefers to ask himself with some skepticism what it means, after all, to be Latin American at the beginning of the twenty-first century"; 39). However, it is a question that no one can answer with certainty, since identity is an ever-evolving process.

In the spirit of his forefathers, and unlike the fictional Berry, Volpi favours cosmopolitan writing that is in dialogue with a global canon:

> lo cierto es que los mejores escritores latinoamericanos han sido, en la mayor parte de los casos, "cosmopolitas." . . . En distintos momentos de la historia [Paz, Fuentes, Elizondo, Arredondo, Pitol, García Ponce] fueron acusados por los nacionalistas de copiar modelos extranjeros y de dejarse

> seducir por las tendencias de moda, cuando en realidad hacían exactamente lo contrario: fundar y preservar la mejor tradición literaria del país, esa tradición que, a fuerza de ser generosamente universal . . . se volvió también ricamente nacional.
>
> the truth is that the best Latin American writers have been, in most cases, "cosmopolitan." . . . At different times in history [Paz, Fuentes, Elizondo, Arredondo, Pitol, García Ponce] were accused by nationalists of copying foreign models and of allowing themselves to be seduced by trends in fashion, when in fact they were doing exactly the opposite: founding and preserving the best literary tradition of the country, that tradition which, by virtue of being generously universal . . . also became richly national. (39)

Volpi, like Carlos Fuentes in *Geografía de la novela*, makes Reyes's proclamation—"Para ser provechosamente nacional, hay que ser generosamente universal" ("In order to be richly national, we must be generously universal"; qtd. in Fuentes 25)—his own. The novelists who started writing during the 1990s are part of this universal tradition, and are resisting a diktat that forces them to be authentic followers of the Latin American style, or rather, proud heirs of the Boom. Although they reclaim some aspects of this production, such as the depth of their texts and literary experimentation, they reject the stereotype of the "Latin American writer," and choose instead to adhere to "la mejor tradición latinoamericana, es decir, la que siempre ha promovido un cosmopolitismo abierto e incluyente" ("the best Latin American tradition, that is, the one that has always promoted an open and inclusive cosmopolitanism"; Volpi, "El fin de la narrative" 40), making them the successors of both Borges and the Boom.

### Rejecting Ideological *realismo mágico*

Along with other authors who emerged in the 1990s, Volpi rises up—in that movement of creative affirmation to which Harold Bloom refers in *The Anxiety of Influence*—against the canonical figures of the 1960s, while also rescuing both their literary exploration and their predecessors' universal perspective.[5] He reformulates the arguments put forth by his precursors and establishes a personal genealogy in which a cosmopolitan perspective is the outstanding criterion. In fact, both in his fiction and in his essays, Volpi rejects nationalism and claims a place in the continental canon while establishing a critical distance from the national and Latin Americanist concerns of the previous generations.

*El insomnio de Bolívar* is another patent example of Volpi's multigeneric prose: it combines political forecast, fantasy literature, and science fiction. The essays raise many questions, several of which remain unanswered, and they cover, among other topics, history, government systems, and the economic problems of Latin America. Each *consideración*—as he entitles each chapter—proposes a reflection on a different aspect of the continent, explores its meaning through the analysis of its past, its present, and its possible and probable future, and concludes, in an ironic manner, that the best thing Latin America could do would be to disappear and merge with North America, à la European Union. Although seemingly an imaginative work of futuristic fiction, *El insomnio de Bolívar* can also be classified as a political essay.

Volpi's reflections on Latin American literature and literary tradition are obviously the most relevant to the present analysis, which is why I concentrate on this specific aspect of the essays. While only the third essay is openly about literary tradition, Volpi's thoughts on literature are scattered throughout the book. One major criticism Volpi makes in *El insomnio de Bolívar*, as well as elsewhere, has to do with the prevalence of magical realism in Latin American literature.[6] Not only is he dissatisfied that it has come to be synonymous with the region's literature, he also resents the fact that it has become an expectation, an "etiqueta sociopolítica" (70) ("socio-political label"). He recalls that

> Como estudiantes de filología hispánica—lo que en México se llama simplemente literatura española—los latinoamericanos éramos asociados, irremediablemente, con García Márquez y el realismo mágico. Poco importaban la tradición prehispánica, los tres siglos de virreinato, el moroso siglo XIX o las infinitas modalidades literarias explo-

radas en América Latina a lo largo del siglo XX: si uno decía "estudio literatura latinoamericana," el 98 por ciento de los oyentes asumía que uno era experto en mariposas amarillas, doncellas voladoras y niños con cola de cerdo. Y ello no gracias al denodado estudio de los entresijos de Macondo, sino a la convivencia diaria con lo maravilloso presente en nuestras tierras.

As students of Hispanic philology—what in Mexico is simply called Spanish literature—we Latin Americans were inevitably associated with García Márquez and magical realism. Little did the pre-Hispanic tradition, the three centuries of viceroyalty, the overdue nineteenth century or the infinite literary modalities explored in Latin America throughout the twentieth century matter: if one said "I am studying Latin American literature," 98 per cent of listeners assumed that one was an expert in yellow butterflies, flying maidens, and children born with pigs' tails. And this was not due to the bold study of the ins and outs of Macondo, but to daily coexistence with the marvelous present in our lands. (21)

This ideological understanding of Latin American literature is *excluyente* and, much like nationalism, confines writers to a very specific space and time period. However, it was the reactions to the publication of *En busca de Klingsor* (1999) that made Volpi realize the extent of the expectations toward Latin American authors: the novel was deemed not Mexican enough, and as a result, some critics argued it should not be called a "Mexican novel"; indeed, Volpi claims that a literary critic even demanded "que se [le] retirara el pasaporte por no escribir sobre México" ("that his passport be revoked for not writing about Mexico"; *El insomnio de Bolívar* 25). While in the first drafts, the protagonist was Mexican, Volpi eventually realized that, for the sake of his credibility in the literary world, he would have to change his nationality; the protagonist therefore became American.[7] While this was a minor change in the narrative, Volpi claims that

Aquella decisión pragmática de transformar a un mexicano en gringo se convirtió en un inesperado manifiesto. Si a ello se suma que, en efecto, al lado de mis amigos mexicanos del *Crack* yo llevaba años renegando del realismo mágico que se exigía a los escritores latinoamericanos—y que nada tenía que ver con la grandeza de García Márquez—, el malentendido estaba a punto. En medio de aquel alud de elogios y ataques, igualmente enfáticos, desperté como un autor doblemente exótico. Exótico por ser latinoamericano. Y más exótico aún por no escribir sobre América Latina (¿cuándo se ha cuestionado a un escritor inglés o francés por no escribir sobre Inglaterra o Francia?). De nada servía aclarar que antes de Klingsor todas mis novelas se situaban en México o que había escrito dos ensayos sobre historia intelectual mexicana: esta novela me transformó en un apátrida literario, celebrado y denostado por las mismas razones equivocadas.

That pragmatic decision to transform a Mexican into a gringo became an unexpected manifesto. If we add to this the fact that, along with my Mexican friends from the Crack, I had been rejecting for years the magical realism that was demanded of Latin American writers—and that had nothing to do with the greatness of García Márquez—the misunderstanding was timely. Amid that avalanche of praise and attacks, equally emphatic, I woke up as a doubly exotic author. Exotic for being Latin American. And even more exotic for not writing about Latin America (when has an English or French writer been called out for not writing about England or France?). It was useless to point out that before Klingsor all my novels were set in Mexico or that I had written two essays on Mexican intellectual history: this novel transformed me into a stateless literary figure, celebrated and reviled for the same wrongheaded reasons. (24–5)

Volpi henceforth found himself in the same predicament as some of the Boom writers. What makes a Latin American author truly Latin American? The fact that the novels take place in the hemisphere? The fact that the author was born on the continent? From Volpi's perspective, literary critics find it quite difficult to see past nationality when it comes to establishing literary belonging:

> Nada detenía la avalancha: en cada entrevista y presentación pública me veía obligado a aclarar mi nacionalidad y a señalar, en vano, que los escenarios no hacen que una obra sea más o menos latinoamericana. Aquella ruidosa querella tuvo, por fortuna, sus ventajas: me hizo enfrentarme a las permanentes contradicciones del nacionalismo y me animó a reflexionar sobre lo que significaba ser mexicano y latinoamericano.
>
> Nothing stopped the avalanche: in every interview and public appearance I was forced to spell out my nationality and point out, in vain, that the setting does not make a work more or less Latin American. That noisy quarrel had, fortunately, its advantages: it made me face the permanent contradictions of nationalism and motivated me to reflect on what it meant to be Mexican and Latin American. (25)

This reflection led him to reject nationalism, based on the fact that it is *excluyente*, both in political and literary terms. Indeed, according to Volpi and many writers of his generation, the so-called Latin American author no longer exists. He maintains that "ninguno se asume ligado a una literatura nacional—Fresán define: mi patria es mi biblioteca—, y ninguno cree que un escritor latinoamericano deba parecer, ay, latinoamericano" ("no one sees himself as tied to a national literature—Fresán stipulates: my homeland is my library—and no one believes that a Latin American writer must appear, alas, Latin American"; 156).[8] He even maintains that "Si bien ninguno reniega abiertamente de su patria, se trata ahora de un mero referente autobiográfico y no de una denominación de origen. A diferencia de sus predecesores, ninguno de ellos se muestra obsesionado por la identidad latinoamericana—y menos por la mexicana, la boliviana o la argentina—aun si continúan escribiendo sobre sus países o incluso los de sus vecinos" ("Although no one openly rejects their homeland, it has now become a mere autobiographical reference and not a designation of origin. Unlike their predecessors, none of these writers are obsessed with Latin American identity—let alone with Mexican, Bolivian, or Argentinian identity—even if they continue to write about their countries or even those of their neighbours"; 168). This is a departure from the literature of both the Boom and the Post-Boom, and a clear rejection of literature conceived in national terms. Moreover, he claims that "Ninguno tiene ni la más remota idea de cuál es el estado actual de la literatura latinoamericana, e incluso alguno duda que la literatura latinoamericana aún exista" ("No one has even the remotest idea of what the current state of Latin American literature is, and some even doubt that Latin American literature still exists"; 162). If neither national nor continental literature exists, what is left is literature understood within a global, or universal, framework. Volpi proposes that authors be radical and venture outside any artificially conceived boundaries to find new ways to tell their stories. If the "Latin American author" does not exist anymore, he does not have to abide by literary dogmas. Volpi thus argues for complete literary freedom:

> Seamos radicales: la literatura latinoamericana ya no existe. Preciso: existen cientos o miles de escritores latinoamericanos o, mejor dicho, cientos o miles de escritores chilenos, hondureños, dominicanos, venezolanos, etcétera, pero un cuerpo literario único, dotado con rasgos reconocibles, no. . . . Y la verdad es que no hay nada que lamentar. La idea de una literatura nacional, dotada con particularidades típicas e irrepetibles, ajenas por completo a las demás, es un anacrónico invento del siglo XIX.
>
> Let's be radical: Latin American literature no longer exists. To be clear: there are hundreds or thousands of Latin American writers or, rather, hundreds or thousands of Chilean, Honduran, Dominican, Venezuelan, etc., writers, but a unique literary body, bearing recognizable traits, no.

> ... And the truth is that there is nothing here to regret. The idea of a national literature, with typical and unrepeatable particularities, completely unrelated to others, is an anachronistic invention of the nineteenth century. (165)

National literature is not the only *anacrónico invento del siglo XIX*—so is nationalism.

## The Global Novel

The two works I study here belong to the category of the global novel, a genre that has yet to be properly defined. Two definitions predominate: scholars either see it as a positive type of literature, since these narratives open up possibilities for authors who would otherwise be confined to their own national markets, or else view it as extremely negative, as novels deemed to belong in this genre lack national elements—discussions that clearly mirror those heard in Latin America and that Volpi considers obsolete. Indeed, the author explained in an interview that "la novela es en el mundo contemporáneo el espacio ideal para las reflexiones globales, fuera de la hiperespecialización de la ciencia y las ciencias sociales" ("the novel is, in the contemporary world, the ideal space for global reflection, outside the hyperspecialization of science and the social sciences"; qtd. in López de Abiada 151). It is, then, but a small step from understanding the novel as the best space to discuss world issues to writing global novels. Héctor Hoyos, in *Beyond Bolaño: The Global Latin American Novel*, also sees the emergence of Latin American novels of this type as positive, since they can discuss universal topics and memory, and thus acquire a "world literary standing" (6). Moreover, they "can contribute to consolidating both the world and Latin America as their chambers of resonance" (7), "cultivate the tension between the global and the local" (22), and show a "profound articulation of globality" (23). For Hoyos, "The global Latin American novel seeks not to flatten, but to give an almost tactile quality to the conflicting forces that define world-consciousness" (23) and as such, it shows a clear "articulation of a global conscience" (24), always of course from a Latin American perspective. I contend that, in their articulation of both Latin America and the world, Volpi's novels depict rooted cosmopolitanism as a positive mode of engagement with the world.

Others disagree with Hoyos's view. According to Tim Parks, the existence of a "world market for literature" means that readers "become part of an international community," in his mind a community that develops around an author's popularity, rather than one based on the quality of that author's work. In this, Parks echoes the fictional Berry of "El fin de la narrativa latinoamericana." He claims that this type of fiction is tantamount to erasing national particularities and renders obsolete "the kind of work that revels in the subtle nuances of its own language and literary culture" (Parks). He fears that some authors, in a conscious attempt to make their material easier to translate and to be understood by foreign audiences, will shy away from using their own linguistic variations, such as Mexican Spanish, and from broaching national topics—which he calls "obstacles to international comprehension" (Parks). The novel, then, by erasing identity markers, would homogenize literature and make narrative a mere product that can be consumed anywhere in the world. This is a valid criticism, as critics and scholars have indeed noted the standardization of language in the production of some authors. However, I contend that this criticism does not apply to Volpi.[9] Parks's comments echo some that members of the Crack made at the beginning of the 1990s—namely, that *literatura light* ought to be confronted at all costs, and readers challenged with dense, complex narratives. As such, an outlook like that of Parks's does not take into consideration the fact that, by having both the world and a national setting as its chamber of resonance, the genre can tackle both national and broader concerns, as well as the tensions between them. Moreover, this outlook ignores the premise of the Crack, which is to challenge readers, regardless of whether a novel uses a national or an international setting. According to Adam Kirsch, "the novel is already implicitly global as soon as it starts to speculate on or record the experience of human beings in the twenty-first century. Global novels are those that make this dimension explicit" (39). In a contemporary world, it is almost impossible for a narrative to confine itself to national concerns, as those are bound to be intertwined with international issues. Whether we like it or not, literature in the twenty-first century has acquired a supranational character. This argument links back to Pheng Cheah's positions, to which I referred in the introduction—namely, that narratives create bonds across borders because, while time and place matter, stories are ultimately about the human experience they (re)present, more than about the settings in which they play out.

Given the political and ideological underpinnings of Volpi's oeuvre, we can now explore how these factors apply to specific novels. The two narratives studied in this chapter are, to date, two of the most explicit of Volpi's novels in terms of cosmopolitanism and globality. In both, key characters concretely tackle world concerns. It would appear that this is Volpi's preferred genre in which to address ideas and the conceptualization of identity at critical moments. Both novels deal openly with universal concerns, pivotal events of the twentieth century, and their effects on individuals. These narratives are also about travelling, be it abroad or at home, and how travel can distance an individual from loved ones, not only physically but also emotionally, and even lead to rejection. They both concentrate on times that were especially charged, from the point of view of politics and the definition—or redefinition—of identity, around the world. While these stories do not take place in a Latin American context, they can still be read as metaphors for events happening across the continent. They create international narrative universes and hybrid characters subjected to the stress of the breakdown of an existing world order. I would even argue that in these novels, events and the processes that result from them are the main characters. Volpi concentrates on defining moments of the twentieth century, portraying them from an ironic distance. Since these life-changing events are the true protagonists of the novels, Volpi's characters appear as empty shells that serve primarily as a pretext for discussing major world events.

## *El fin de la locura*: Cosmopolitanism and the Global Intellectual

*El fin de la locura* (*The End of Madness*; 2003[10]) recounts the European and Latin American trajectory of Mexican psychoanalyst Aníbal Quevedo, from the Paris of 1968 to Carlos Salinas de Gortari's Mexico in the 1990s. He moves through various revolutionary movements to the emblematic moment of the triumph of neo-liberalism and contemporary discourses concerning the end of ideologies. The novel presents cosmopolitanism from the perspective of a Europeanized character in order to parody the

Latin American intellectual of the twentieth century, and explores global madness, understood as the widespread ideas of revolution and utopian thought. These are interpreted as a totalitarian impulse, one that ultimately leads to various failures. *El fin de la locura* addresses Latin American history obliquely, analyzing it in the broader context of both global and intellectual history. It also shows how this intersection in turn influences both the region and the world. With its oblique fictionalization, as well as its use of parody, intertextuality, and irony, the novel critically tackles issues pertaining to the recent history of Latin America, concentrating on the flaws and failings of the intellectual. I see this as Volpi's criticism of the political situation in Mexico at the turn of the twenty-first century, and the failure of the intellectual in the twentieth. For this reason, I find this novel particularly valuable when it comes to studying the evolving relationship between history and fiction in contemporary Latin American novels.

*El fin de la locura* showcases two major characters in a constant ideological battle: the Mexican psychoanalyst Aníbal Quevedo and his ever-disappearing French love interest, Claire. Quevedo is crazy about Claire, and is prepared to go to great lengths to make her fall in love with him. Claire, a French university student, is involved in a variety of social revolutionary movements, indeed she "está obsesionada con América Latina" ("is obsessed with Latin America"; 190) and the Cuban Revolution. She is an idealist and a true revolutionary. Quevedo, for his part, does not share her enthusiasm, but is willing to commit himself to revolution if it wins him Claire's love. But whereas Quevedo still questions revolutionary movements, Claire stays true to them until the end.

The novel is divided into two major parts: the "Primera parte" takes place in France during the revolutionary movements of May 1968, while the "Segunda Parte" takes place mostly in Mexico. The first part is itself divided into two major sections, "Amar es dar lo que no se tiene a alguien que no lo quiere" ("To love is to give what one does not have to someone who does not want it")—which recounts Quevedo's arrival in France and meeting Claire, who rejects his love time and again—and "Si Althusser permanece en cura de sueño, el movimiento de masas va bien" ("If Althusser remains in sleep therapy, the mass movement is going well")—which recounts Quevedo's first foray into revolutionary movements. The second part is also divided into two sections, "Quevedo por Quevedo" ("Quevedo by Quevedo")—which recounts Quevedo's disenchantment with revolution, and "Microfísica del poder" ("Microphysics of power")— which concentrates on the downward spiral that leads to his suicide in 1989, as a new world order is emerging.

*El fin de la locura* is at the intersection of two literary genres. Like most of Volpi's multi-generic prose, the novel assumes a hybrid form: it is a collection of essays, both literary and critical, of correspondence between various characters, interviews, psychological analysis, and personal journal entries, compiled by an editor—a key figure of the historical novel (Pons 48)—who confronts the reader with complementary points of view.[11] The use of various sources highlights the fact that both as a writer and a psychoanalyst, Quevedo does not seem to have his own style. His incompetence, doubled with his desire to learn from the best, means that every time he encounters a seminal intellectual figure, he ends up imitating their way of thinking and writing, mimicking the colonial mindset and passively reproducing it: the intellectual from the periphery copying the metropolitan discourse and style, instead of producing his own. The texts of Quevedo's personal file, compiled by a publisher who remains unknown until the end of the novel, emulate the theoretical production of philosophers. For example, the texts of the third part, following Barthes's style, are fragmentary and chaotic, while the fourth and last part, consisting of various manuscripts, newspaper clippings, interviews, and letters, is reminiscent of Foucault's archivist type. Each section of the novel is structured around the life of a French structuralist—Lacan, Althusser, Barthes, and Foucault—and besides painting the European intellectual context of the 1960s and the '70s, the narrative portrays the life story of each thinker. In this way, the novel moves from intellectual history to the history of intellectuals, with some artistic license (Areco 307).

Aníbal Quevedo, given his initials, already alludes to *Don Quijote*, particularly Alonso Quijano and his famous *locura*.[12] He wakes up one day in Paris suffering from amnesia: "Sin saber cómo, un buen día había despertado en París, sin memoria de los días anteriores; por lo visto llevaba allí una buena temporada y, cuando al fin [se] había atrevido a pasear por la ciudad, [se] encontr[ó] en medio de una batalla campal entre policías y estudiantes" ("Without knowing how, one fine day he had awakened in

Paris, without any memory of the previous days; apparently he had been there for a good while and, when at last [he] had dared to walk around the city, [he] found himself in the middle of a pitched battle between the police and students"; Volpi, *El fin de la locura* 31). Quevedo claims not to remember anything from his past life: "Al despertar, los murmullos se habían desvanecido, pero seguía sin saber por qué estaba lejos de mi hogar, de mi familia, de mi consultorio. Mi mundo se había desvanecido para siempre. Como si hubiese renunciado a la cordura, ahora yo era incapaz de distinguir la fantasía de la realidad" ("When I woke up, the murmurs had faded, but I still didn't know why I was far away from my home, my family, my office. My world had disappeared forever. As if I had given up on sanity, I was now unable to distinguish between fantasy and reality"; 22). One of the few things he does remember is his *consultorio*, his clinic, which justifies his pursuit of the key figures of French psychoanalysis. The lack of memories from his previous Mexican life allows him to slowly become French. Quevedo ends up meeting and conversing with his role models, and travelling to Cuba to psychoanalyze Fidel Castro and to Chile, where he provides the same treatment to Salvador Allende. These encounters have a great impact on him: "en vez de enloquecer[lo] leyendo novelas de caballerías, [lo] enloquece con tratados de marxismo y maoísmo" ("instead of driving himself mad reading novels of chivalry, he drives himself mad with treatises on Marxism and Maoism"; Volpi, "Política y literatura" 76). Quevedo embodies the subordination of the Latin American intellectual to foreign models—namely, the European one, which he not only absorbs, but later brings back with him to Latin America.

*El fin de la locura* is, in fact, a history of the many failures that push the protagonist toward his own end. At the global level, it is the failure of the revolutionary utopia of 1968, in both Paris and Mexico. On a personal level, it is the failure of Aníbal Quevedo, first as an intellectual and as a psychoanalyst, then as a Mexican intellectual and revolutionary. In the novel, Volpi analyzes, in addition to the debates generated by the student movements of the period, the psychoanalytic, Marxist, and structuralist theories prevalent on the left at the time, and criticizes the role of Latin American intellectuals inside and outside their countries or continent in recent decades, so as to provide various examples of failures that defined, according to the novel, the last decades of the twentieth century.

Another global aspect explored in the novel is that of the intellectual as a key figure in public life in the twentieth century, notwithstanding national categorization.

The protagonist is the archetypical anti-hero. Quevedo has big ambitions but lacks the personality to succeed. As a fallible individual, he is aware of his flaws as a human being; in retrospect, about his flight from Mexico he says: "Si salí de mi patria fue porque en ella me sentía atrapado, porque un paciente demostró de modo brutal mi incompetencia, porque tal vez ya no soportaba a mi familia" ("If I left my homeland it was because I felt trapped in it, because a patient demonstrated my incompetence in a brutal fashion, because perhaps I could no longer stand my family"; 289). His move to France, which was initially presented as accidental, becomes a way to start over. Quevedo has two major reasons to escape from Mexico. First, he feels *atrapado* (trapped) within the borders of his country, which he believes to be lacking a proper psychoanalytical culture. Second, he feels *atrapado* by his family, which he abandons and never sees again. By travelling to Paris, the quintessential cosmopolitan city, he rejects those closest to him, which makes his cosmopolitan project flawed from the start. This reveals the ambiguities of Quevedo's discourse: first, he claims to be suffering from amnesia and not to remember much of his past life, but later on, in the section allegedly written around 1980, he refers to leaving Mexico of his own volition.

Once in France, he tries to restart his career as an intellectual. He spends time with Lacan, Althusser, Barthes, and Foucault, so as to learn everything he can from these great masters. Foucault is the thinker that he emulates and works with the most, yet he does not find his place with him either. Nor does he find it with struggling students who fight within several revolutionary movements based on the ideas of the structuralists. Although she keeps rejecting him, Quevedo wants to prove himself to Claire, his Dulcinea, and enters the Parisian student movement. After several confrontations during which members of Claire's revolutionary cell are jailed, the group decides to start a hunger strike in "La capilla de Saint-Bernard, en plena estación de Montparnasse" ("the Saint Bernard chapel, in the centre of Montparnasse station"; 181). At first, Aníbal attempts to convince Claire of the madness of her plan—"¡Una huelga de hambre!—me aterroricé—. Claire, ¿no te parece que exageras?" ("A hunger strike! I panicked. Claire, don't you think you're going too far?"; 179)—but in an effort to seduce her, "no [le] qued[a] otra alternativa que sumar[se] a ella" ("he doesn't have any other option than to join it"; 181). Claire is an idealist who believes that she can actively take part in changing the world; according to Quevedo, "Lo único que la mantenía lúcida era la idea de que, a pesar de la inquina y los errores, aún era posible modificar las reglas del mundo" ("The only thing that kept her lucid was the idea that, despite the grievances and mistakes, it was still possible to change the rules of the world"; 179). Claire, a true revolutionary, believes in the power of the hunger strike because she is convinced it can change the world—although, conveniently, her physician does not allow her to take part in it. Quevedo, however, only wants to please her: he takes part in the strike through no will of his own, making his commitment to Claire hypocritical.

It does not take long for the young revolutionaries to become "esqueletos revolucionarios, *zombis*" and "moribundos" ("revolutionary skeletons, zombies" and "at death's door"; 181). Quevedo claims that his love for Claire has brought him too close to "degradación," a state in which he does not wish to persevere for long. He tries to convince his fellow strikers that "[fingir] la inanición sin llegar a padecerla" ("faking starvation without getting to the point of suffering from it"; 182) would be a better option and achieve similar results without any suffering. He argues that they could fight more effectively if they ate, but the group rebukes him. He is told that they are "revolucionarios honrados" ("honourable revolutionaries"; 182), which only offends Quevedo even more. Since "la perspectiva de matar[se] de hambre [le] parec[e] muy poco atractiva" ("the prospect of dying of hunger held little appeal for him"; 182), he finds a way out of the chapel every night and dines on éclairs and *petits-fours* while hiding in the bathroom of the subway station. He believes that "no cometía ninguna infracción contra la causa, simplemente [se] rendía a las inquebrantables leyes de la supervivencia" ("he was not betraying the cause, he was simply surrendering to the unbreakable laws of survival"; 183). Although nobody sees through his revolutionary disguise, Quevedo has some remorse; he is aware of his moral failure and lack of ethics. While his comrades are willing to starve to death to defend their revolutionary cause, Quevedo does not understand why so much suffering is needed, and he fails as a revolutionary.

On top of the madness caused by these student movements, Quevedo is faced with his own folly in the form of the role of the Latin American intellectual who ends up far away from his country and continent. He is the embodiment of the Latin America intellectual of the nineteenth and early twentieth centuries who travels to France—in certain cases, to England—and all of a sudden forgets his origins and appropriates a different world view. Quevedo, then, is not a special case in Latin American history. Indeed, he reproduces the model forged by many artists who were trying to emancipate themselves from their national context and ended up merging—in a metaphorical manner—with the metropole. In *Littératures et cultures en dialogue* (*Literatures and Cultures in Dialogue*), French sociologist Daniel-Henri Pageaux defined this behaviour as *manic*—that is an attitude according to which

> la réalité culturelle étrangère est tenue par l'écrivain . . . comme absolument supérieure à la culture 'nationale,' d'origine. Cette supériorité affecte tout ou partie de la culture étrangère. La conséquence pour la culture d'origine, regardante, est qu'elle est tenue comme inférieure par l'écrivain. . . . À la valorisation positive de l'étranger, correspond la vision dépréciative de la culture d'origine.
>
> foreign cultural reality is held by the writer . . . as absolutely superior to the "national" culture of origin. This superiority involves either all or a part of the foreign culture. The consequence for the original, observing culture is that it is held as inferior by the writer. . . . With the valorization of the foreign comes a corresponding disparaging image of the culture of origin. (47)

This explanation of manic behaviour summarizes well Quevedo's attitude, since during his first years in Europe he values, to the detriment of his Mexican culture, French culture and philosophy. He is, then, an allegory for intellectuals of his era, one which Volpi harshly criticizes. As Pageaux explains,

> on peut dire que cette attitude maniaque a prévalu dans les rapports culturels entre Europe et Amérique Latine jusqu'au début du XXᵉ siècle: tous les artistes et hommes de lettres latino-américains avaient les yeux rivés sur les modes et révolutions culturelles parisiennes si bien que les productions nationales latino-américaines ont très longtemps été subordonnées aux schémas et techniques élaborés dans la capitale française.
>
> this manic attitude prevailed in cultural relations between Europe and Latin America until the beginning of the twentieth century: all Latin American artists and writers were fixated on Parisian cultural fashions and revolutions, and Latin American national productions were, for a very long time, subordinated to the patterns and techniques developed in the French capital. (*Littératures et cultures en dialogue* 294)

This subordination leads to blind acceptance and the imitation of foreign models, which ultimately turn into the denial of one's cultural roots.

Quevedo's only link to Mexico is through his friend Josefa, whom he likes but judges through the eyes of a French local, even though they share the same origin. When Josefa succeeds in developing an intimate relationship with Althusser—no small accomplishment, since the philosopher does not often like to see people—Quevedo becomes jealous: he does not understand why his spiritual master has no interest in discussing philosophical matters with him. Angered by the fact that his Mexican friend—whom he deems lacking in the intellectual capacities Quevedo finds necessary—has a privileged access to the philosopher, he violates her sanctuary—her bedroom—and, analyzing its contents, claims that "Su habitación reflej[a] los gustos y las manías de la clase media mexicana: pequeñas reproducciones de cuadros impresionistas, un par de vasijas con enormes flores secas, una imagen de la Virgen de Guadalupe junto a un recorte de Elvis Presley" ("Her room reflected the tastes and predilections of the Mexican middle class: small reproductions of Impressionist paintings, a pair of vases filled with huge dried flowers, an image of the Virgin of Guadalupe next to a clipping of Elvis Presley"; Volpi, *El fin de la locura* 171). He criticizes the Mexicanness of some of Josefa's belongings and behaves in a condescending manner toward her, for in his view she does not have the necessary clout to have a romantic relationship, as well as an intellectual one, with Althusser. What Quevedo fails to see is that Althusser loves Josefa *because* she is authentic and does not reject her roots. He calls her "mi añorada estrella mexicana" ("my long-awaited Mexican star"; 176) and "jirafa mexicana" ("Mexican giraffe"; 185)—terms of endearment that emphasize, rather than erase, her origins.

While Josefa keeps alive her ties with her homeland, Quevedo seems to have a complicated relationship with his Latin American identity. The massacre of the Plaza de las Tres Culturas in October 1968 in Mexico City, also known as the Tlatelolco massacre, saddens him, but he admits, albeit unwillingly, that these dead are not his:

> La tarea era espantosa y aburrida: ninguna información paliaba mi dolor. Una aciaga casualidad me había conducido a París y ahora me resultaba imposible sentir verdadera indignación ante aquellos muertos lejanos, mis muertos. Las imágenes de la manifestación del 2 de octubre, las luces de bengala en el cielo, del tiroteo, los heridos y los cadáveres lucían como simples manchas en el papel: no me concernían. Sentí ganas de vomitar. Lo peor no era mi incapacidad para odiar a Díaz Ordaz y a sus secuaces, sino la falta de un odio verdadero. Yo también estaba muerto, tan muerto como los jóvenes atravesados por las balas de los militares en Tlatelolco.

> The task was frightening and boring: no information could alleviate my pain. A fateful coincidence had led me to Paris and now it was impossible for me to feel real indignation for these distant dead, my dead ones. The images of the demonstration on October 2, the flares in the sky, the shooting, the wounded and the corpses looked like simple stains on paper: they did not concern me. I felt like vomiting. The worst was not my inability to hate Díaz Ordaz and his henchmen,

but the lack of true hatred. I was also dead, as dead as the youth shot down by the soldiers' bullets in Tlatelolco. (141)

Quevedo rejects anything that has to do with national identity, but feels sympathy for the students who fight in France. He universalizes the fight of the Mexican students without empathizing with them. This national death is symbolic, and does not mean that Quevedo has rid himself of all aspects of his Mexican identity. According to Steinberg, even if Tlatelolco is mostly absent from the narrative, it remains central to the book's development. The critic posits that

> An image travels from Mexico to become the sign that drives Quevedo's future. If, on one level, Tlatelolco initiates and organizes the protagonist's stated emancipatory desire, then on the other, more formal, level, Tlatelolco initiates and organizes the narrative's disenchantment of this desire, that is, transition, turning on the decline of the Mexican state's national-popular form and its reconfiguration in the neo-liberal era. (267)

Although Quevedo declares he is as dead as the students at the heart of Mexico City, the massacre serves as a first step in his conversion to leftist ideologies, the first step into his *locura*, although it must be noted that it is also a first step into the reaffirmation of some aspects of his identity. After Tlatelolco, he makes a point of correcting his interlocutors when they overlook his Mexican identity.

When Lacan sends him to meet Althusser, he explains to Quevedo that getting close to the philosopher should be easy:

> —Yo le enviaré una nota diciéndole que usted está muy interesado en conócerlo. . . . ¿Qué le parece si le decimos que usted prepara una memoria sobre marxismo y psicoanálisis? Además, como usted es sudamericano . . .
>
> —Mexicano . . . lo interrumpí.

—Además, como usted es *mexicano*—corrigió con enfado—, y él mantiene unos lazos especialmente afectuosos con colegas de esa parte del mundo, estoy seguro de que no dudará en recibirlo.

"I will send him a note telling him that you are very interested in meeting him. . . . How about we tell him that you are preparing a memoir on Marxism and psychoanalysis? Furthermore, as you are a South American. . ."

"—Mexican" . . . I cut him off.

"Also, since you are a Mexican," he corrected himself angrily, "and he maintains especially friendly ties with colleagues from that part of the world, I am sure he will not hesitate to meet with you." (Volpi, *El fin de la locura* 151)

In this very moment, Quevedo—although *afrancesado* ("Gallicized")—reclaims his Mexican identity. He wants to be known for his country, not for a continent. He also laughs at Claire's lack of understanding of Latin America, as she, much like Lacan, lumps together the whole region:

Estuve a punto de contarle mi experiencia posterior al dos de octubre, pero preferí seguirla escuchando; Claire me reveló entonces que ella no había estado muy lejos del lugar de la masacre y que no había dejado de pensar en mí . . .

—¿Estuviste en México?—salté.

—No, en Venezuela.

—¡En Venezuela!

Poco importaba que entre Caracas y Tlatelolco hubiese miles de kilómetros de distancia: para ella América Latina carecía de fronteras.

> I was about to tell her about my experience after October 2, but I preferred to continue listening; Claire then revealed to me that she had not been very far from the scene of the massacre and that she had not stopped thinking about me...
>
> "You were in Mexico?"
>
> "No, in Venezuela."
>
> "In Venezuela!"
>
> It mattered little that between Caracas and Tlatelolco there were thousands of kilometres: for her, Latin America had no borders. (164)

Like most Europeans, Claire does not perceive the regional differences among various Latin American cultures and nations; rather, she understands the continent as one unified element, which forces Quevedo to re-evaluate his own sense of identity.

Moreover, while a major part of the narrative takes place in Paris, the ideal city for any revolutionary endeavour in 1968, several characters ironize this fact and comment on the literary process:

> —El gran problema de este libro es que la mayor parte de las acciones se desarrollan en París—me sanciona Josefa—. ¿Sabes cuántas novelas latinoamericanas se sitúan en esta ciudad? Centenares, Aníbal, centenares...
>
> —¿Y qué quieres que haga, Josefa? ¿Que me vaya a vivir a Varsovia o a Bogotá para no incomodar a los críticos? ¿No te parece una concesión suficiente el que yo sea mexicano?
>
> "The big problem with this book is that most of the action takes place in Paris," Josefa sanctions me. "Do you know how many Latin American novels are set in this city? Hundreds, Aníbal, hundreds..."

> "And what do you want me to do, Josefa? Should I go live in Warsaw or Bogota so as not to inconvenience the critics? Don't you think that the fact that I'm Mexican is concession enough?" (305)

Once again, a Gallicized Quevedo reclaims his Mexican identity. He is aware that he fits into the stereotype of the Latin American writer in Paris.

While Quevedo realizes that he embodies a stereotype, Claire is unaware that she behaves similarly by perceiving Latin America as lacking borders. She also sees the region as the perfect playground for her revolutionary ideals; she claims that "Al fin cumplí mi sueño de hacer la revolución en América del Sur" ("Finally I achieved my dream to be a revolutionary in South America"; 164), as if she was checking off something on a bucket list. During her stay abroad, she becomes "una campesina" ("a peasant"; 164) who is accepted by the "guerrilleros locales" ("local guerrillas"; 164), who treat her as one of their own. Claire is blinded by her revolutionary fervour the same way Quevedo is blinded by his love for her. In search of Claire, Quevedo travels to Cuba, where he is first greeted by the director of the Casa de las Américas, the national publishing house, with whom he discusses the role of the revolutionary. He listens attentively to the claims that "No basta con adherirse verbalmente a la revolución para ser un intelectual revolucionario; ni siquiera basta con las acciones propias de un revolucionario. . . . Ese intelectual está también obligado a asumir una posición intelectual revolucionaria" ("It is not enough to verbally adhere to the revolution to be a revolutionary intellectual; even the actions themselves of a revolutionary are not enough. . . . This intellectual is also obliged to adopt a revolutionary intellectual position"; 195), but Quevedo is not convinced by the speech, although he feigns interest for personal gain. Indeed, by agreeing with the director, he is offered a place on the jury of the Premio Casa de las Américas, one of the most prestigious literary prizes in Latin America. He takes his task very seriously: "Más que discernir un premio, nos aprestábamos a definir el futuro de la humanidad" ("More than awarding a prize, we were getting ready to define the future of humanity"; 198), for whatever book is awarded the prize will receive a lot of attention and have a great impact on the way the Cuban Revolution is perceived throughout the world. His trip to Cuba also serves as a pretext to attempt to cure Fidel Castro of insomnia, to no avail. His meetings with Castro also highlight the role of literature in Cuba, or in any authoritarian regime: writers are "arribistas sin compromiso... ratas" ("careerists without commitment... rats"; 212), and words, useless, except when they promote the revolution. Again, Quevedo, although at ease in these intellectual circles, is not convinced. "La autocrítica de Padilla [le hace] repensar por completo [sus] convicciones revolucionarias" ("Padilla's self-criticism [makes him] completely rethink [his] revolutionary convictions"; 223), and he realizes that "siempre que alcanzaba el poder, la revolución se pervertía. ... Cuba no era un lugar para nosotros" ("any time it came to power, the revolution was perverted.... Cuba was not a place for us"; 224)—thoughts that spur his expulsion from the island for being anti-revolutionary and rejecting the influence of authority figures such as Castro.

Although Quevedo openly judges Josefa for her Mexicanness, she remains indispensable in his life. In fact, it is with Josefa that he wants to return to Mexico after seventeen years in France. Eventually, Quevedo, now certain of his potential as an intellectual leader, travels back to Mexico: in a letter, Claire comments that "después de estos años de aprendizaje en Francia, llegó el momento de completar tu camino. Como cualquier héroe, debías regresar a Ítaca para poner en práctica tus conocimientos, tu saber" ("after these years of training in France, it was time to complete your journey. Like any hero, you had to return to Ithaca to put into practice your knowledge, your wisdom"; 320). Having acquired all the knowledge in the metropole, he can now go back to the periphery and mimic behaviours acquired abroad. He seems so accustomed to his life in France that Claire is very surprised by his return to Mexico. Indeed, she is shocked that he left Europe, and even more shocked that he continues to remain in his native land. Staying put appears unrealistic for someone like Quevedo, who had thus far been ambivalent in most aspects of his life:

> Me cuesta trabajo imaginarte allá, tan cerca de tu infancia y tan lejos de ti mismo (del hombre que eres hoy), extraviado en una ciudad que, como dices, ya no puede ser tuya. México: qué significante más extraño, tan árido y al mismo tiempo tan solemne. Un lugar de cuyo nombre no querías

> acordarte.... Cuando te marchaste pensé que no resistirías y que terminarías por regresar a Europa.
>
> I find it hard to imagine you there, so close to your infancy and so far from yourself (from the man you are today), lost in a city that, as you say, can no longer be yours. Mexico: what a strange signifier, so arid and, at the same time, so solemn. A place whose name you didn't wish to recall.... When you left I thought that you would not be able to resist and that you would end up returning to Europe. (320)

However, Quevedo does not have to be in Europe, for he brings his European experience and intellectual history to Mexico. While much of the ensuing story takes place in Latin America, the physical setting is not equivalent to the intellectual space. The intellectual mindset in which Quevedo evolves is still European. Once established in Mexico, he continues to reproduce the cultural and intellectual models that he has integrated. When his daughter, whom he has not seen in years, goes to a book signing to meet him, she gets to see the extent to which he has become a stranger and is disconnected from Mexico: indeed, she says "sentí como si mi padre estuviese dormido.... Y no tuve el valor de despertarlo" ("I felt like my father was asleep.... And I didn't have the courage to wake him"; 336).

Despite the fact that he creates successful magazines such as *Tal Cual*, an imitation of *Tel Quel*, the French magazine of literary theory and criticism, and has a certain prestige in Mexican intellectual circles, he is met with only modest results. He is awarded a prize for the "peor libro del año" ("worst book of the year") by some literary critic, who rejects him both as a writer and an intellectual; his research on murder in Chiapas—copied on Foucault's *Surveiller et punir*—does not reach any concrete conclusions; and rumours of government corruption after his psychoanalysis sessions with President Salinas de Gortari abound. All these setbacks bring Quevedo to conclude that it is impossible to be an *intellectuel engagé* in Mexico:

¿Es posible ser un intelectual comprometido en México? Esta cuestión me atormenta desde mi regreso.... Hasta los pensadores más críticos necesitan del poder para subsistir. Basta repasar la triste historia de la mayor parte de los escritores mexicanos de este siglo para desanimarse por completo. Al parecer, sólo existen dos opciones: mantener una posición independiente hasta las últimas consecuencias, y entonces sufrir la persecución o el silencio—acaso la peor de las condenas—, o bien plegarse a los caprichos de la clase política y guardar una obligada discreción ante los excesos del PRI y del gobierno.

Is it possible to be a committed intellectual in Mexico? This question haunts me since my return.... Even the most critical thinkers need power to survive. Just reviewing the sad history of most of the Mexican writers of this century is enough to be completely discouraged. Apparently there are only two options: maintain an independent position to the bitter end, and then suffer persecution or silence—perhaps the worst sentence—or bow to the whims of the political class and maintain a compulsory discretion before the excesses of the PRI and the government. (322)

"Demolido" ("destroyed"; 13) by the corruption rumours emanating from the *Salinista* administration, and since Claire cannot be convinced of his intellectual integrity, Quevedo commits suicide while the Berlin Wall falls, thus embodying "el fracaso de [las] ilusiones" ("the failure of the illusions"; 12) of the revolutionary left and the end of utopias. The ending of the novel does not make clear if Quevedo was actually corrupted by power—embodied by President Salinas de Gortari—or if he fell victim to a conspiracy led by those in power. The government of Salinas de Gortari wins over the intellectual figure Quevedo, eliminates dissent, and reiterates the victory of neo-liberalism as a system. His death on 9 November 1989, at the very moment when "Tras más de setenta años de locura, el mundo se apresta a volver a la razón" ("after seventy years of madness, the world is preparing to return to reason"; 472), confirms that he represents the end of that long trajectory.

The last part of the novel, "El diario inédito de Christopher Domínguez" ("The Unpublished Diary of Christopher Domínguez"), echoes this finality:

> La historia de este siglo es la historia de una gigantesca decepción. Su ruina representa el ansiado fin de la locura. Después de incontables esfuerzos, se ha podido comprobar que, como muchos de nosotros habíamos advertido, la revolución fue un fiasco. Detrás de sus buenos deseos, su ansia de mejorar el mundo y su pasión por la utopía, siempre se ocultó una tentación totalitaria.
>
> The history of this century is the history of a gigantic disappointment. Its ruin represents the long-awaited end of madness. After countless efforts, it is clear that, as many of us had warned, the revolution was a fiasco. Behind its good intentions, its desire to improve the world and its passion for utopia, there always lay a hidden totalitarian temptation. (448–9)

In the end, Quevedo's fight was pointless. The end of madness spells the end of Quevedo's understanding of the world as he knew it, and his own demise, for he cannot go on living now that he sees the futility of revolution.[13] The fall of the Berlin Wall is but a symbol of Quevedo's own fall from grace. As the Wall and the ideological struggles it represents come to an end, Quevedo suddenly *recobra la cordura* ("recovers his sanity") and in a last attempt at justifying himself, turns toward Claire. He questions everything he had taken for granted until then: their shared interests, protests, even their complicated love affair. His own demise is a metaphor for that of the revolutionary movements, something with which he has come to terms. In his suicide letter, addressed to Claire, he asks: "¿De qué te sirvió contemplar el fin de la revolución, el penoso trayecto de este siglo, el sanguinario envejecimiento de nuestra causa? Si algo aprendimos en esta era de dictadores y profetas, de carniceros y mesías, es que la verdad no existe: fue aniquilada en medio de promesas y palabras" ("What was the point of you contemplating the end of the revolution, the painful journey of this century, the bloody aging of our cause? If we have learned anything in this era of dictators and prophets, of butchers and messiahs, it is that truth does not exist: it was annihilated amid promises and words"; 12). Revolutions, after all, were based on words and very few actions, fuelled by utopian visions but not grounded in reality. Whereas Claire thrives on utopias—"Yo soy la desquiciada, la violenta, la rebelde, ¿lo recuerdas? Oigo voces. Siempre me mantengo en pie de guerra. Y nunca transijo. Lo siento, Aníbal: a diferencia de ti, yo no pienso renunciar a la locura" ("I am the deranged, the violent, the rebellious one, remember? I hear voices. I always stay on a war footing. And I never compromise. I'm sorry, Aníbal: unlike you, I don't plan to give up on madness"; 462)—Quevedo realizes that the revolutionary calls for action were but a farce. He criticizes Claire harshly:

> Me equivoqué doblemente: primero, al creer que era posible armonizar la independencia y el compromiso y, luego, al asumir que antepondrías nuestro pasado común a tus ideales. O quizás sería mejor decir que ambos erramos o nos confundimos en esta época dominada por la falta de certezas. . . . Nuestro caso resulta tan trágico e ilusorio, banal y esperpéntico como el propio siglo XX. . . . ¿Entonces por qué asumes que eres mejor que yo? Tú me convenciste de sumarme a ese gigantesco espejismo que fue la izquierda revolucionaria y ahora te arrogas una integridad que, siento decirlo, no posees. ¿Qué buscas? ¿Comprobar que soy un traidor o un embustero? ¿Denunciar mis tratos con el poder? ¿Revelar mi debilidad, mi incongruencia, mi avaricia? Tal vez ha llegado el momento de volver a la cordura. ¿Y si en nuestros días fuese imposible luchar sin transigir? ¿No esconderá tu ansia de pureza una ambición aún mayor que la mía? Dime: ¿quién es el mentiroso: yo, eternamente afligido por mis dudas, o tú, que nunca dudaste de tu fe?
>
> I was doubly wrong: first, by believing that it was possible to combine independence and commitment, and then, by

assuming that you would put our shared past ahead of your ideals. Or perhaps it would be better to say that we both erred or were confused in this age dominated by the lack of certainty. . . . Our case is as tragic and illusory, banal and gruesome as the twentieth century itself. . . . So why do you assume you are better than I am? You convinced me to join that gigantic mirage that was the revolutionary left and now you assume an integrity that, I am sorry to say, you do not possess. What are you looking for? To prove that I am a traitor or a liar? To denounce my dealings with power? To reveal my weakness, my inconsistency, my greed? Maybe the time has come to return to sanity. What if in our time it was impossible to fight without compromising? Does your craving for purity not hide an ambition even greater than mine? Tell me, who is the liar: me, eternally assailed by doubts, or you, who never doubted your faith? (12–13)

He paints Claire as a fanatic who never doubted her revolutionary commitment, someone blinded by faith who believes that staying true to her ideals makes her better than Quevedo, who was never able to commit fully to revolution. Claire's *locura*, then, makes her superior to Quevedo, whose newfound *cordura* turns him into a traitor to their cause. Quevedo also admits his own shortcomings—namely, the fact that he believed he could find a middle ground between logic and pragmatism, and revolution. He realizes, albeit a little late, that a compromise is impossible to find in such extreme circumstances, with such extreme interlocutors.

This discourse about *locura* and *cordura* echoes the fictional Michel Foucault's words about the role of madness in human life. The character describes it as a role to play: "Por el juego del espejo y por el silencio, la locura está llamada sin descanso a juzgarse a sí misma. Además, es juzgada a cada instante desde el exterior; juzgada no por una conciencia moral o científica, sino por una especie de tribunal que constantemente está en audiencia" ("Through mirror images and through silence, madness is tirelessly called to judge itself. Furthermore, it is judged at every moment from the outside; judged not by a moral or scientific conscience, but by a kind of tribunal that is constantly in session"; 143). Claire embodies both *locura* and *tribunal*, a character who can judge others according to her fervour.

The topic of the relationship between intellectual figures and power—or, to be more precise, the criticism of the relationship between intellectuals and power—stands out in Volpi's works, whether in his essays or his novels. In his article "El fin de la conjura" ("The End of the Conspiracy"), he argues that although the tight-knit relationship between intellectuals and the state goes back to the beginning of the twentieth century, "el poderoso y el intelectual en México siguen unidos por la costumbre y un preocupante desconocimiento mutuo" ("the powerful and the intellectual in Mexico are still united by habit and by a worrisome mutual lack of understanding"). In Volpi's view, this is a relationship based on a dichotomy:

> Dominado por un impulso irracional, el poderoso escucha las opiniones de los intelectuales con la convicción de que poseen una influencia—una sabiduría—peligrosa. A partir de ahí, no se le ocurre más que clasificarlos en dos categorías: si las ideas que expresa el intelectual en turno son favorables a sus políticas, se trata sin excepción de un *lamesuelas*, una especie de empleado oficioso al cual debe pagar sus servicios por medio de prebendas, honores o dinero (o las tres cosas); si, en cambio, cuestionan, invalidan o de plano se oponen a sus actos, el poderoso no tarda en reconocer en él a un *conjurado*, un delincuente en potencia que sirve a "oscuros intereses," al cual debe intimidar, cortejar, perseguir, o, en un caso extremo, eliminar (lo que resulte más barato).

> Dominated by an irrational impulse, the powerful listen to the opinions of intellectuals with the conviction that they possess a dangerous influence and wisdom. From that, they can think of nothing more than to classify them into two categories: if the ideas expressed by a favoured intellectual agree with their policies, he is without exception a bootlicker, an officious employee who must be paid for his services with privileges, honours, or money (or all three); if, on the other hand, they question, invalidate or outright oppose

their acts, the powerful soon recognize in them a conspirator, a potential delinquent who has "dark interests," someone whom they must intimidate, court, pursue, or, in the extreme case, eliminate (whichever is cheaper). ("El fin de la conjura")

In the article, Volpi explains that there are four generations of intellectuals in Mexico: the so-called generation of 1915, whose members created the first parties opposed to the Partido Revolucionario Institucional; the generation of 1929, which includes figures such as Octavio Paz; the generación de Medio Siglo, defined by the Cuban Revolution and the Cold War, which includes figures such as Gabriel Zaid and authors such as Elena Poniatowska and Carlos Fuentes; and finally, the generation of 1968, whose most famous members are Enrique Krauze and Héctor Aguilar Camín. Volpi's objective in re-examining the various generations is to propose new possibilities for twenty-first-century intellectuals:

> En primer lugar, habría que reconocer su verdadera dimensión en una sociedad democrática. A partir de ahora los intelectuales ya no debieran ser vistos por el poder como esos admirados enemigos de antes. . . . El intelectual, así, debe ser visto como lo que es: un profesional independiente, como cualquier otro, cuya misión es opinar sobre los asuntos de interés público para ayudar a modelar la opinión general sobre temas de importancia.

> First, their true dimension in a democratic society should be recognized. From now on, intellectuals should no longer be seen by those in power as the admired enemies of old. . . . Intellectuals, therefore, must be seen for what they are: independent professionals, like any other, whose mission it is to express an opinion on matters of public interest to help shape general opinion on important issues. ("El fin de la conjura")

He also maintains that the role of intellectuals must evolve over time, and that they cannot expect to be acknowledged by authority figures, which is the mistake Quevedo makes, for he wants to be acknowledged at all costs. Volpi concludes with the idea that "la transparencia debe ser la nota dominante en las relaciones entre el poder y los intelectuales" ("transparency must be the key element in relations between those in power and intellectuals"); such *transparencia* is absent from Quevedo's relationships. He is aware that associating with power is dangerous for one's reputation, so he does it in secret. Similar to Vargas Llosa, Volpi plots in fiction concerns he expresses in his essays and columns. The writer Ignacio Padilla has stated that Volpi's views were but a roadmap for the Crack members' own role as Mexican intellectuals in the twentieth century (218–19). Reading *El fin de la locura* as a roadmap makes obvious the role intellectuals ought to play in the development of a global consciousness.

*El fin de la locura* is also a political novel, a sub-genre of the historical novel, by virtue of the fact that the issues at hand are eminently political. It raises the idea of the end of the leading role of intellectuals in general, of the end of the Latin American intellectual forged by his European stay, and of the end of revolutionary ideas. This idea of *the end*, ironically qualified as dementia in the title itself, evokes other discourses about the end of history. The American political scientist Francis Fukuyama, in "The End of History" (1989), hypothesized that the world had reached the end of history. In this article, and then in the book of the same title, Fukuyama argued that humanity had reached the end of history as understood as a clash between competing ideologies about the economic and political organization of the world. Fukuyama argued that the failure of communism had allowed liberalism to become the universal and uncontested form of human organization. Therefore, the end of history had happened with the fall of the Berlin Wall, an event that symbolized the end of ideology. In *El fin de la locura*, Quevedo also represents the end of the intellectual and the guiding ideas of past decades.

As with other discourses on temporal change, the novel has a personal dimension. This echoes comments made by Noé Jitrik in *Historia e imaginación literaria* (*History and Literary Imagination*), where he argues that the historical novel he calls *cathartic* allows authors to address recent problems in their relationship with a past they experienced themselves.

These works tend to seek "una definición de la identidad que, a causa de ciertos acontecimientos políticos, est[á] fuertemente cuestionada" ("a definition of identity that is highly questioned due to certain political events"; 17). Volpi offers a critical view of intellectuals and of Mexican and Latin American intellectual history more broadly, and he ironically advocates in favour of emancipation from the European codes of his own precursors. His view aligns with that of Edward Said, who, in *Representations of the Intellectual*, claimed that "one task of the intellectual is the effort to break down the stereotypes and reductive categories that are so limiting to human thought" (xi). Quevedo is a caricature of Latin American intellectuals of the past. His depiction serves as a counter-example to what an intellectual in Mexico should be—namely, someone who rejects the old binary between the core and the periphery and can thereby have a true worldly standing. This is how Volpi himself conceptualizes his own role as an intellectual.

According to Roberto González Echevarría, "La 'locura' que Volpi exorciza y ayuda a los intelectuales latinoamericanos a exorcizar es la imitación servil del pensamiento y estética europeos" ("The 'madness' that Volpi exorcises and helps Latin American intellectuals to exorcise is the servile imitation of European thought and aesthetics"; 147). In Volpi's understanding of literature, national traditions are not limits to creation—not his own, not foreign traditions. A well-rounded intellectual should be open to the whole of the world's intellectual tradition, for it can help in shaping one's critical thinking. Here lie Quevedo's mistakes: not only does he absorb another intellectual model, but he abides by that model alone. He dismisses other traditions that could complement his philosophical positions. Consequently, Quevedo's goals cannot be construed in cosmopolitan terms. From the beginning of his journey to France, he betrays not only the cosmopolitan impulse, in that he solely focuses on the world, but also the commitment necessary for the articulation of cosmopolitanism. Indeed, he only concentrates on what the world can bring him, and not on what he can bring to the world. Quevedo is not committed to changing the world or tackling universal issues; he merely wants to acquire the philosophical standing necessary to be recognized as a great intellectual figure. This is contradictory to what Said argues; indeed, "the purpose of intellectual activity is to advance human freedom and knowledge"

(*Representations of the Intellectual* 17). By replicating the works of various French philosophers, Quevedo does not advance either human freedom or knowledge: he is not free to think by himself, does not come up with new ideas, and his bringing back French philosophical articulations to Mexico does not free the Mexican people, for they remain subordinated to the metropole. Moreover, Quevedo's rejection of those closest to him is twofold. First, he rejects the life he had built in Mexico, abandoning his wife and daughter. Indeed, even when he returns, he does not seek to rekindle his relationship with them. Second, he dismisses the whole of Mexican culture: intellectually, he does not identify with it, rejecting it as a defining characteristic of identity when in France, and never reclaiming it once back on Mexican soil.

In every aspect of his life, then, he betrays the precepts of both cosmopolitanism and intellectualism. He cannot articulate a true global consciousness, for he denies one aspect of globality—home. This failure to incarnate cosmopolitan tenets also highlights his failure as an intellectual. Indeed, in Said's interpretation, the intellectual must be truly universal and embody "the interaction between universality and the local" (xiii), as well as question all aspects of society. Quevedo does not embody the interaction between the universal and the local, but rather the relationship between the periphery and the core, a situation he does not question. He lacks the critical distance and ethical commitment necessary to put his own situation into perspective: Quevedo is blinded by his desire to learn from his masters. Said also states that "the role of intellectuals is supposed to be that of helping a national community feel more a sense of common identity, and a very elevated one at that" (29), another task at which Quevedo fails. Indeed, he only succeeds in uniting people against him, in their common repudiation of him as a Mexican intellectual.

Often, historical novels fictionalize the past that its authors believe their nation to have overcome, only to criticize it and make it theirs (Pons 62). By placing Latin American history in a global context, *El fin de la locura*, a hybrid novel, shares aspects of the historical novel and the global novel, and as such, it is a striking example of a metafictional work that uses literature as a weapon to reflect on and criticize the Latin American intellectual past in a global setting. On numerous occasions, Quevedo filters his understanding of global events through a national lens, which is also problematic. He is unable to universalize a Mexican's situation, and to truly commit to global changes. For instance, he fails both as a revolutionary and as an intellectual during the May 1968 protests in France, and cannot conceive of the October 1968 massacre in Mexico City as part of a global event. He does not "tak[e] a risk in order to go beyond the easy certainties provided by [his] background, language, nationality," which shield him "from the reality of others" (Said, *Representations of the Intellectual* xiv). Not only does Volpi criticize the *Latin American intellectual* as a global category, he also criticizes the *Mexican intellectual* in relation to both Tlatelolco and the Salinas de Gortari government. Indeed, "in dark times an intellectual is often looked to by members of his . . . nationality to represent, speak out for, and testify to the sufferings of that nationality" (43). Quevedo, by not taking a stand—worse, by feeling nothing after the massacre of October 1968—tacitly sides with the Díaz Ordaz government (1964–70).[14] Later, in 1988–89, by helping the Salinas de Gortari administration, he does not voice the public's concerns about the neo-liberal policies implemented by the government. By not acting, Quevedo becomes an accomplice who fails in his commitment to his fellow Mexicans, both as an intellectual and a cosmopolitan.

Even by portraying a failed Mexican intellectual and by engaging the Latin American setting obliquely, Volpi still proposes a reflection that is relevant to his continent of birth. As he has said in an interview, "se necesita ser muy poco avezado en prácticas literarias como para no darse cuenta que en cualquier caso, un mexicano escribiendo sobre Alemania o sobre Rusia o lo que sea, incluso no metafóricamente, hay una correspondencia con lo que estás viviendo" ("you need very little experience of literary practice not to realize that in any case, with a Mexican writing about Germany or Russia or whatever, even unmetaphorically, there is a connection with your life"; qtd. in Areco 300). This *correspondencia* to which Volpi refers has to do with the events on which his novels concentrate—that is, global events that had an impact on a national as much as an international scale. The narrative is written from the perspective of rooted cosmopolitanism and presents models that are problematic and need correcting, precisely for their lack of articulation of an ethical local and global consciousness. Quevedo is anything but an exemplary personification of a rooted cosmopolitan: he does not commit to those close to him, nor to the larger world.

His various travels serve to enrich him only. Lessons drawn from his behaviour can be applied to Mexico, Latin America, or the world—it has global implications about universal commitment. As a global novel, *El fin de la locura* not only articulates both the world and Latin America as its chambers of resonance, but also proposes a cosmopolitan consciousness through the depiction of intellectual counter-examples of the twentieth and early twenty-first centuries.

## *No será la Tierra*: The Fate of Cosmopolitanism in the Neo-liberal World Order

Jorge Volpi has said that *No será la Tierra* (*Season of Ash*[15]) is "the most pessimistic novel I have written" (qtd. in Corral et al. 103). It is also, incidentally, his most global novel, in terms of territory covered, to date. *No será la Tierra* is a prime example of a novel in which events are given more importance than characters. I contend that the narrative is about the fanaticism of characters who emerge from a world of extremes, to use Eric Hobsbawm's description of the century in *The Age of Extremes* (1994), and who, filled with doubts in a world that they identify correctly as totalitarian, have oscillated to embrace opposite ideologies. My analysis shows that *No será la Tierra* represents a criticism of nationalism and of the excesses that arise from this political position, as well as a pessimistic view of cosmopolitanism in contemporary times, in which one relates to people from another continent but forgets one's family. The novel also showcases how globality can be synonymous with uprootedness and disengagement. I concentrate on two characters, the Russian Arkadi Granin and the American Allison Moore, as well as on their families, to explore Volpi's representation of the failures of both the nationalist and the cosmopolitan position. Moreover, I show that political polarities destroy as much as the nuclear weapons against which these characters fight. While both characters try to reconcile their family life with their universal concerns, both fail in their attempts to achieve a balanced approach to their projects. They feel propelled by their ideals to engage primarily with the universal, which leads them to disengagement from the local; in this way, each betrays the precepts of rooted cosmopolitanism, which reconciles love and responsibilities for one's nation with a universal commitment toward others. In fact, inasmuch as they deny to varying degrees their cultural roots, their cosmopolitan engagements do not promote dialogue among cultures, which, in my proposed conceptualization, is a basic tenet for the articulation of a universal community. Rooted cosmopolitanism, after all, is universalism plus difference (Appiah, "Cosmopolitan Reading" 202). Their disengagement from their own cultural milieu makes their projects flawed from the outset.

According to Volpi, the narrative is structured like an opera:[16] a prelude recounts the events of the Chernobyl nuclear disaster of 1986—and sets the tone for a novel about human hubris and the end of ideologies—and is then divided into three *actos*: the first act, "Tiempo de Guerra ["War Time"] (1929–1985)," starts with the 1929 Black Thursday and concludes with Ronald Reagan's 1985 Star Wars military project; the second, "Mutaciones ["Mutations"] (1985–1991)," spans the years leading to the fall of the Soviet Union; and the third, "La esencia de lo humano ["The Essence of the Human"] (1991–2000)," concentrates on the aftermath of market liberalization in post-Soviet Russia. In other words, the novel covers, in great detail, the global events that shaped the 1929–2000 period on every continent.

The narrative intertwines the lives of eight major characters, as well as those of their respective relatives, reinforcing my reading that the novel is more about global events than it is about individual characters.[17] Journalist Yuri Mijáilovich Chernishevski recounts the events from his prison cell, where he sits after being convicted of murder. Chernishevski is the narrator of what appear to be, at first sight, three disparate subplots, which converge toward the end of the novel. The three main protagonists are "tres mujeres" ("three women"), as is reflected in the title of a subsection of the novel: Jennifer Moore, Irina Gránina, and Éva Halász. Their relatives and acquaintances, though less fleshed out, are as important—if not more—to the plot's development. Indeed, it is through the interaction of members of their respective families that the three women eventually meet.

Jennifer Moore is the eldest daughter of a member of the US Senate. She is a very sensible and determined person. After graduating college with honours, she sets her mind on becoming one of the students of Canadian-born American economist and diplomat John Kenneth Galbraith. Henceforth, her unwavering ambition and dedication leads her to success. She eventually secures an important position at the International Monetary Fund (IMF), where she is put in charge of key projects. Jennifer is married to Jack Wells, a failed entrepreneur who cheats on her regularly. Blinded by capitalism, Wells pursues risky trading ventures. Jennifer is unable to have children; she gets to experience motherhood thanks to her younger sister, Allison, the black sheep of the family, who abandons her son to her sister. Allison resents the fact that their father has always shown a clear preference for Jennifer, and during her teenage years, Allison does everything in her power to cause trouble. As a young adult, she distances herself from her family, and becomes involved in various anti-globalization movements. Her son, Jacob, becomes the object of Jennifer's motherly love. Allison meets the narrator, Chernishevski, during the 1999 Seattle World Trade Organization protests.

Irina Gránina is a Soviet scientist who has little interest in human relationships; she has, however, taken a keen interest in the bacteria she studies in her laboratory. She believes that the whole world can be understood through science, as it is more stable than human interactions. She does not question the Soviet regime nor does she take an active part in it. Her only desire is to dedicate herself to science. Her life changes when she meets fellow scientist Arkadi Granin; they soon marry and have a daughter, Oksana. Arkadi is the incarnation of the perfect Soviet citizen, until a bacteriological incident, for which he feels responsible, results in him being sent to the Gulag. His imprisonment, unsurprisingly, embitters him and leaves him disenchanted with communism. When he is freed years later, Oksana does not recognize her father. A troubled child under Irina's care, she becomes an ever more disturbed teenager. She resents her father and the work he does, turning to poetry to exorcise the pain she feels for not having a defined national identity. She expresses her condition eloquently: "Desde hoy me considero apátrida. Nací en una nación muerta, en un territorio que perderá su nombre, en un tiempo vacío que el mundo se obstina en olvidar. Me considero ciudadana de la Nada, ostento un pasaporte de Ninguna parte, tal vez yo ya tampoco existo, soy una ilusión o un error de cálculo, un daño colateral—así los llaman—una ruina" (Volpi, *No será la Tierra* 362) ("Beginning today, I consider myself a stateless person. I was born in a dead nation, in a territory that will lose its name, in an empty time the world insists on forgetting. I consider myself a citizen of Nothingness, I can flash a passport for Nowhere, perhaps I too no longer exist. I'm an illusion, a mistake, collateral damage—that's what they call it—a ruin"; *Season of Ash* 277–8). She even claims to be "un *anacronismo*" (362) ("an anachronism"; 278). She eventually escapes her parents' care and resurfaces in Vladivostok, where she turns to prostitution and is killed by a man known as "el coreano" ("the Korean"). Whereas Irina is crushed by the death of her daughter, Arkadi does not feel anything. Out of spite and grief, Irina shares Oksana's diaries and poems, and her life story, with Chernishevski.

The last female protagonist is Éva Halász, a gifted scientist. Born in Hungary, she is raised in the United States, where she attends prestigious universities. A depressed figure, she only cares about artificial intelligence; she insists that the reproduction of human intelligence is science's final frontier. Throughout the novel, she repeats her claim that humans are not as evolved as machines, and that feelings are a waste of time. Her dismissal of the importance of feelings is exemplified by the fact that Éva has many lovers—Jack Wells, husband of Jennifer Moore, and the narrator Chernishevski, among others—none of whom stay in her life for very long. Like Irina, her sole interest is science. However, whereas Irina works on concrete projects within the borders of her nation, Eva has but one goal in mind, to map the human genome, and her research takes her around the globe. For instance, she spends some years in Berlin, where she witnesses the fall of the Wall. Much like Oksana, Éva does not feel she has a stable national identity—"Éva no poseía un hogar, era húngara y estadounidense y alemana (o más bien berlinesa), y no era nada de eso" (360) ("Eva had no home; she was Hungarian, American, and German [well, actually a Berliner] and none of those things"; 276)—her identity is tied solely to her profession as a scientist. Éva represents the most extreme incarnation of globality—neither territory nor human beings are important to her, she only thrives through science. She eventually dies at the hands of the narrator, Chernishevski, which spurs the writing of the novel within the novel.

Benedict Anderson, in *Imagined Communities* (1983), describes nationalism as "the pathology of modern developmental history, as inescapable as neurosis in the individual . . . and largely incurable" (5).[18] This definition is consistent with the vision of the Communist Bloc put forward by the narrator Chernishevski. He explains that after the October Revolution of 1917, the Soviet Union developed a political program focused on the creation of the *homo sovieticus*, "un nuevo tipo de ser humano, alejado de los yerros, la torpeza, la avaricia, y la mezquindad propia de nuestra especie" (Volpi, *No será la Tierra* 54) ("a new type of human being, free of the errors, awkwardness, avarice, and meanness of our species"; *Season of Ash* 35), and, finally, on the spread of nationalism at all costs. Although Soviet officials were aware of their shortcomings and mistakes—as in the Chernobyl tragedy, a symbol of communist decadence—it was unpatriotic to admit it. Chernishevski goes even further than comparing the USSR to a lie: "Chernóbil desveló el secreto: la Unión Soviética era una ficción" (221) ("Chernobyl revealed the secret: The Soviet Union was a fiction"; 166), an imagined country.

The character of Arkadi Granin fits neatly into this narrative plot created by the state. Granin, a Russian scientist specializing in bacteriological warfare, begins his life as a perfect student aware of the role he has to play to satisfy both his family's and the state's expectations. The two are conflated in the mind of the character, for the state makes clear that everything must be done for the greater good of the motherland. From an early age, Arkadi is also aware that his life is relatively easy when compared to that of the average Soviet, for "a diferencia de la mayor parte de los internos, él se había beneficiado de los privilegios de la élite, había disfrutado de una vida llena de comodidades y ni siquiera había sufrido las penurias del estalinismo" (149) ("unlike most of the prisoners, he had benefited from the privileges of the elite, had enjoyed a life full of comforts, and hadn't even suffered the shortages of the Stalin era"; 109). The easy life that he has led, a result of his ignorance of the shortcomings of the USSR, ultimately conditions him to believe in the utopian project that is communism/socialism, since he has never seen how terribly it affected large groups of people. Consequently, at nineteen years of age, he is quite different from his classmates, who for the most part have more reasonable dreams and expectations. When his best friend asks him why he chose medicine, Arkadi confesses to dreams bigger than himself:

> ¿y por qué no? Ésa no es una respuesta, Arkadi Ivánovitch. Entonces porque sí. *Reductio ad absurdum*. A los 19 años cualquier discusión se volvía trascendental: para salvar a la

> humanidad, concluyó Arkadi. . . . Una frase típica de Arkadi que reflejaba la diferencia entre ambos: él quería estudiar medicina para ayudar a unos pocos individuos de carne y hueso, mientras que Arkadi sólo podía soñar con el género humano. (57)

> Why not? That's not an answer, Arkady Ivanovitch. Well, just because. *Reductio ad absurdum.* When you're nineteen, any discussion becomes transcendent: to save humanity, concluded Arkady. . . . A typical Arkady statement, which reflected the difference between the two of them: He wanted to study medicine to save a few real people, Arkady could only dream about the human race. (37–8)

Arkadi expresses strong cosmopolitan concerns. He wants to *salvar a la humanidad* ("save humanity"), a dream that does not appear beyond reach when construed in Soviet terms. Indeed, Arkadi is blinded by the discourse that posits communism as the best ideological stance. *Salvar a la humanidad* is, then, a twofold process: first, it can be accomplished through medicine and the development of strong medical practices and scientific discoveries, which are possible thanks to the superiority of the USSR, and second, through the spread of communism, once other nations recognize the superiority of that system. Arkadi's interest in a humanity that is not confined to the borders of the Soviet Union seems suspicious to the administration of the Central University of Moscow and to some sections of the Communist Party. It is said that Arkadi "No tiene raíces. Flirtea con el Occidente. Es un traidor" (63) ("They have no roots. They flirt with the West. They're traitors"; 43) and that "tiene que reparar en sus inclinaciones cosmopolitas" (63) ("he had no choice but to renounce his friendship"; 43) if he wants to thrive in the USSR. For a time, his dream of becoming a doctor is stronger than his humanist ambitions. Although at first the thought of having to distance himself from his best friend, Vsevolod Birsten, when he is accused of being a "perro judío" (62) ("Jew bastard"; 42), is unbearable, he eventually does so when he is himself accused of being a "cosmopolita como Vsevolod: sólo los traidores eran amigos de los traidores" (63) ("a *cosmopolite* like Vsevolod: Only traitors were friends of traitors"; 43). Being cosmopolitan can mean being sent to the Gulag, something everyone dreads. Arkadi rationalizes his decision in the following way: "Si pretendía continuar su ascenso, no le quedaba más que renegar de su amistad" (63) ("If he wanted his rise to continue, he had no choice but to renounce his friendship"; 43)—what does it matter if you sacrifice one person if you can save millions? He refuses to ground his cosmopolitan pretensions in reality—standing by a friend. He prefers the abstraction of utopia—the possibility to save millions. He denies the importance of kith and kind in the name of his cosmopolitan project, which makes it flawed from the outset.

Arkadi lets himself be convinced by the state, "seguro de ser un elegido de los dioses" (68) ("certain he was one of the chosen of the gods"; 46), and, as a young adult, is the perfect embodiment of the *homo sovieticus* who thrives within the system. Supported by his wife Irina, he rises to an important position in a state company and is very successful until a serious accident occurs with anthrax bacillus, causing the death of a hundred innocent people. This event is the turning point in the evolution of his character. His faith in the party starts to falter, never to return. Indeed, instead of acknowledging the tragic accident, the party finds scapegoats who are later sent to the Gulag or before a firing squad. At all times, the narrative set up by the USSR must hold, and the death of a handful of citizens is no reason to challenge the established order. Arkadi is disgusted by this attitude: he became a scientist to save lives, not to see them destroyed by a state he believes in. He needs for his "trabajo sea útil, salvar vidas, no acabar con ellas" (141) ("work to be useful, to save lives, not end them"; 102). While his wife Irina cannot conceive that the world is different outside the borders of the country, does not believe "en la propaganda oficial que insist[e] en la amistad entre los pueblos" (48) ("the propaganda that insisted on the friendship between the two nations"; 30), and gladly admits that "el mundo exterior sólo le provo[ca] indiferencia" (48) ("the exterior world only aroused her indifference"; 30), Arkadi returns to the humanist ambitions of his nineteen-year-old self and wants to get away from the *nomenklatura*, or party apparatus, creating frictions in his marriage. Irina, without being a fervent communist, does not share the universalist ideals of her husband and only believes in the importance of applied science, not human beings. She also fears, rightfully, that Arkadi's newfound rebellion will affect those closest to him—his wife and daughter. And sure enough, the party disapproves of the change in Arkadi's political position, and exiles him while also tormenting Irina and Oksana. In jail, Arkadi has all the time that he needs to reflect on communism, and to develop a pure hatred toward the system he once admired.

When Arkadi is released five years later, he is a changed man. He has become anti-national to the extreme, and has assimilated the universalist doctrine and the cosmopolitan view of the globalization/capitalist discourse. He only thinks "en el modo de salvar a su patria" (239) ("and thought about how to go about saving the nation"; 182) from communism. *Salvar* is, then, a leitmotiv in his life, notwithstanding the ideology by which he is blinded. He cannot stand the idea that communism and its misleading ideals are still thriving in the Soviet Union, and is adamant that "él, y sólo él, tenía una misión que cumplir" (239) ("he, and only he, had a mission to carry out"; 182). He feels invested with a mission, and becomes driven by a messianic spirit, the same spirit that made him choose medicine as a young adult. He calls for open markets during the period of *Perestroika* ("restructuring") led by Russian leaders Mikhail Gorbachev and later Boris Yeltsin. Irina disapproves of this position, and agrees with many members of their group who "deploraban de su radicalismo" (255) ("deplored his radicalism"; 192). He has gone from the extreme of communism to that of capitalism, each time blindly believing its gospel. Although Irina is glad of the fall of communism, she notes that new dogmas—Western capitalism and the Orthodox Church—appeared in its wake, each as extreme as its predecessor:

> La Unión soviética había sido una pesadilla, una fuente de opresión y de tortura, pero a Irina le resultaba imposible imaginarse en el desierto, no toleraba la ciega voluntad de borrar el pasado que animaba a los reformistas. . . . Otorgarle poder a esos ancianos incultos y anacrónicos le parecía un síntoma inequívoco de la demagogia imperante; se llenaba el vacío ideológico dejado por el comunismo con otra fe absurda: antes Lenin, ahora Cristo. (332)

The Soviet Union had been a nightmare, a source of oppression and torture, but Irina could not imagine herself in the desert: She couldn't stand the blind will to erase the past that animated the reformers. . . . To grant power to those ignorant, anachronistic old men seemed to her an unequivocal sign of the current demagoguery. The ideological void left by Communism was being filled by another absurd faith: First it was Lenin, now Christ. (252–3)

History repeats itself, as one ideology has been replaced by another.

Arkadi, meanwhile, calls for the democratization of the country and internalizes Western influence without realizing that he shifts from one extreme to another, from communist nationalism to American capitalism; "se había convertido en un liberal tan autoritario como sus enemigos" (334) ("had become a liberal and was as authoritarian as his enemies"; 254) and "Su odio al comunismo lo había convertido en un fanático del mercado" (429) ("his hatred of Communism had turned him into a free market fanatic"; 333–4). He has converted to a new faith, and is aware of major changes in his personality, but does not resent them: "Arkadi Ivánovich no podía ni quería contenerse, ya no podía volver atrás, la revolución de su mente y de su cuerpo era irrefrenable. Sí, ahora era violento; sí, ahora era intransigente; sí, ahora era brutal. Era el precio que había pagado, y no se conformaba con las mijagas de libertad que le concedía Gorbachov, pastor de hombres" (276) ("Arkady Ivanovich could not hold back, didn't want to, couldn't go back. The revolution of his mind and body was now unfettered. Yes, now he was violent; yes, now he was intransigent; yes, now he was brutal. That was the price he'd paid, and he wasn't going to settle for the crumbs of freedom conceded to him by Gorbachev, shepherd of men"; 210). The flow of consciousness makes the reader privy to Arkadi's most intimate thoughts. He longs for complete individual liberty, and his disgust for communism makes him profess his faith to a new god, America, which he associates with freedom and democracy. However, he has an idealistic view of America. Once there, he cannot believe the type of capitalism displayed in New York is the right one. He is disappointed with the concrete incarnation of his dream: "El capitalismo no era aquella obscena proliferación de productos, marcas, colores y sabores, sino algo superior, casi metafísico: una forma de vida abstracta, una metáfora de la libertad que apenas se correspondía con su encarnación real" (410) ("Capitalism was not that obscene proliferation of products, brands, colors, and tastes but something superior, something almost metaphysical: an abstract kind of life, a metaphor for freedom that barely corresponded to its real incarnation"; 318). Once again, reality disappoints him, much like the concrete praxis of communism that led him to rebel against it. The abstraction about which he dreams is not what he finds in the United States, nor what his business associate Jack Wells is promoting. He associates with Wells, Jennifer's husband, who is eventually accused of fraud. Arkadi cannot find the middle ground between these two irreconcilable positions. However, he does not see that this new position is as destructive as the former, for anything seems to be better than communism.

Irina is not surprised by her husband's demise. In fact, the reader is privy to her thoughts, which she shares with the narrator in an interview included in the third part of the novel. Although at first, when Arkadi refuses to keep working for a system that scapegoats its citizens, Irina "no ponía en duda la repentina toma de conciencia de su marido" (146) ("never doubted her husband's sudden attack of conscience"; 106), she doubts the purity of his intentions: "creía que su frustración profesional también había resultado determinante. Para Arkadi el anonimato era la peor de las condenas" (146) ("she believed that his frustration also played a role. For Arkady, anonymity was the worst sentence he could receive"; 106). Communism tried to annihilate individual identity, much like the extreme articulation of globality does with local cultures. Irina even believes that somehow being jailed and exiled was his endgame, for his only desire was to be "el centro del mundo" (147) ("the center of the world"; 107), which he effectively becomes once the government tries to rid itself of its once best example of *homo sovieticus*.

Like Arkadi, Allison Moore is another major character. She, too, goes to the extremes of her ideologies, and she also does it for what she deems to be the greater good. She is the black sheep of a prominent American family who grew up in an environment protected by her father's money, knowing only the best society has to offer. Expected to act as a daughter of a good family would (103–4), she rebels during her adolescence, during which "no busc[a] divertirse sino cambiar el mundo" (91) ("instead of trying to amuse herself, [she] attempted to change the world"; 66), only to become what her family, conservative Republicans, hates. After she is expelled from her private high school, she attends university only sporadically, preferring instead to become involved in the protests against the Vietnam War and in the Flower Power movement. Allison has a chaotic relationship with her older sister, Jennifer, who is her polar opposite. While Jennifer "odi[a] o más bien despreci[a] a los liberales como su hermana por su doble moral" (173) ("hated liberals like her sister because of their double standard"; 130), Allison cannot stand her sister talking about her "irritante[s] experiencia[s] [por el mundo] trufada[s] con estereotipos y quejas" (232) ("irritating experiences, complete with stereotypes and complaints"; 175), seeing the IMF, for which Jennifer works, as the only way to save the Third World. Allison believes that Western organizations are but meddlers trying to impose a way of life instead of trying to understand the cultural framework of the countries they arguably fail to help. She is angered when Jennifer claims that "el único modo de ayudar a 'esa gente' (la del Tercer Mundo, por supuesto) era obligándola a acatar las disposiciones del Fondo" (232) ("the only way to help 'those people' [of the Third World, of course] was by forcing them to respect the policies of the IMF"; 175), and swears that her sister is wrong, for she embodies, through her position at the IMF, the very neo-liberal policies against which she fights. Jennifer has the very same opinion of her sister as Allison has of her. Jennifer sees Allison as an idealist with little to no understanding of the socio-political struggles of the countries she wants to help. Jennifer is irritated by the fact that the groups to which Allison belongs present themselves as "defensores de los débiles y los desheredados," but who are "incapaces de buscar soluciones reales a sus problemas. Ella, republicana orgullosa—*conservadora compasiva*, se definía—no se creía mejor que nadie, no pensaba en guiar a los pobres, los enfermos o los lisiados, pero hacía más por ellos que todos esos progresistas de salón" (173) ("defenders of the weak and abandoned, but they were unable to find real solutions for their problems. She, a proud Republican, did not think she was better than anyone, did not think about guiding the poor, the sick, or the disabled, but she did more for them than these armchair progressives"; 130). Ironically, the two sisters have the same objective: to improve the living conditions of the less fortunate, albeit through different means.

Allison's humanitarian concerns begin early on, and never waver: she is "decidida a consagrarse a lo único que le importaba: los otros" (200) ("intent on dedicating herself to the only thing that mattered to her: other people"; 151). She even puts her own needs—for love, stability, and security—behind those of the rest of the world. However, like Arkadi Granin, she cannot reconcile her universalist concerns with her own family, which eventually disintegrates. While her sister Jennifer travels a lot for work, Allison gets involved with different organizations and lives all over the planet: San Francisco, Auckland, Palestine. Although both are committed to helping their fellow human beings, their ways of doing so could not be more different. Jennifer wants to help the developing countries—Zaire (now the Democratic Republic of Congo), Mexico, Russia—to improve their economies, but she comes with an American imperialistic mentality. Instead of trying to understand the rules governing the systems of these other countries, she just imposes her own. For instance, when she travels to Mexico City with the IMF in 1986, she claims that while it is not Zaire, "se le parecía" (221) ("it seemed like it"; 166), and that it was "un país tan hospitalario como opaco" (212) ("a country as hospitable as it was opaque"; 159). The Mexican public servants she meets are not helpful, nor are they dedicated to redressing the economic situation of the country. She also travels to Africa, the "corazón de las tinieblas" (157) ("the heart of darkness"; 116), a continent where "se concentran todas las taras de la colonización y barbarie" (162) ("we have concentrated here all the defects of colonization and barbarism"; 120) to "civilizar a esos salvajes" (156) ("to civilize those savages"; 116). She is so extreme in her approach that she drives her team of analysts, and herself, to the verge of exhaustion. She considers it her duty to help them surmount the economic misery in which they live, and she experiences the IMF's failures to redress these economic woes as personal failures. Like her sister, she is a utopian, in that she really believes she can have an impact wherever she goes. She sees herself as "la punta de lanza de ese cambio" (161) ("the advanced guard for that change"; 119), and sincerely embodies the ideals of the IMF and the powers the institution grants her. Like Arkadi, she is also extremely self-centred and wants to be acknowledged for the work she does:

Ella podría bien estar en América, paseando por Central Park o comprando vestidos de piel en Saks, alimentando su colección de joyas y abrigos de piel, despreocupada de la misera, y en cambio prefería el calor, la inseguridad y los mosquitos de Kinshasa, con el único objetivo de ayudar a sus roñosos habitantes. Lo menos que esperaba de ellos era que se mostrasen comprensivos con sus cambios de humor. (164)

She could easily have been in the United States, augmenting her collection of jewels and fur coats, unconcerned about poverty, but instead she preferred the heat, insecurity, and mosquitoes of Kinshasa. Her only objective was to help its mangy inhabitants. All she expected from them is that they show some understanding for her mood shifts. (122)

She feels "the white man's burden," and has a dire need to be acknowledged for her efforts, be they in helping foreign countries or trying to have a functional life back in the United States.

Allison, however, cannot divide her attention as well as her sister does. Idealistic, she gives herself body and soul to a cause, whether it is with Greenpeace or Earth First, and she struggles to reconcile her universal concerns with her family life. During her period with Earth First, with whom she feels she has finally "encontrado su lugar" (242) ("found her place"; 184) after years of soul-searching, she falls in love with a fellow protester, Zak, whom she calls her "pequeño paraíso" (273) ("little paradise"; 207). Zak turns out to be an undercover FBI agent, sent to thwart the organization's plans. On 31 May 1989, members of Allison's cell are arrested and jailed. She later realizes that she is pregnant with Zak's child (294), something that Jennifer takes as a personal affront (296). Much like Irina, who sees Arkadi's need to be the centre of the world as egotism, Jennifer hurls abuse at her sister and calls her decision to keep the child "un puro gesto de egoísmo" (297) ("a pure act of egoism"; 225), for she doubts Allison will set aside her various projects to raise a child. Unsurprisingly, Allison eventually has Jennifer take care of her son, Jacob, while trying to save the lives of other children in Palestine, something Jennifer resents deeply. During one of their numerous fights, Jennifer tells Allison that she should "Deja[r] de salvar al mundo y ocupa[rs]e de la única persona que de verdad te necesita" (341) ("forget saving the world and look after the only person who really needs you"; 261), her son. She never does, because Allison knows that Jennifer is better at raising Jacob than she would be.

Allison dies defending others, without worrying much about her own life (508). Ironically, while Allison has a truly universalist desire to help others, as opposed to the US-centred perspective of her sister, Jennifer enjoys a relative degree of success balancing her commitment to all aspects of her life. However, as her death nears, Allison partially comes to terms with her role in the world, and is aware that she can only do so much:

> Allison tomó al pequeño en sus brazos y lo cubrió de besos. ¿Qué importaba lo que sucediese con el resto de la humanidad? Ella sola jamás lograría eliminar la brecha entre ricos y pobres, entre poderosos y desheredados, pero al menos podía ocuparse de que cinco o diez personas, acaso veinte o treinta, tomasen conciencia de su situación y aprendiesen a sobrevivir por sí mismas. (447)

> Allison took the boy in her arms and covered him with kisses. What did it matter what happened to the rest of humanity? Alone, she would never manage to eliminate the gap between rich and poor, between the powerful and the disinherited, but she at least could see that five or ten people, maybe twenty or thirty, could become aware of their situation and learn to survive on their own. (349)

She reframes her commitment to others, and her universalist pretensions. It is still global, in the sense that she is far from home, but she narrows down her field of action. She has, in Said's words, "creat[ed] an environment in which [she] feel[s] that [she] belong[s]" (*The World, the Text, and the Critic* 14), having replaced filiation, the natural bonds of family, with affiliation, the bonds of "culture and society" (20). She has made the "transition from a failed idea or possibility of filiation"—her strained relationship with her father and her confrontational rapport with Jennifer—to what Said calls a "compensatory order . . . that provides men and women with a new form of relationship"—namely, affiliation (19). Although she dies and cannot expand on that understanding of her place in the world, she has acknowledged that she could only act on a smaller scale. Ironically, even in death, she is the character who finds the greatest closure.

*No será la Tierra* is fundamentally a novel about death, strictly and metaphorically speaking. First, the narrator is writing his story as he sits in jail after his conviction for the murder of Éva Halász. Second, the death of a loved one is both the start and end of every subplot. At the beginning of the novel, Jennifer learns of Allison's death, Irina of Oksana's, and the narrator's killing of Eva prompts the very writing of the narrative. At the end of the novel, Jennifer must tell Jacob that his mother passed away— Jennifer comments that Jacob "está a punto de perder la inocencia" (508) (is "about to lose his innocence"; 398)—and Irina and Arkadi struggle to come to terms with their daughter's death, which marks the metaphorical death of their marriage. Third, the novel is about human hubris, and if not its death, at least its consequences. The novel begins with the Chernobyl tragedy, the beginning of the end for the USSR, and concludes on the eve of the new millennium, when it is apparent that Russia has failed in its attempts at liberalization. The novel also emphasizes quite eloquently how the capitalist system is broken; this is conveyed through the character of Wells, his association with Granin, and Oksana's sexual exploitation and murder in Vladivostok.

Like *El fin de la locura*, the novel is a work of metafiction, although it must be noted, less ironic and parodic in tone. First, the narrator, Chernishevski, acts as the editor of the novel, a key figure for this type of fiction. Second, this narrator is reminiscent of Volpi himself. Indeed, the journalist has become famous for his novel *En busca de Kaminski* (*In Search of Kaminski*), a political thriller set in the USSR. Chernishevski explained that he enjoyed the writing of this novel very much: "Al principio se trató de un entretenimiento o un juego para olvidar las horas; luego la tarea se volvió tan absorbente que los días se desvanecían mientras trazaba la historia de Jodorkovski que era también la historia del final de la Unión Soviética y la historia del triunfo del capitalismo en Rusia" (434) ("At first, it was an amusement, a pastime. Then the work became so absorbing that tracing Khodorkovsky's history, which was also the history of the end of the Soviet Union and the history of the triumph of capitalism in Russia"; 338), much like Volpi's *En busca de Klingsor* recounts the end of Nazi Germany, and *No será la Tierra* the end of communism and the—mostly failed—implementation of capitalism in Russia. *En busca de Kaminski* is, then, a fictional work reminiscent of two of Volpi's works. Chernishevski also recalls how his "vida se paralizó" (436) ("life stopped"; 339) after the publication of the novel: "Durante meses mi existencia se redujo a hablar una y mil veces, en distintas ciudades y lenguas—a veces era incapaz de reconocerlas—, del infame Vladímir Kaminski, quien no sólo terminó por carcomer o suplantar a Jodorkovski, sino a mí mismo" (436) ("For months, my existence was reduced to speaking a thousand and one times in different cities and languages—at times I couldn't even recognize what they were—about the infamous Vladimir Kaminski, who not only consumed Khodorkovsky but did the same to me"; 339), much like that of Volpi after the publication of *En busca de Klingsor*, and the polemics that followed. Third, the very title, *No será la Tierra*, is the title of a collection of poems by Oksana. Irina, Oksana's mother, discovers the poems after burying her daughter. She reads and shares them with Chernishevski, who then uses the same title for the novel he writes about the events. Finally, the narrator uses a variety of apocryphal texts, such as newspaper articles, briefing notes, conversations he had with various characters, and the previously mentioned collection of poems. The novel also has some characteristics of the new historical novel: real-life figures, such as American president Bill Clinton and Soviet leader Joseph Stalin, are turned into characters, though never given a central role. History is circular and repeats itself through various cycles.

*No será la Tierra* is also universal in scope, although it must be said that some countries and continents only play a minor role in the narrative, which I contend is essentially a comment on globality itself; by covering too much ground, one eventually loses oneself. Jennifer Moore, for instance, travels to Zaire, Mexico, and Russia for the IMF, but never develops a sense of belonging to these countries. In contrast, her sister Allison travels to New Zealand and Palestine, and develops a sense of belonging abroad that she never feels at home in the United States. Even if these countries play what appears to be, at first sight, a lesser role—in terms of the narrative space dedicated to the events that take place there, or the time the character spends in these countries—they are the most important in the development of her global awareness. For instance, the explosion of the *Rainbow Warrior* in the port of Auckland, and the subsequent death of a colleague, cement her revolutionary beliefs, and her time spent in Palestine helping children makes her come to terms with the failure of her universalist dream.

My analysis has shown that the novel is about the embrace of opposite, yet equally extreme, ideologies. Through its plotting of characters who fail to reconcile their commitment to their family and the world, *No será la Tierra* is about ideological extremes; neither nationalism nor cosmopolitanism, the characters learn, fulfils universal human needs, for they are at opposite ends of the spectrum. Whereas Allison is eventually able to reframe her commitment to others, albeit in global terms that still alienate those closest to her, Arkadi ultimately alienates everyone in his life. Although he tries to reconcile the plight of those closest to him—family, friends, and colleagues—he ends up dedicating all his efforts to humanity. These characters, who embody ideas and intellectual positions, are not rooted cosmopolitans: their universal concerns and attempts to tackle the world's problems are thwarted by their betrayal of the local aspects of their lives. Only Jennifer, by maintaining a critical perspective close to rooted cosmopolitanism, partially succeeds.

## Conclusion

In my investigation of *El fin de la locura* and *No será la Tierra* I have interpreted these two texts as global novels that plot cosmopolitanism proper, and advocate for rooted cosmopolitanism. Yet it is worth noting that neither book shies away from arguing in favour of this position through the use of counter-examples that highlight the difficulties of espousing such a position. Indeed, neither Quevedo nor Claire, neither Allison nor Arkadi, are rooted cosmopolitans, and not one of them finds full redemption.

Quevedo turns his back on his Mexican roots to adopt a European intellectual identity that he later brings back to Mexico; he becomes rooted in his milieu—claiming a Mexicanness he rejected some years before—while also remaining foreign to it. Claire's only interest is in revolutionary movements, be they in France or abroad; their physical location matters little, only the praxis of revolution. She is blinded by her belief in the revolutionary gospel and refuses to admit that as the Berlin Wall is falling, so are the revolutionary movements of the 1960s and '70s. Neither Quevedo nor Claire is a rooted cosmopolitan; their ideology, be it psychoanalysis or revolution, makes them impervious to a balanced commitment to their immediate surroundings and the world.

Allison is eventually able to come to terms with the fact that her universalist pretensions are setting her up for failure, and she reconceptualizes her role in the world; she nevertheless abandons those closest to her, who were never part of her cosmopolitan ideals from the start. Like Claire, the only thing that matters is that some sort of greater good be achieved outside of her national territory. Allison is similar in this regard to Quevedo, for both, toward the end of their lives, grasp and acknowledge some of their shortcomings. However, Allison is allowed a partial atonement by the narrative voice, for she realizes, to a certain extent, the error of her ways. She is judged harshly for abandoning her son, but given credit for being able to reconceptualize her universal concerns on a smaller scale. Unlike Quevedo, she is not the object of ridicule.

Arkadi dreams of the world, but constantly abandons his friends, family, and colleagues. He, too, is blinded by his faith in ideology. Arkadi resembles Claire in terms of ideological extremes, but unlike Claire, whose faith never wavers, Arkadi moves from communism to capitalism. Claire and Arkadi remain on the extremes of the ideological spectrum, but Arkadi moves from one extreme to another when he loses faith in the USSR. Arkadi is also similar to Quevedo—they both feel they have a mission to save their country—and to Allison, for they each had a sheltered childhood that allows them to develop universalist ideals.

Only Jennifer Moore can be seen to embody rooted cosmopolitanism, with some difficulty. Contrary to Allison, who has no roots, Jennifer always returns to her husband in the United States and tries to make her marriage function. Appearances must be maintained, at all costs. Although she does not succeed in every project—her attempts to fix Third World economies are failures, and she has a hard time maintaining close-knit work relationships and friendships—Jennifer is the closest example to a rooted cosmopolitan in the novel. She tries her best in everything she attempts, be it helping the less fortunate or taking care of Allison's son. Her self-centredness and her striking US-centred perspective are two aspects that keep her from fully embodying the ethos of rooted cosmopolitanism.

The global novels studied in this chapter are two of the most explicit articulations of both cosmopolitanism and globality in Volpi's oeuvre, since they represent characters compelled to address the world's concerns. Indeed, all characters studied above actively take part in trying to change the world. Quevedo and Claire participate in various revolutionary movements that aim to undo real or perceived authoritarianism, both at home and abroad, and try to give a voice to subalterns, be they workers and students during the May 1968 protests, or Indigenous populations through Subcomandante Marcos in the Lacandon Jungle. Allison Moore tries to undo the legacy of colonialism and neo-liberalism, both at home and abroad; her travels to Palestine and her participation in the so-called Battle of Seattle of 1999 are but two examples of her dedication to improving the world. Arkadi Granin fights against communism by turning to capitalism, which he sees as the solution to the irreparable issues of the USSR's political and social structure. Jennifer Moore tries her best to tackle the world's problems—the fact that she does so in a problematic manner, trying to impose a Western economic vision on Third World countries, does not take away from the fact that she acts. Even Irina Gránina, through her interviews with the narrator and her handing in of the various writings that are the basis for the novel, can be seen to tackle the world's problems: she wants the story of her family, and Arkadi's ideological conversion, to be exposed so that the world can learn about not only their shortcomings, but also the state's. She wants to ensure that the same mistakes will not be made again, and that history does not repeat itself. Even if all characters fail in their Sisyphean task of changing the world order, they do attempt to confront its ills, thus embodying a universal impulse that the novels critically dissect and condemn for its shortcomings.

As I have demonstrated, Volpi's novels are framed in historicity and are pedagogical in nature. The extensive investigation the author undertakes before writing each of his novels indicates a detail-oriented writer who seeks to reproduce the historical context of the characters in the most accurate way possible (Lukács), and his protagonists are historical characters who discuss philosophical ideas (Menton). Volpi's novels are global novels, but they could also be read as novelized essays, which is a departure both from Lukács and Menton. Rafael Lemus commented as follows about *No será la Tierra*: "el reseñista intenta comprender: ¿por qué esta novela? Porque Volpi cree, acaso válidamente, que la novela es, ante todo, un instrumento al servicio de la inteligencia" ("the reviewer tries to understand: Why this novel? Because Volpi believes, perhaps with good reason, that the novel is, above all, an instrument at the service of intelligence"). Chávez Castañeda and Santajuliana further comment in their "Diccionario Volpi" ("Volpi Dictionary"), for the Mexican author "la literatura no se cierra en un fin en sí mismo. Narrar le supone un medio de conocimiento . . . y esta exploración del mundo siempre queda 'grabada' con mayor o menor sutileza en sus libros, convirtiéndoles en un híbrido entre la novela y el ensayo" ("literature is not an end in itself. Narrating is seen as a means of acquiring knowledge . . . and this exploration of the world is always 'recorded' with more or less subtlety in his books, making them a hybrid between the novel and the essay"; 93). These novels "con una pesada carga documental . . . viene[n] a ser una enciclopedia de sus pasiones intelectuales" ("with their heavy documentary content . . . become an encyclopedia of his intellectual passions"; 93). These intellectual passions are, in *El fin de la locura*, French philosophical and political thought, and, in *No será la Tierra,* economics, politics, and science. This hybridity of genre is a departure from the Latin American historical novel. Still, some characteristics, such "the cyclical nature of history," "the conscious distortion of history," and "the utilization of famous historical characters as protagonists" (Menton 22–3), are also an integral part of the narratives. However, these characteristics are but a starting point that Volpi rearticulates in an ironic manner. History is not only cyclical: the circularity of history allows for the realization that failure is the only logical ending. *El fin de la locura*'s Quevedo participates in various revolutionary movements, only to die when he becomes aware that revolutions are doomed. Moreover, a disillusioned Quevedo comments on the absurd nature of both his life and the twentieth century. History repeats itself: Quevedo courts Claire and is rejected time and again, until he commits suicide—which could arguably be seen as his biggest failure—and revolutionary movements arise one after the other, in various regions of the world, but consistently fail in living up to their "promesas y palabras" ("promises and words"; Volpi, *El fin de la locura* 9). *No será la Tierra*'s Allison Moore is part of various failed social movements, but she keeps trying to bring social change to the less fortunate parts of the world; she dies doing so. Arkadi Granin fights communism, seeing it as the terrible ideology that destroyed his career as a scientist, but fails to see that his blind faith in capitalism destroys his marriage and causes his daughter's death. Through the character of Irina, it is also suggested that capitalism in Russia is a failure, and although it is not explicit, one can see beneath Irina's concerns that she fears that a different type of authoritarianism is looming.

In both novels, history is distorted so as to give more importance to events than to characters. Moreover, the historical characters that are fictionalized in both novels are but empty shells, and eventually they become the object of ridicule. They do not take an active role in the narrative; they are, rather, but a pretext for the protagonists to face the embodiment of their (bygone) ideals. Quevedo meets with Castro and Allende; both these figures and their devotion to their respective ideologies are ridiculed. The same happens in *No será la Tierra*, where Soviet leaders are portrayed at their weakest: Stalin, a shadow of his former self, is about to die and cannot be associated with the idea of power anymore; and Gorbachev is mocked for his idealism and incapacity to deliver on his promises to make Russia a better place through *Perestroika* (restructuring) and *Glasnost* (openness).

The two works, although close to the new historical novel, are a rearticulation of the canonical genre. Both the traditional historical novel, as theorized by Lukács, and the new historical novel, as theorized by Menton, focus on the history of great events. However, as María Cristina Pons notes, "la reciente producción de novelas históricas se caracteriza por la relectura crítica y desmitificadora del pasado" ("the recent production of historical novels is characterized by a critical and demystifying rereading of the past"; 16), which "marca un cambio radical en el género" ("marks a radical shift in the genre"; 15) since "la novela histórica contemporánea tiende a presentar el lado antiheroico o antiépico de la Historia; muchas veces el pasado histórico que recuperan no es el pasado de los tiempos gloriosos ni de los ganadores de puja histórica, sino el pasado de las derrotas y fracasos" ("the contemporary historical novel tends to present the antiheroic or anti-epic side of History; often the historical past that they recover is not the past of glorious times nor of the winners of the historical struggle, but the past of defeats and failures"; 17). Both *El fin de la locura* and *No será la Tierra* are about failures: the failure of revolutionary movements, and the failure of both communism and various social movements in the face of neo-liberalism. Quevedo fails in his pragmatic approach to his role as an intellectual who aims to give advice to heads of state; Claire—although she never admits it—fails to reap the fruits of her revolutionary labour; Allison fails to be balanced in her approach to cosmopolitan concerns; Jennifer fails to save her sister from herself; Arkadi fails to save his country, replacing one dogma with another; and both Irina and Arkadi fail as parents.

Furthermore, the literary form of the novel reflects Volpi's political vision in the choice of narrators and implicit authors. Failure is also suggested by the personality of the very narrators, who are problematic narrative voices. *El fin de la locura*'s Aníbal Quevedo is an amnesic liar, and *No será la Tierra*'s Yuri Mijáilovich Chernishevski is writing from his prison cell, having previously been convicted of murder. Also, the erasure of the identity of the editors, which is only revealed late in the narratives, is symptomatic of the erasure of identity in an ever more globalized world. In *El fin de la locura*, ideas are more important than people—a metaphor for the pervasiveness of ideologies. In *No será la Tierra*, events are more important than people as well—the characters are puppets to global events. Both novels are about ideological extremes; neither nationalism nor cosmopolitanism fulfills universal human needs, only rooted cosmopolitanism, as partially embodied by Jennifer, can. In the end, all the characters fail in their endeavours because they believe in utopias without grounding them in reality, or put differently, their universal impulse divorces them from engagement with kith and kin.

Both *El fin de la locura* and *No será la Tierra*, albeit indirectly and in a global manner, engage the Latin American context. To this end, Ignacio Padilla claimed that

> La mayor parte de las novelas escritas por los firmantes de aquel manifiesto transcurren en México, si bien en todas ellas y para todas ellas hemos reivindicado nuestro derecho a situar nuestras historias en el lugar del mundo o del inframundo donde mejor podamos expresar ese relato concreto, siempre, eso sí, en esa patria nuestra que desde siempre ha

> sido la lengua española. (Volpi et al., "Postmanifiesto del Crack" 17)

> For the most part, the novels authored by the signatories of this manifesto involve Mexico, but in all of them and on behalf of all of them, we have maintained our right to set our stories on the world's (or underworld's) stage, where we can best express these particular stories which, yes, have always been at home in the nation we know as the Spanish language. (200)

This is a comment about the place Latin America now occupies on the world stage, and it reflects Volpi's conceptualization of his role as a cosmopolitan Mexican writer and public intellectual, as well as his understanding of Latin America's reality as globalized and decentralized. In *El fin de la locura*, the Mexican intellectual is ridiculed, and in *No será la Tierra*, Mexico is almost completely absent. Mexico, part of the global community, does not escape this state of affairs. Both novels are also a comment on Mexico at the end of the twentieth century, and the role of globalization, understood as a deterritorialized tackling of both national and wordly concerns, which has to this point been a failure.

In the short essay "Yo soy una novela" ("I Am a Novel") Volpi expounds on his vision of literature, which is articulated in cosmopolitan terms—even if the word itself is never mentioned. First, "Los humanos somos rehenes de la ficción" ("We human beings are hostages to fiction") for it is a human characteristic to produce it, a part of being human, which gives fiction a universal character. Second, even if narratives, by definition, lie, "las vivimos con la misma pasión con la cual nos enfrentamos a lo real. Porque esas mentiras también pertenecen al dominio de lo real" ("we live them with the same passion with which we face the real world. Because those lies also belong to the realm of reality"). It is, then, logical that

> la ficción cumple una tarea indispensable para nuestra supervivencia: no sólo nos ayuda a predecir nuestras reacciones en situaciones hipotéticas, sino que nos obliga a representarlas en nuestra mente—a repetirlas y

> reconstruirlas—y, a partir de allí, a entrever qué sentiríamos si las experimentáramos de verdad. Una vez hecho esto, no tardamos en reconocernos en los demás, porque en alguna medida en ese momento ya somos los demás.
>
> fiction fulfills an indispensable task for our survival: it not only helps us to predict our reactions in hypothetical situations, but it forces us to represent them in our minds—to repeat and reconstruct them—and, from there, to glimpse what we would feel if we actually experienced them. Once this is done, it does not take us long to recognize ourselves in others, because to some extent we are already the others. (*Nexos.com*)

He emphasizes that fiction makes human beings *reconocerse en los demás*, which is the very basis of the cosmopolitan reading that I have grounded in Appiah's philosophy. Not only do we, as readers, see ourselves *en los demás*, we become *los demás*—acquiring a sense of universality that only narrative allows. Through synecdoche, human beings are able to universalize their fellow human beings' experience. Fiction helps us to "ensanchar nuestra idea de lo humano. Con ella no sólo conocemos otras voces y otras experiencias, sino que las sentimos tan vivas como si nos pertenecieran" ("broaden our idea of the human. With it we not only come to know other voices and other experiences, but we feel them as being as alive as if they belonged to us"). Fictions helps one experience the lives of others, but more importantly, develop new values: "Vivir otras vidas no es sólo un juego . . . sino una conducta provista con sólidas ganancias evolutivas, capaz de transportar, de una mente a otra, ideas que acentúan la interacción social. La empatía. La solidaridad" ("Living other lives is not just a game . . . but a behaviour equipped with solid evolutionary gains, capable of transporting, from one mind to another, ideas that accentuate social interaction. Empathy. Solidarity"). Narratives allow us the possibility of becoming better human beings, for they force readers to feel and develop emotions that, I posit in this case, are the very basis of cosmopolitan engagement: empathy and solidarity.

As the works studied in this chapter show, novels, by providing readers with the opportunity both to develop new values and recognize the dangers of ideologies, also serve a social function: "Una novela . . . me transmite información social relevante—la literatura es una porción esencial de nuestra memoria compartida. Y se convierte, por tanto, en uno de los medios más contundentes para asentar nuestra idea de humanidad" ("A novel . . . conveys relevant social information to me—literature is an essential portion of our shared memory. And it becomes, therefore, one of the most powerful means of establishing our idea of humanity"). Narratives, through their universality, also erase identity markers: "Frente a las diferencias que nos separan—del color de la piel al lugar de nacimiento, obsesiones equivalentemente perniciosas—, la literatura siempre anunció una verdad que hace apenas unos años corroboró la secuenciación del genoma humano: todos somos básicamente idénticos. Al menos en teoría, cualquiera podría ponerse en el sitio de cualquiera" ("Faced with the differences that separate us—from skin colour to birthplace, two equally pernicious obsessions—literature has always anticipated a truth that, just a few years ago, the sequencing of the human genome confirmed: we are all basically identical. In theory at least, anyone could trade places with anyone else"). Literature should not be bound either by nationality or nationalism, which are *obsesiones perniciosas*, for they distort the very idea of literature as universal. If literature is about seeing ourselves in other peoples' lives and experiences so as to universalize their situation, it appears logical that Volpi shies away from dwelling exclusively on national settings and problems, and prefers instead to engage issues and settings in universal terms. In the "Postmanifiesto del Crack," the authors argue that there is "Nada más pernicioso que el nacionalismo—un adjetivo europeo, por cierto—para la novela. El nacionalismo es una mentira y la novela odia, aborrece la mentira. La novela entraña una búsqueda de la verdad literaria. Dentro de sus páginas, todo lo que ocurre es absolutamente verdadero. El *Crack* es una novela sin adjetivos y sin nación" (Volpi et al. 18) ("When it comes to the novel, nothing is more pernicious than nationalism, which is a European modifier, of course. Nationalism is a lie, and the novel hates lies. In fact, it abhors them. The novel is about the search for literary honesty. Everything that happens within its pages is absolute truth. And the Crack is a novel without modifiers, without a nation"; 199).

This affirmation reinforces my contention that *El fin de la locura* and *No será la Tierra* are about a universalizing position.

In conclusion, I have shown that Volpi's novels posit rooted cosmopolitanism as the best way through which to engage humanity and tackle the world's issues, and that this is reflected precisely in the fact that his narrative worlds dissect the difficulties of this position. His rearticulation of the historical novel allows him to discuss cosmopolitanism, ideologies, intellectual and political engagement, and globalization and its shortcomings. Under the guise of historical metafiction, the reader can learn from the characters' behaviours, for they are harshly criticized and presented as counter-examples in opposition to an ethos of rooted cosmopolitan for the global era. Ultimately, both *El fin de la locura* and *No será la Tierra*, through their complex articulation of globality, are global novels that, in line with the prerogatives of this literary genre, articulate a global consciousness.

# Conclusion

*Belonging Beyond Borders* underlines as a point of departure the traditionally contentious relationship between Latin America and cosmopolitan thought. In literature, from *Modernismo* through to the Boom, cosmopolitanism was the subject of many debates and tensions. Nationalist circles understood cosmopolitanism as a foreign influence that, through aesthetic means, was diluting the exploration and expression of Latin American culture. For cosmopolitan artists, however, this ethos was a way to break Spanish America's perceived asynchronicity with the rest of the world—be it through Spanish, French, British, American, or other worldly influences. They did not believe that their *deseo de mundo* was incompatible with the creation of a strong national culture. They believed that by integrating the best elements that other literatures had to offer, they could only create a better, stronger national tradition, one that was capable of engaging the world. Beginning in the mid-1960s as the Boom was in full swing, the erosion of nation-states and the rise of neo-liberal globalization have enabled Spanish Americans to reframe their relationship with cosmopolitanism. While these concepts and their effects remain disputed, it is now harder to completely shut off cosmopolitanism and globalization, not to mention the other cultural influences they bring about. Whether nationalists like it or not, the world is now one, and it is impossible to live in it without being exposed to cultural otherness. Interconnectedness is now a *fait accompli*. For Latin Americans more specifically, the fact that current articulations of cosmopolitanism give equal standing to locality and globality in the creation of a cosmopolitan identity has opened up new possibilities. After years of being wrongly perceived as a menace to national cohesion, cosmopolitanism is now a political tool that can be used to reframe the continent's relationship with the world.

The novels I have studied in this book—Elena Poniatowska's *La "Flor de Lis,"* Mario Vargas Llosa's *El Paraíso en la otra esquina* and *El sueño del celta*, and Jorge Volpi's *El fin de la locura* and *No será la Tierra*—closely mirror the opening of Spanish America to political cosmopolitanism in the twentieth century, and they exemplify the conceptual shift that took place in Spanish American literature, from aesthetic cosmopolitanism and the rejection of political cosmopolitanism in favour of other concepts, to its acceptance, affirmation, and promotion in the global era. Previous studies of earlier periods of Spanish American literary production concluded that cosmopolitanism had always been a part of the continent's artistic production. It was either the object of much critical debate, which always led to its displacement (Rosenberg), or the expression of a *deseo de mundo* (Siskind). Here, I have established the existence of a shift, a transformation in the literary treatment of cosmopolitanism from its displacement to a new articulation; and from the *deseo de mundo*, expressed in aesthetic terms, to engagement with the world through rooted cosmopolitanism.

Examining five narratives published between 1988 and 2010 has enabled me to show that the representation of cosmopolitanism is intimately tied to the intricate and ever-evolving circumstances that bind the nation to the world, and local politics to geopolitics. This has also allowed me to identify a shift in the treatment of cosmopolitanism in Spanish American literature, from the rejection of cosmopolitanism, understood as intertwined with an imperialist world view in Poniatowska, to its acceptance and promotion, understood as a philosophy reconcilable with an individual's national identity in Vargas Llosa and Volpi. This shift is explicitly political.

I have developed a methodological framework that I call cosmopolitan reading. This approach is predicated on an exploration of the ways these novels plot human experience across cultures, and on an evaluation of the specific Latin American cultural and historical concerns in which these texts are grounded. My cosmopolitan reading is also premised on the universality of narrative. Indeed, the novel appears to be one of the genres most suited to a cosmopolitan reading, since the complex worlds it portrays serve to reveal our common humanity across space and time. As readers, we can associate with characters, develop empathy and solidarity with them, and in so doing can turn narratives into spaces of universality.

I detected the emplotment of cosmopolitanism in the novels studied here; by identifying travel, residence in multiple localities, and the experience of global events, we can point to the articulation of a cosmopolitan proposition at work in these texts. Each plots travel as the impulse that brings the characters to adopt different perspectives, which leads them to commit to their localities and the world, a departure from the previous generations of Latin American literary production, where cosmopolitanism was mostly an aesthetic proposition.

Even if travel allows them to develop a cosmopolitan consciousness, none of the characters studied in *Belonging Beyond Borders* succeed in being rooted cosmopolitans in the strictest sense of the term. This failure on their part further highlights the difficulty of holding this position in the perilous cultural and political circumstances of the modern and postmodern worlds. Mariana develops a transcultural identity, deeply rooted in Mexico, and Casement discovers his Irish roots through his exposure to colonized people. Both characters evolve because they espouse a national identity based on that of their mother. Luz rejects Mexico, which brings Mariana to become Mexican, and Casement's mother, an Irish Catholic forced to pretend to be a British Protestant, brings Casement to live his Irishness out in the open. Flora Tristán, Paul Gauguin, Aníbal Quevedo, Allison Moore, and Arkadi Granin thrive on universalizing projects. This desire to take part in endeavours bigger than themselves drives them to reject the people closest to them, and to abandon or irremediably damage their families. Only Jennifer Moore finds some balance in her commitments, yet she does so with an imperial mindset, which makes her stances flawed.

All of these characters show, at one moment or another, a desire to be world citizens. And yet few succeed. Rooted cosmopolitanism, as embodied by such characters as Flora, Casement, and Jennifer, is a celebration of diversity. By combining universalism and difference, their rooted cosmopolitanism allows for their national culture and the new cultures they encounter to flourish and enrich one another. In spite of their shortcomings, it is precisely because they embrace diversity that Tristán and Casement are redeemed by the narrative voice, that Allison gets closure before her death, and that Jennifer's dream of having a child materializes. They are deeply flawed characters, but through rooted cosmopolitanism are rendered open to the world, and are willing to share in the human experience. Characters such as Gauguin, Quevedo, and Irina are not offered redemption, since they never demonstrate any openness to diversity, nor do they try to establish a meaningful connection with other human beings. It is the treatment of these characters, their ultimate fates, that, among other elements, clearly points to the ways in which the notion of rooted cosmopolitanism permeates the novels.

In four of the novels studied, childhood has a major impact in the development of the characters' cosmopolitan commitment. Indeed, Flora and Paul are expelled from their childhood paradise; this is portrayed as the basic impetus for their subsequent development. The same can be said of Casement; after his parents die, he dreams only of travelling, which eventually triggers the development of his cosmopolitan conscience, but also his nationalist sentiment. Both are associated with his childhood, through the figures of his British father and his Irish mother. This is also the case for Arkadi and Allison, who develop, respectively, a strong ethical commitment to others and a rejection of one's birth country in their childhoods. While it is a happy childhood that leads Arkadi to want to save the world, it is (what she thinks of as) a sad one that leads Allison to reject the United States to embrace the world. Much like Mariana, who rejects the elitism associated with her mother's cosmopolitanism and Eurocentredness, Allison rejects the vision the United States promotes on the world stage, which she conflates with her father, who, she believes, has not given her enough attention. Childhood, then, appears to be the moment when a global conscience and/or a cosmopolitan commitment to others are born. This is consistent with current theoretical approaches in cosmopolitanism studies. Indeed, scholars such as Martha Nussbaum, in *For Love of Country: Debating the Limits of Patriotism*, posit that childhood is the best moment in an individual's life to breed a cosmopolitan sentiment, to cultivate humanity, and to develop empathy and compassion—both of which are integral to cosmopolitan citizenship.

By discerning the way in which cosmopolitanism is plotted in the novels, and by analyzing the new narrative recourses at work, as well as the novels' inscription in literary and intellectual history, I underscored the political aspects in the representation of cosmopolitanism. Poniatowska's *La "Flor de Lis"* takes place in the 1950s, when nationalist discourses were at their height in Mexico, and at a moment when the Latin

American-coined concept of transculturation gained increased discursive currency. Mariana's mother Luz embodies cosmopolitanism and its imperial connotations. The novel conceives cosmopolitanism as a tool of cultural imperialism that has the power to undermine the articulation of a liberating cultural identity. In a way, cosmopolitanism is perceived as a step backward. Indeed, after having fought for the country's emancipation from European and American investors, and their cultural hegemony, Mexicans cannot conceive of turning back to Europe yet again. In *La "Flor de Lis,"* the controversy surrounding cosmopolitanism in Spanish America is represented as a rejection of the complex hybrid culture that emerged out of conquest and colonization. Although cosmopolitans such as Luz have an extensive cultural repertoire, unlike rooted cosmopolitans, they lack the perceptiveness and commitment to frame it in harmony with the repertoire of their national setting.

Whereas my allegorical reading of Elena Poniatowska's novel shows how cosmopolitanism was displaced in favour of transculturation, and in this view, is very much aligned with the political discourse of mid-century Mexico, Mario Vargas Llosa's and Jorge Volpi's works plot political cosmopolitanism, advocate for rooted cosmopolitanism, and imagine characters who take an active role in tackling the world's problems. The novels engage in discussions about conceptions of cosmopolitanism and its articulation, as well as the articulation of a global consciousness. Vargas Llosa's and Volpi's novels embrace the contemporary view that aims to deconstruct the dichotomy that pits cosmopolitanism against nationalism. However, while Vargas Llosa is obsessed with plotting cosmopolitanism in stark opposition to nationalism—which highlights the dichotomous relationship his generation has had with the latter—Volpi, who belongs to a generation that has experienced the increasing porosity of the nation-state and the emergence and consolidation of globalization, has transcended it. Indeed, his emplotment of cosmopolitanism goes beyond the traditional binary opposition, and his fictions, especially *No será la Tierra*, construct narrative worlds where characters are deeply immersed, as global citizens, in the world.

In Vargas Llosa's *El Paraíso en la otra esquina* and *El sueño del celta*, political cosmopolitanism is plotted as a means to abolish inequality—namely, through the representation of Flora Tristán's and Roger Casement's trajectories. The novels place cosmopolitanism at the intersection of rooted cosmopolitanism and liberalism. As cosmopolitans, the two activists have a cultural repertoire that allows them to connect to others across cultures. They see a glimpse of success when they find balance in their commitments both to their national setting and to the world, but fail when they choose one extreme—humanity for her, the Irish people for him. The character of Paul Gauguin is also applicable to an examination of Vargas Llosa's take on cosmopolitanism, for he embodies the binary opposition at its fullest, and never finds a middle ground like Tristán or Casement do. He is the counterpoint to rooted cosmopolitanism. It is because he never develops a balanced approach that Gauguin is not redeemed in the end.

Cosmopolitanism is represented as the best way to fight for the improvement of the oppressed, and by setting these novels in the distant past, Vargas Llosa participates in a discussion about nationalism and cosmopolitanism in the contemporary world. In this manner, a cosmopolitan reading reveals the novel as a space of universality that also transcends the past and informs the present. Not only does the novel highlight the failure of various ideologies in the nineteenth and twentieth centuries, but my analysis has shown that Vargas Llosa is also commenting on today's society. In numerous instances, the narrative voice comments on the downfalls of nineteenth-century globalization, interventions that echo similar indictments of globalization today.

Volpi's *El fin de la locura* and *No será la Tierra* plot political cosmopolitanism as a means to address conflicted identities, and to attempt to overcome the deterritorialization brought about by neo-liberalism in the twentieth century. Through the representation of characters such as Quevedo, the Moore sisters, and the Granin family, the two novels articulate cosmopolitanism on both a local and a global scale. In Volpi's works, the cosmopolitan is someone who concretely tackles the world's problems, even if in most instances these efforts are flawed from the outset. All the characters fail in their endeavours because they cannot embody the precepts of cosmopolitanism. Quevedo is always turning toward Europe, even when he is back in Mexico; Arkadi and Allison thrive on universal projects that leave little space for their local settings—and consequently alienate their family—and Irina and Jennifer are too anchored in their local settings to give enough credit to how the rest of the world could help them shape their outlook on life. No one embodies rooted cosmopolitanism; they all occupy a different place on the spectrum from nationalism to cosmopolitanism, some being too nationalist, and others too universalist or disengaged. I have argued that the novels thus reveal a conception of cosmopolitanism as a means to have a concrete impact on other people's lives, in the truest sense of world citizenship.

I have also pointed out that these novels are a new step in the development of a Spanish American literary tradition. They reflect the contemporary ethos, our relationship with increasing globalization. The new politics of cosmopolitanism showcased in the novels thus inform aesthetic transformations. The novels are, on the one hand, framed within the Spanish American literary tradition, for they are part of a popular subgenre, while on the other, they propose a rearticulation of that tradition. Poniatowska uses the traditional genre of first-person narrative to consider the experience of a female immigrant—a departure from that very genre. By reworking the codes of the historical novel, and through his use of documents produced by real-life Flora Tristan and Roger Casement, Vargas Llosa produces novels that are pedagogical in nature. They highlight the difficult position in which the characters find themselves, but they also advocate for the acceptance of this very position. For Vargas Llosa, literature is a means to fight against *las insuficiencias de la vida*; I conclude that his historical novels constitute a concrete stand in this direction. Though the novels do not propose a solution to overcome the possible failures, they are an attempt to explore the complexities and contradictions of characters with a global consciousness. Historical novels have traditionally served to discuss national identity and fill the void in official histories; Vargas Llosa's rearticulation of the canonical genre, by contrast, expands on the notion of cultural identity and its inscription in institutional discourses of the nation-state, for his novels frame it in global terms.

For his part, Volpi embeds his narratives with extensive research, turning them into *novelas ensayos*, hybrids between the historical novel, historiographical metafiction, and intellectual research. Moreover, while the new Latin American historical novel generally focuses on the history of individual Latin American countries, Volpi deliberately moves away from this tradition and incorporates international settings in his narratives. Volpi's rearticulation of historiographical metafiction—which generally serves to reassess national history using irony and parody—on a global scale expands on the possibility of re-evaluating Latin American history in global terms. The fact that most of his characters are removed from Mexico or Latin America allows for the plotting of global events and issues in which Mexico and Latin America took part, but in which they did not occupy centre stage. Volpi's global novels rearticulate Latin America's relationship with the world: his country, his continent, and the world are transformed into chambers of resonance for the issues discussed in the novels.

Rooted cosmopolitanism is clearly at work in the novels of Vargas Llosa and Volpi, and such a position is not surprising given the long history of Latin American cosmopolitan authors—from Reyes and Borges to Paz and Fuentes, among many others—who have always deconstructed the faulty perception of cosmopolitanism as dangerously alienating and foreign. Moreover, ideas about the decolonization of cosmopolitanism are precisely what explain its displacement in Poniatowska; at a time when the concept still carried an imperial connotation, transculturation was the only concept capable of reconciling the local and global aspects of an identity.

Despite the current stances on cosmopolitanism, there are still many readers, scholars, and politicians who criticize Spanish American cosmopolitan authors who choose to set their novels abroad or discuss issues that are deemed not Spanish American enough and who, in short, do not abide by the dogma that dictates what and how a Spanish American author ought to write. The argument is invariably the same—these critics associate cosmopolitanism with a lack of commitment to the nation. Although current articulations of cosmopolitanism, and the novels that inscribe themselves within this new thinking, try to undo the dichotomy that pits cosmopolitanism against nationalism, people believe that this binary opposition still exists. The *Modernistas*, the *Vanguardistas*, and the authors of the Boom were all called cosmopolitans in a reductive and derogatory manner, as are two of the novelists studied in *Belonging Beyond Borders*. Vargas Llosa and Volpi have each been called out and criticized for their supposed lack of allegiance to the nation; Vargas Llosa is despised due to his engagement as a public intellectual defending cosmopolitan ideals and globalization, while Volpi has been criticized because his novels are deterritorialized. Both authors have also been condemned by the Peruvian and Mexican nationalist intelligentsias because they are often highly critical of their native countries.

Beyond these perennial debates, I would counter this criticism with the argument that these Spanish American authors are now engaging, as never before, in the global cosmopolitan conversation, and thus expanding the traditional loci of enunciation of the concept, an exercise that, in light of Walter Mignolo's proposal to deconstruct Western cosmopolitanism, can be construed as taking part in a decolonial project. Spanish American authors are now proposing their own conceptualizations of rooted cosmopolitanism, and discussing its implications, which is a concrete way to tackle the world's problems.

In this context, a promising line of inquiry is to expand on the study of cosmopolitanism in Latin American literature by investigating not only other contemporary authors, but also by exploring specific cosmopolitan positions in Spanish American intellectual and literary history more broadly, both critical tasks that, given the scant traditional interest in this increasingly important area of inquiry, are still pending. I have explored my conception of cosmopolitanism, but it is a multi-faceted concept, and there are other perspectives beyond those of the authors studied here. To this end, a project I would like to develop is the study of the articulation of rooted cosmopolitanism in the literary output of *McOndo* and the Crack, to which I alluded in the introduction. I believe it would be of particular interest to study the evolution of the ideas on cosmopolitanism put forward by the writers of both movements, how these ideas intersect with discourses of globalization and the rise of new nationalisms in the current world order, and their responses to the current situation in the United States.

# Notes

INTRODUCTION

1. Unless otherwise noted, translations from the original Spanish (and in some cases French) are my own. Where I have quoted from a published English translation, I have used an endnote to indicate the source on first occurrence.

2. I use *mestizaje* and miscegenation interchangeably.

3. This translation comes from p. 219 of the 1970 edition of Borge's *Labyrinths*, translated by James Irby and published by Penguin.

4. From p. 23 of Lysander Kemp and Margaret Sayers Peden's translation of *The Siren and the Seashell*, U of Texas P, 1976.

5. In Argentina, Roberto Arlt is a prominent example of this literary experimentation. Another key figure is the young Jorge Luis Borges, who spent his early adulthood in Spain, where he was exposed to the Spanish Ultraist movement, which he later brought back to Buenos Aires in his twenties. In Mexico, the poet Manuel Maples Arce was the *figure de proue* of the *Estridentistas*, a movement that was both artistic and political, its proponents having experienced the Mexican Revolution (1911). José Carlos Mariátegui imported the *Vanguardistas* to Peru, and in 1926, created the journal *Amauta*, to which César Vallejo was a major contributor. For a thorough review of national Avant-Garde movements, see Ramírez and Olea.

6. While it is true that Latin American authors aspired to be published in Spain, they mostly longed for Paris. In fact, the most important literary review promoting the Boom, Rodríguez Monegal's *Mundo Nuevo*, was published in the French capital. Vargas Llosa describes it at length in *La tía Julia y el escribidor*, to which I refer in chapter 2. In fact, the protagonist, Varguitas, discusses how Peru lacked any sort of literary system, and Peruvian authors and journalists, intellectual autonomy. His integration into the already well-established European literary market—be it in Spain or France, where all Boom authors spent time—meant the affirmation of the very possibility of his role as a *creador* who was no longer expected to mimic the production of other European or Latin American countries.

7. The publication and subsequent popularity of Boom authors in the metropole raises paradoxes, which can be explained by the very question of modernity to which I referred earlier. In the late 1950s and early '60s, Spanish cultural elites were eager to

*219*

enter their own modern framework. After twenty years of dictatorship under Franco, who condemned everything foreign for fear it would dilute the Spanish national essence, there was a frantic search for foreign cultural products. Contact with the Boom writers was an injection of both modernity and cosmopolitanism for the Spaniards. The Boom was as useful for Latin Americans as it was for Spaniards: emerging writers from the periphery received international attention, and readers from the metropole were finally allowed to access reading materials from outside their national area. For Spain, Latin America represented modernity versus its own cultural and intellectual backwardness; for Latin America, Spain represented the undoing of coloniality, and reaching contemporaneity with the rest of the world—ironically so, since Spain was itself at the periphery of Europe's intellectual scene.

8   Most of the authors published in *McOndo* received a cosmopolitan education since they were raised or lived abroad during their youth. The paradigm through which to study this movement should be globalization rather than cosmopolitanism, which is why I have not included *McOndo* in *Belonging Beyond Borders*. *McOndo* novels portray characters in a global world, but do not concern themselves with the ethics of living in one. In the "Presentación del País *McOndo*," the preface to *McOndo*, Fuguet and Gómez hint at the fact that Latin America has now moved past Rama's *arritmia temporal*, even if being synched with the rest of the world now means having access to things such as MTV Latina, CNN in Spanish, NAFTA, and Mercosur (9).

9   Appiah is but one of many scholars to advocate in favour of rooted cosmopolitanism. Some authors refer to the same idea using a slightly different terminology: Dallmayr's "anchored cosmopolitanism" (2003), Baynes's "situated cosmopolitanism" (2007), Erskine's "embedded cosmopolitanism" (2008), and Werbner's "vernacular cosmopolitanism" (2006) all express similar ideas.

10  Mignolo advocates in favour of decoloniality, which he describes as a movement that confronts "the colonial matrix of power" (*The Darker Side of Western Modernity* xxvii). The main objective of decoloniality is to erase all aspects of coloniality and rearticulate history as stemming from multiples locations, not only Europe. As much as rooted cosmopolitanism is "an actually existing" type of cosmopolitanism (Calhoun 1), decoloniality is a concrete practice that aims at undoing the—according to decolonial scholars such as Mignolo—ever-growing effects of colonialism and its recent incarnation, globalization. Decoloniality is particularly used in relation to Latin America, where decolonial theorists argue that post-coloniality is mostly an intellectual movement, while decoloniality is an actual praxis.

11  In Appiah's conceptualization, "what makes the cosmopolitan experience possible—in reading as elsewhere—is not that we share beliefs and values because of our common capacity for reason: in the novel, at least, it is not 'reason' but a different human capacity that grounds our sharing: namely, the grasp of a narrative logic that allows us to construct the world to which our imaginations respond" ("Cosmopolitan Reading" 223).

CHAPTER 1

1. The English comes from p. 72 of Katherine Silver's translation of *Tinísima*. U of Mexico P, 1995.

2. According to Teresa M. Hurley, in "Mother/Country and Identity in Elena Poniatowska's *La 'Flor de lis*,'" the novel is a "female novel of awakening" (152) rather than a *Bildungsroman*, since Mariana is a woman: "The novel of awakening is similar to the apprenticeship novel in some ways: it also recounts the attempts of a sensitive protagonist to learn the nature of the world, discover its meaning and pattern, and acquire a philosophy of life, but she must learn these lessons as a woman. The protagonist's growth results typically not with an 'art of living,' as for her male counterpart, but instead with a realisation that for a woman such an art of living is difficult or impossible: it is an awakening to limitations" (Rosowski in Hurley 152). I disagree with this position. As we shall see, while Mariana does discover some limitations caused by her being born abroad, once she overcomes them and becomes a transcultural Mexican, she is sure of where she belongs and does not experience limitations due to her gender.

3. *Massacre in Mexico*, about the events at Tlatelolco, was published in English in 1975, and *Nothing, Nobody: The Voices of the Earthquake*, about the aftermath of the 1985 earthquake, in 1995. *La noche de Tlatelolco* recounts the events that marked Mexico shortly before the opening of the 1968 Olympic Games. On 2 October 1968, between 30 and 300 students were killed by the police and the military in the Plaza de las Tres Culturas, in downtown Mexico City. They were protesting numerous decisions taken by the government of Gustavo Díaz Ordaz. After the massacre, Poniatowska gave voice to the people who lived through the events and compiled a series of testimonials from Mexicans who were in favour of, as well as some who opposed, the student movement. The chronicle was published in 1971. Many historians consider the Tlatelolco massacre the first in a lengthy series of events that led to the defeat of the PRI in 2000. *Nada, nadie—Las voces del temblor* focuses on the impact of the 1985 earthquake that cost the lives of about 26,000 people. For weeks, the government denied the extent of the disaster and it was Mexicans themselves who saved their countrymen buried in collapsed buildings. In this chronicle, Poniatowska weaves her earthquake experience into the testimonies of people who were present to show the consequences of this drama on a human scale. Poniatowska has often spoken about her commitment to the subaltern and how her work as a *cronista* ("chronicler") became intertwined with her career as a journalist: "lo que sucedió con el periodismo es que fui comprometiéndome cada vez más, no sólo con el periódico, sino también con las personas a quienes entrevistaba" ("what happened with journalism is that I became more and more committed, not only to the newspaper, but also to the people I was interviewing"; *Nada, nadie* 26).

4. From p. 98 of Harriet de Onís's translation of *Cuban Counterpoint: Tobacco and Sugar*, Duke UP, 1995.

5. From pp. 86–7 of Lysander Kemp's translation of *The Labyrinth of Solitude*, Grove Press, 1961.

6. From p. 88 of the Kemp translation.

7   Despite the fact that her Mexican grandmother is of primary importance in Mariana's development, she never mentions her first name. At the beginning of the novel, Mariana makes a distinction between her European grandmother and her Mexican grandmother, referring to the latter as *la nueva abuela*, the new *abuela*. As she grows accustomed to her new setting, the protagonist only uses the term *la abuela*.

8   In *Me lo dijo Elena Poniatowska*, Poniatowska addresses this very event and acknowledges that her grandmother was not as prejudiced as she is portrayed as being in the novel:

> mi abuela paterna, se llamaba Elizabeth Sperry Crocker, era norteamericana y hablaba mal el francés—lo conjugaba mal—, nos quería mucho a Kitzia y a mí. Ella fue la que más se opuso a que viniéramos a México. Por las noches nos enseñaba una revista, la *National Geographic Magazine*, donde aparecían hombres y mujeres con huesos atravesados arriba de la cabeza, las tetas caídas, los labios deformados con platos. Mientras las hojeábamos nos decía: "Miren niñas, esto es México." Nos contaba que llegando allá nos iban a sacar la sangre y nos iban a comer crudas. Por eso cuando llegué a México yo tenía mucho miedo por todo lo que mi abuela nos había dicho, pero obviamente la abuela lo decía porque no quería que la dejáramos (14).

> My paternal grandmother, her name was Elizabeth Sperry Crocker, was an American and spoke French poorly—she conjugated it poorly—she loved Kitzia and me very much. She was the one most opposed to our coming to Mexico. At night she would show us a magazine, the *National Geographic*, where men and women appeared with bones pierced above the head, sagging tits, lips deformed with plates. As we leafed through them, she would tell us: "Look at it girls, this is Mexico." She told us that when we got there they would drink our blood and eat us alive. That's why when I arrived in Mexico I was very afraid, because of everything my grandmother had told us, but obviously Grandma said it because she didn't want us to leave her.

9   Glantz compares Magda to La Malinche, and claims that "con ella entran a la casa las leyendas, los servicios, la segunda lengua: como Malinche, es la que interpreta la realidad, la transforma, le da sentido, la organiza" ("with her legends, services, the second language enters the house: like Malinche, she is the one who interprets reality, transforms it, gives sense to it, organizes it"; "Las hijas de la Malinche" 87). La Malinche, Doña Marina, or *la lengua*—the tongue—was the young Indigenous woman gifted to Hernán Cortés in 1519. Her mastery of Indigenous languages and Spanish enabled her to act as a mediator and translator, a role resembling Magda's in Mariana's life. The formative process fostered by the Indigenous *nana* is a recurring trope in Mexican post-revolutionary literature. For instance, in Rosario Castellanos's 1957 novel *Balún Canán*, the privileged daughter of a landowner gets acquainted with Indigenous and lower-class Mexicans through her Indigenous nanny. Unlike in *La "Flor de Lis*," both the child narrator and the *nana* are nameless, thus highlighting their relative lack of importance in the family.

10  In the essay "A Question Mark Engraved on My Eyelids," Poniatowska claims that she "absorbed Mexico through the maids. . . . I discovered Mexico through them, and not even Bernal Díaz del Castillo had better guides. Surrounded by Malinches . . . I was able

to enter an unknown world, that of poverty and its palliatives.... Without realizing it the maids provided me with a version of Benito Juárez; they were all like Benito Juárez. Like him they vindicated themselves: 'Dirty foreigners.' Like him they defended Mexico, as stubborn as mules" (99–100).

11  By her own admission, this is something that Poniatowska took to heart: "desde joven, por mi propia formación pensaba: 'Bueno, yo le tengo que ser útil a mi país.' Pero, ¿cómo le puedo ser útil? Denunciando lo que vea, observando, escribiendo acerca de los problemas de cada día y dándoles voz a gente que simplemente me la pide" ("from when I was young, all by myself, I thought: 'Well, I have to be useful to my country. But how can I be useful? By denouncing what I see, by observing, by writing about everyday problems, and by giving a voice to people who simply ask me for it"; *Me lo dijo Elena Poniatowska* 27). This resonates with her body of work, whether we think of *La noche de Tlatelolco* or *Hasta no verte Jesús mío* (*Here's to You, Jesusa!*).

CHAPTER 2

1  All English renderings of Vargas Llosa's Nobel speech come from Edith Grossman's translation, available at https://www.nobelprize.org/prizes/literature/2010/vargas_llosa/25162-mario-vargas-llosa-nobel-lecture-2010/.

2  Vargas Llosa has written extensively on the function of literature, and has also stated in various essays that the very act of writing also serves as a way to settle the score with reality and history, reimagining, or rather improving, some of its aspects. In *Cartas a un joven novelista* (*Letters to a Young Novelist*; 1997), for instance, he argues that the very act of writing is an act of rebellion. In "The Power of Lies" (1987), he argues that "the real world, the material world, has never been adequate, and never will be, to fulfil human desires. And without that essential dissatisfaction with life which is both exacerbated and at the same time assuaged by the lies of literature, there can never be any genuine progress" (30).

3  In my analysis of *El Paraíso en la otra esquina*, I use the same spelling as Vargas Llosa to refer to the character of Flora Tristán, whereas I use the spelling "Flora Tristan" (absent the tilde) to refer to the historical figure.

4  The other Latin American authors who won the Nobel Prize for Literature are Chilean poet Gabriela Mistral in 1945, Guatemalan novelist Miguel Ángel Asturias in 1967, Chilean poet Pablo Neruda in 1971, Colombian novelist Gabriel García Márquez in 1982, and Mexican intellectual Octavio Paz in 1990.

5  Indeed, most of his novels, even the deterritorialized ones, revisit Peru, whether we think of *El hablador* (*The Storyteller*; 1987) or *Travesuras de la niña mala* (*The Bad Girl*; 2006). More recently, after a series of novels that took place in a global environment, he has returned to Peruvian settings in such novels as *El héroe discreto* (*Discreet Hero*; 2013), which is set in Lima and Arequipa, and *Cinco esquinas* (*The Neighbourhood*; 2016), which focuses on Lima and is set during the Fujimori regime.

6  Page numbers here and below refer to Helen Lane's translation of *Aunt Julia and the Scriptwriter*, Farrar, Straus and Giroux, 1982.

7   The publication of *El héroe discreto*, in 2013, and of *Cinco esquinas*, in 2016, seems to shake, at least partially, the foundations of this theorization, since the novels take place in Lima and Arequipa, two Peruvian cities that embody the idea of *peruanidad* in Vargas Llosa's works. *Cinco esquinas* also deals with so-called Peruvian themes, more specifically with the Fujimori regime. *El héroe discreto* does not openly discuss either cosmopolitanism or nationalism, but it does broach universal topics, such as corruption, greed, and family roots. The characters in *El héroe discreto* are not cosmopolitans by value—they show no moral commitment, and I would even argue that both protagonists display behaviour close to Gauguin's much-criticized individualism in *El Paraíso en la otra esquina*. *Cinco esquinas* also deals with such themes, which are, if not cosmopolitan, at least universal.

8   While Vargas Llosa's first *maître à penser* was Jean-Paul Sartre, a second reading of Camus's *L'homme révolté* (*The Rebel*; 1951) in 1962, as Vargas Llosa was starting to have doubts about the Cuban Revolution, allowed the Peruvian author to detect similarities between his still developing ideas and those of Camus. In the essay, Camus criticizes revolutions, which, according to him, fail because they end up betraying their precepts. This second reading allowed Vargas Llosa to conclude that the fight against injustice was moral rather than political, and not political rather than moral, as it was conceived by Sartre. This articulation planted the seeds of Vargas Llosa's rejection of Cuba after the Padilla Affair, and later his turn to liberalism.

9   The George Lengvari Sr. Lecture was given in English at the Institut économique de Montréal, then translated into French and Spanish. I'm quoting here from the trilingual French-English-Spanish publication entitled *Mon itinéraire intellectuel/My Intellectual Journey/Mi trayectoria intelectual*.

10  However, Giudicelli also claims that as a young author, Vargas Llosa had a tendency to write about what he knew: "Avec la prudence qu'impose une oeuvre en devenir, on peut souligner deux aspects qui marquent un cheminement. Par rapport aux premiers romans de l'aire liméenne, en prise directe avec une réalité connue, vécue et subie, et avec tout juste quelques années d'écart seulement, les oeuvres suivantes marquent une approche du fonds historique avec davantage de recul, que ce soit dans l'implication directe, personnelle, ou que ce soit dans le temps historique" ("Notwithstanding the necessary caution when considering a writer's early works, we can distinguish two aspects that mark a progression. When compared to the first novels of the Limean era, which are grounded in a known and lived experience, and with just a few years between them, the works that follow treat their historical source material with greater perspective, whether it be through the lens of personal experience or of a historical setting"; 191).

11  In his study, Menton defines historical novels as "novels whose action takes place completely (in some cases, predominantly) in the *past*—arbitrarily defined here as a past not directly experienced by the author" (16). Of course, Menton's definition is highly arbitrary. Following this reasoning, Vargas Llosa's *La fiesta del Chivo* (2000), among others, would not be a historical novel.

12  Other than the ones previously mentioned, characteristics of the new historical novels include metafiction, intertextuality, and the "Bakhtinian concepts of the *dialogic*, the

*carnivalesque*, parody, and *heteroglossia*" (Menton 23–4), all characteristics that apply to the Jorge Volpi novels I study in the next chapter.

13   Vargas Llosa first expressed interest in Flora Tristan in his biography, *El pez en el agua*. He later realized that he would need another character to balance the narrative, and the figure of Tristan's grandson, Paul Gauguin, prevailed, for "they had very similar personalities: stubborn, a propensity towards idealism, utopian constructions, very courageous in trying to materialize their utopias, even though they were very different ones" (qtd. in Rangel 11).

14   To this end, Sabine Köllmann has argued that "the frequent shifts from third-person to second-person-singular narrative voice and back do not hide but, on the contrary, underline the strong presence of the omniscient narrator in the background" (247). The use of *tú*, doubled with the fact that the narrator refers to Tristán as Madame-la-Colère, could be read as somewhat condescending. The narrator seems to diminish women. Although this is a legitimate reading of the narrative voice, I contend it leaves aside the fact that the novel celebrates Tristán's obstinacy. Moreover, unlike Gauguin, she is redeemed at the end of the novel. In "Arabesques: Mario Vargas Llosa et Flora Tristán," Stéphane Michaud puts forth the hypothesis that the Peruvian author took this narrative tool directly from the historical Flora Tristan's writings, for she used to talk of herself as *Florita* or *l'Andalouse* (the Andalusian), two nicknames the second-person-singular narrator uses when present. Vargas Llosa, for his part, responds to Michaud's argument by stating that his main objectives were to provide intimacy and to reproduce internal monologues: "Si vous utilisez la deuxième personne grammaticale, vous introduisez un narrateur ambigu. On ne sait pas directement si c'est le narrateur impersonnel qui parle ou si c'est le personnage qui se parle à lui-même, en se dédoublant, comme nous faisons couramment quand nous réfléchissons. . . . Dans ces petites parenthèses, il laissait le personnage se parler à lui-même, en montrant cette intimité qui introduit une perspective pas seulement subjective, mais aussi un peu ironique, établit une espèce de distance entre un personnage et sa propre expérience" ("If you use the second grammatical person, you introduce an ambiguous narrator. It is not immediately evident whether it is the impersonal narrator who is speaking or if the character is in fact talking to himself as though he were someone else, as we commonly do when we are trying to think. . . . In these brief interludes, he would let the character speak to himself, and portray this intimacy to introduce a perspective that is both subjective and ironic, and which sets a character at a distance from his own experience; qtd. in Michaud and Bensoussan 224–5). According to Daniel Lefort in "Mario Vargas Llosa, de la *Fête* au *Paradis*: fictions de l'histoire et pouvoirs de l'écrivain" (Mario Vargas Llosa: From *Feast* to *Paradise*: Fictions of History and the Writer's Powers), this feature of Vargas Llosa's writings appeared for the first time in *La fiesta del Chivo*; it is thus a feature of the third cycle in his writing.

15   Page numbers refer to Natasha Wimmer's translation of *The Way to Paradise*, Farrar, Straus and Giroux, 2003.

16   This affirmation echoes that of Mariana in *La "Flor de Lis,"* who says "Soy de México porque quiero serlo, es mi país" ("I am from Mexico because I want to be, it's my country"; 74).

17  Vargas Llosa relies heavily on Flora Tristan's writings and books, such as *Pérégrinations d'une paria*, to create her character. In fact, the novel's depiction of her experience in Peru is supported by her travel accounts.

18  This technique is common in Vargas Llosa's work. Indeed, as pointed out by Weldt-Basson, the Peruvian author has a "tendency to metaphorize one historical context through another" (231). For instance, *La guerra del fin del mundo* discusses fanaticism in Canudos and obliquely criticizes "Castro's curtailment of freedom of artistic expression in Cuba" (231), while *La fiesta del Chivo* (2000) is both a critique of Trujillo's regime and Alberto Fujimori's regime in the late 1990s.

19  Gauguin's quest for perfection, for an *escurridizo lugar*, is a recurring topic throughout the novel. Near death, he remembers having chased it most of his life: "Su música llenaba los vacíos del espíritu, lo sosegaba en las crisis de exasperación o abatimiento, y, cuando estaba enfrascado en un cuadro o una escultura—rara vez, ahora que tenía la vista tan mala—, le daba ánimos, ideas, algo de la antigua voluntad de alcanzar la escurridiza perfección" (Vargas Llosa, *Paraíso* 391) ("Music filled the empty places in his soul, soothing him at moments of frustration or discouragement. When he was immersed in a painting or a sculpture—rarely now, since his sight was so bad—it gave him energy, ideas, something of his old will to achieve elusive perfection" 363).

20  I quote in this chapter from Edith Grossman's translation of the *Dream of the Celt*, Farrar, Straus and Giroux, 2012.

21  This is not the first time that Vargas Llosa writes about Roger Casement. In the chapter titled "*El corazón de las tinieblas*—Las raíces de lo humano" ("*Heart of Darkness*—The Roots of Humankind") in *La verdad de las mentiras*, he referred to the historical Casement as one of the first people to have denounced King Leopold II's abuses in the Congo. He states that "quienes, a base de una audacia y perseverancia formidables, consiguieron movilizar a la opinión pública internacional contra las carnicerías congolesas de Leopolodo II fueron un irlandés, Roger Casement, y el belga Morel. ... Ambos merecerían los honores de una gran novela" (38) (those "who, showing extraordinary bravery and perseverance, were mainly responsible for mobilising international public opinion against Leopold II's butchery in the the Congo, were an Irishman, Roger Casement, and a Belgian, Morel. Both deserve the honours of a great novel")—in this way foreshadowing his own work. (The English here is from p. 34 of John King's translation of Vargas Llosa, *Touchstones: Essays on Literature, Art, and Politics*, Farrar, Straus and Giroux, 2007.)

22  According to Kristal, "The novel might also be loosely inspired by a Jorge Luis Borges story, 'Tema del traidor y del heroe,' 1944, in which an Irishman is remembered as a hero because his people want to remember him as such, even though he was deeply flawed" ("From Utopia to Reconciliation" 141).

23  *Heart of Darkness*'s narrator, Charles Marlow, recounts a trip up the Congo River in the Congo Free State, and epitomizes the civilization/barbarism dichotomy, implying that the white man is as barbaric as the African native populations (as perceived by Europe at the time). Although very popular and still required reading in high school and college, *Heart of Darkness* has been harshly criticized by eminent scholars in post-colonial studies, who argue against its dehumanization of Africans. Published in 1975, Chinua Achebe's "An Image of Africa: Racism in Conrad's *Heart*

*of Darkness*" maintains that the novella "projects the image of Africa as 'the other world,' the antithesis of Europe and therefore of civilization, a place where man's vaunted intelligence and refinement are finally mocked by triumphant bestiality" (3), where Africans are depicted as "dumb brutes" and cannibals who grunt (7). Vargas Llosa addresses Achebe's paper in his essay "*El corazón de las tinieblas*—Las raíces de lo humano." While he does not dispute Achebe's claim, he maintains that the novel is "pese a las severísimas condenas que lanzó contra ella el escritor africano Chinua Achebe acusándola de prejuiciada y salvajemente racista *(bloody racist)* contra los negros, una dura crítica a la ineptitud de la civilización occidental para trascender la naturaleza humana, cruel e incivil" (43) ("without doubt, and despite the strong criticism launched at it by the African writer Chinua Achebe who condemned it for being prejudiced and 'bloody racist,' a trenchant critique of Western civilisation's inability to transcend cruel and uncivilised human nature"; 37-38). In the novel, Casement and Conrad meet for the first time in Congo, and later in 1903 after the publication of *Heart of Darkness*. Conrad makes clear that he owes a lot to Casement, and tells him that he should have appeared "como coautor de ese libro . . . Nunca lo hubiera escrito sin su ayuda. Usted me quitó las legañas de los ojos. Sobre el África, sobre el Estado Independiente del Congo. Y sobre la fiera humana" (*Sueño* 74) ("You should have appeared as co-author of that book, Casement. . . . I never would have written it without your help. You removed the scales from my eyes. About Africa, about the Congo Free State. And about the human beast"; 52). Later on, in jail, Casement discusses the novel with the historian Alice Stopford Green, to whom Vargas Llosa gives the part of Achebe: "Esa novela es una parábola según la cual África vuelve bárbaros a los civilizados europeos que van allá. Tu *Informe sobre el Congo* mostró lo contrario, más bien. Que fuimos los europeos que llevamos allá las peores barbaries" (76) ("That novel is a parable according to which Africa turns civilized Europeans who go there into barbarians. Your Congo report showed the opposite. That we Europeans were the ones who brought the worst barbarities there"; 54). Casement, for his part, speaks the words of Vargas Llosa and sees the novel as a metaphor for the original sin ("*El corazón de las tinieblas*—Las raíces de lo humano" 38; *Sueño del celta* 76).

24  A quotation like this one reveals the work and preparation Vargas Llosa put into the writing of the novel. The expression "incorregible irlandés" is taken from a 1907 letter Casement sent to Alice Stopford Green, one of his closest friends: "I had accepted Imperialism—British rule was to be extended at all costs, because it was the best for everyone under the sun, and those who opposed that extension ought rightly to be 'smashed' . . . Well the [Boer] War gave me qualms at the end—the concentration camps bigger ones—and finally when up in those lonely Congo forests where I found Leopold I found also myself—the incorrigible Irishman" (qtd. in Ó Síocháin 1).

25  In "*El sueño del celta*: Postcolonial Vargas Llosa," Helene Carol Weldt-Basson criticizes the fact that "at times the reader has the sense that the novel's most pressing point is not the denunciation of colonization in Africa and South America, but rather the criticism of Ireland's colonial status in the early twentieth century. The character Roger Casement, although a clear denouncer of colonialist abuse both in the Congo and in the Putumayo region, interprets these geographical regions from a Eurocentric perspective and seems at times more concerned with European politics and his own nationalist agenda, than with Third-World realities" (234). She maintains that while the novel

"exposes the economic motivation of colonialist 'civilizing' discourse, [it also] falls into the colonialist trap of de-emphasizing national peculiarities in favour of a generalizing discourse that runs the risk of being racist and essentialist through eliding ethnic, racial, and social differences between nations and favouring the European 'First-World' problematic versus the Third-World reality" (236).

26   *Travesuras de la niña mala* (2006) is quite cosmopolitan too, but in a very broad understanding of cosmopolitanism, where it is only associated with travels, and not articulated as a philosophical position.

27   According to Vargas Llosa, "The reconstruction of the past through literature is almost always misleading in terms of historical objectivity. Literary truth is one thing, historical truth another. But, although it may be full of fabrication—or for that very reason—literature presents us with a side of history which cannot be found in history books. For literature does not lie gratuitously. Its deceits, devices, and hyperbole all serve to express those deep-seated and disturbing truths which only come to light in this oblique way" ("Power of Lies" 28).

## CHAPTER 3

1   Even if he has been criticized for not being Mexican enough, Volpi's first novels tend to prove this affirmation as false. *A pesar del oscuro silencio* (*In Spite of the Dark Silence*; 1992) concentrates on the life and works of Mexican poet Jorge Cuesta; *Días de ira* (*Days of Wrath*; 1994) is inspired, from a narrative and thematic perspective, by Salvador Elizondo's *Farabeuf*; and *La paz de los sepulcros* (*Peace in the Graves*; 1995) is perhaps the most Mexican novel of all, since it was written in Mexico, has a Mexican narrator and protagonist, and is about Mexican events.

2   Julio Cortázar talks at length of his cosmopolitan vocation in his letter-essay "Situación del intelectual latinoamericano" (1967), directed at the Cuban thinker Roberto Fernández Retamar, who had rather conflicted views when it came to the internationalization of the Latin American author. Cortázar confesses that his years in France made him discover his true Latin American self, which he puts in perspective on a global scale: "¿No te parece en verdad paradójico que un argentino casi enteramente volcado hacia Europa en su juventud, al punto de quemar las naves y venirse a Francia . . . haya descubierto aquí, después de una década, su verdadera condición de latinoamericano? Pero esta paradoja abre una cuestión más honda: la de si no era necesario situarse en la perspectiva más universal del viejo mundo, desde donde todo parece poder abarcarse con una especie de ubicuidad mental, para ir descubriendo poco a poco las verdaderas raíces de lo latinoamericano sin perder por eso la visión global de la historia y del hombre" ("Doesn't it seem really paradoxical to you that an Argentine almost entirely turned toward Europe in his youth, to the point of burning his bridges and coming to France . . . had discovered here, after a decade, his true condition as a Latin American? But this paradox leads to a deeper question: whether it was unnecessary to place oneself in the most universal perspective of the old world, where it seems that everything can be encompassed by a kind of mental ubiquity, in order to discover little by little the true roots of Latin Americanness, without losing as a result the global vision of history and mankind"; 269–70). In Cortázar's

understanding, locality and globality go hand in hand, in that they both help a writer become more aware of the tradition to which he belongs, but also drive him to discover more about himself. Cortázar also mentions having received negative comments since "vivir en Europa y escribir 'argentino' escandaliza a los que exigen una especie de asistencia obligatoria a clase por parte del escritor" ("living in Europe and writing as an 'Argentine' scandalizes those who demand a kind of compulsory classroom attendance by the writer"; 275), but he remains "dispuesto a seguir siendo un escritor latinoamericano en Francia" ("willing to continue being a Latin American writer in France"; 277).

3   They claimed that "Ahí hay más bien una mera reacción contra el agotamiento; cansancio de que la gran literatura latinoamericana y el dudoso realismo mágico se hayan convertido, para nuestras letras, en magiquismo trágico; cansancio de los discursos patrioteros que por tanto tiempo nos han hecho creer que Rivapalacio escribía mejor que su contemporáneo Poe, como si proximidad y calidad fuesen una y la misma cosa; cansancio de escribir mal para que se lea más, que no mejor; cansancio de lo *engagé*; cansancio de las letras que vuelan en círculos como moscas sobre sus propios cadáveres" ("Manifiesto Crack" 5) ("There is, of course, a reaction against exhaustion; weariness of having the great Latin American literature and the dubious magic realism converted, for our writing, into tragic magicism; weariness of the patriotic speeches which, for a long time, have made us believe that Rivapalacio wrote better than his contemporary Poe, as if proximity and quality were one and the same thing; weariness of writing poorly in order to be read more [but not better]; weariness of the engagé; weariness of the letters that circle like flies over corpses). This English rendering comes from Cecilia Bartolin and Scott Miller's translation of the "Crack Manifesto," included in Jaimes (2017).

4   Page numbers here and below are from Ezra Fritz's translation of the "Crack Postmanifesto," in Jaimes (2017).

5   One could argue that Berry's stand on the integration of a Latin American canon, as well as how to ensure one's legitimacy and longevity in literature, can be tied to that of Harold Bloom and his seminal *The Anxiety of Influence*. Bloom associates literary tradition with authors who have a certain influence over others, and says that "Every disciple takes away something from his masters" (6), whether consciously or unconsciously. In addition, Bloom proposes a gradation to explain the development of what he calls the "strong poet." He posits that such poets maintain an ambiguous relationship with their predecessors and with the literary canon, since their influence creates a feeling of anxiety in the new poet. Bloom considers that as long as the works of his precursors inspire the young poet, he is doomed to produce works that are unoriginal and weak. Therefore, the poet must forge a personal poetic vision for himself, in order to ensure his survival in the literary world, and eventually his inclusion in a new canon.

6   While Volpi applauds García Márquez's skills, and does not deny that magical realism had a tremendous impact on Latin American literature, he laments that it has become some sort of brand that is expected from Latin American authors. He also claims that the fact that magical realism is seen as the defining characteristic of a whole continent is inevitably reductive, for it erases large parts of Spanish America's literary history,

"desde los balbuceos del siglo XIX hasta algunos de los momentos más brillantes de nuestras letras, incluidas las vanguardias de principios del siglo XX, Borges y Onetti, la novela realista o comprometida posterior—en especial la novela de la Revolución mexicana—, las búsquedas formales de los cincuenta y el contagio de la cultura popular de los sesenta. . . . Y, acaso lo más grave, ha exacerbado el nacionalismo frente a la rica tradición universal de la región" ("from the babbling of the nineteenth century to some of the brightest moments in our letters, including the Avant-Garde of the early twentieth century, Borges and Onetti, the later realist or socially engaged novel— especially the novel of the Mexican Revolution—formal searches in the 1950s and the contagion of popular culture in the 1960s. . . . And, perhaps most seriously, it has heightened nationalism despite the region's rich universal tradition"; *El insomnio de Bolívar* 69–70). He also despises the hypocrisy of some critics, who were fast to attack the Boom for its use of foreign literary devices, but who eventually changed their mind when García Márquez and other Boom writers' novels became successful: after the publication of *Cien años de soledad* "el realismo mágico© fue elevado a paradigma y, de ser tachados de vendepatrias, los miembros del Boom pasaron a encarnar la esencia misma de América Latina" ("magical realism© was elevated to a paradigm and, after being tarred as traitors to the nation, members of the Boom came to embody the very essence of Latin America"; 70). Volpi uses the copyright sign—©—to highlight how magical realism has been turned into a brand.

7   Volpi explained that he never intended to portray an American physicist, but that the authenticity of the novel depended on it: "A fines de 1998 comprendí que había algo ridículo en que un mexicano, y para colmo físico, se dedicase a cazar nazis en Alemania. Sólo entonces decidí, por una simple cuestión de verosimilitud, cambiar la nacionalidad de mi personaje, que se tornó estadounidense y pasó a llamarse Francis Bacon, como el filósofo isabelino" ("At the end of 1998 I understood that there was something ridículous about a Mexican, and on top of that a physicist, devoting himself to hunting down Nazis in Germany. Only then did I decide, simply as a matter of plausibility, to change the nationality of my character, who became an American renamed Francis Bacon, like the Elizabethan philosopher"; *Insomnio* 24). Volpi even shared, in an interview with Areco, that the first portrayal of Bacon was named Jorge Cantor, a wink to the German mathematician Georg Cantor. For an analysis of Volpi's supposed lack of national allegiance, see Christopher Domínguez Michael's various interventions in *Letras Libres*.

8   Rodrigo Fresán is an Argentinean author and journalist. He now lives in Spain. He was a close friend of Chilean Roberto Bolaño, with whom he shares a tendency to write hybrid narratives that make use of different media. He is openly influenced by American fiction, which has obviously caused some commotion in Argentina, where his writings are deemed by some insufficiently national.

9   Volpi addresses this very criticism in *El insomnio de Bolívar*. He says, in an ironic manner, that "un español me acusó de usar un lenguaje desprovisto de localismos para conquistar el mercado mundial (que un oficial nazi dijese 'me lleva la chingada' me parecía una simple falta de sutileza)" ("a Spaniard accused me of using language devoid of local turns of phrase in order to appeal to the world market [that a Nazi officer would say 'fuck me' seemed to me a simple lack of subtlety]"; 25).

10  *El fin de la locura* has yet to be translated into English.

11  Toward the end of the novel, the reader learns that the editor of the novel is none other than Jorge Volpi. In a section entitled "Peor libro del año" ("Worst book of the year"), journalist Juán Pérez Avella provides a devastating critique of "*El fin de la locura*, de Aníbal Quevedo (edición a cargo de Jorge Volpi, Seix Barral, 2003)" ("*The End of Madness*, by Aníbal Quevedo [edited by Jorge Volpi, Seix Barral, 2003]"). The criticism presented in this section is twofold. First, in an ironic manner, Volpi questions journalists and literary critics who are still interested in a literary tradition that would mostly be of a national sort, and who dislike this "intensa—y estéril—globalización" ("intense—and sterile—globalization") that does not bring about great literature. Second, he mocks openly the supposed identity of the novel at hand, calling it "un libro francés escrito en español" ("a French book written in Spanish"), which, according to literary critics well versed in national tradition, cannot make it Mexican (451).

12  The intertextual references to Miguel de Cervantes's *Don Quijote* are obvious throughout the novel: Josefa Ponce, whose last name sounds like that of Sancho Panza, acts as a helper to Quevedo; the psychoanalyst publishes his work with a publishing house called Rocinante; and he spends the major part of his life trying to seduce Claire, whom he calls his Dulcinea.

13  Volpi already alluded to this state of affairs in the "Manifiesto Crack": "parafraseando a Nietzsche, el fin de los tiempos no ocurre fuera del mundo, sino dentro del corazón. Más que una superstición decimal o una necesidad del mercado, el fin del mundo supone un particular estado del espíritu, lo que menos importa es la destrucción externa, comparada con el derrumbamiento interior, con ese estado de zozobra que precede a nuestro íntimo Juicio Final" (9) ("paraphrasing Nietzsche, the end of time does not happen outside the world, but inside the heart. More than a mere superstition, the end of the world supposes a particular state of the spirit; what matters less is the external destruction when compared to the inner collapse, this state of anguish that precedes our internal Judgment Day"; 188).

14  Quevedo's behaviour is the polar opposite of that of great intellectual figures like Carlos Fuentes, Octavio Paz, and José Revueltas, who openly criticized the government. For instance, Fuentes never stopped denouncing the massacre in various *revistas*, both in Mexico and abroad; Paz renounced diplomatic service in solidarity with the protesters; and Revueltas was jailed after being accused of being the brains behind the protest.

15  The English title comes from Alfred MacAdam's translation of *No será la Tierra*, Open Letter, 2009. All page references in the English quotations in this section come from this edition.

16  In an interview entitled "Jorge Volpi: Quiero dedicarme a la música" ("I want to dedicate myself to music"), the author explained that "*No será la tierra* ... empieza como una ópera, tiene una obertura en donde se presentan los temas que se van a desarrollar, y luego son tres actos. Los personajes se desarrollan de una manera operística" ("*Season of Ash* begins like an opera, it has an overture where the themes to be developed are presented, and then there are three acts. The characters develop in an operatic way"; 34). In the same interview, Volpi also describes the novel as a "novela rusa" ("Russian novel"; 34).

17  The novel is unique in terms of characters, who, as in some operas, are classified in very strict categories according to occupations ("Los científicos," "Los economistas," "Los ecologistas," "Los poetas"), countries ("En Hungría," "En Afganistán"), cities ("Chernóbil," "San Francisco"), nationalities ("Los soviéticos," "Los estadounidenses"), and the projects with which they are identified ("Iniciativa de defensa estratégica," "El genoma") (*No será la Tierra* 517–23).

18  Nationalism is a topic with which the narrator is well acquainted. Before moving to Moscow, he lives in Baku (now the capital of Azerbaijan), where he gets to experience it for himself. In 1988, "el pasado se volvió presente y dio inicio a la guerra" (Volpi, *No será la Tierra* 263) ("the past became present and war broke out"; 199). Consequences of *glasnost* and *perestroika* are "la exacerbación de las disputas y rencillas nacionales, aplacadas por la fuerza durante más de siete décadas" (263) ("the exacerbation of national disputes and quarrels, all of which had been held in check for more than seven decades"; 199). People are killed in various skirmishes, which only exacerbates the tensions. In his diary, he notes that "Los fantasmas pretéritos reaparecen, otra vez se instala aquí la muerte, otra vez entramos en la Historia" (265) "Ghosts of the past are reappearing. Once again we have death, once again we're entering History"; 200). He speaks of the "virus nacionalista" (266) ("nationalist virus"; 202) that has contaminated his wife and his family.

# Works Consulted

Achebe, Chinua. "An Image of Africa." *Research in African Literatures*, vol. 9, no. 1, Spring 1978, pp. 1–15. *JSTOR*, https://www.jstor.org/stable/3818468?seq=1.

Aching, Gerard. *The Politics of Spanish American* Modernismo: *By Exquisite Design*. Cambridge UP, 1997.

Ágreda, Javier. "El celta de Vargas Llosa." *Vargas Llosa y la crítica peruana*, edited by Miguel Ángel Rodríguez Rea, Universidad Ricardo Palma Editorial Universitaria, 2010, pp. 257–8.

Allemand, Roger-Michel. *L'utopie*. Ellipses, 2005.

Anderson, Benedict R. *Imagined Communities: Reflections on the Origin and Spread of Nationalism*. Verso, 1991.

Anderson Imbert, Enrique. "Discusión sobre Jorge Luis Borges." *Revista Megáfono*, vol. 3, no. 11, August 1933, pp. 13–33.

Appiah, Kwame Anthony. *Cosmopolitanism: Ethics in a World of Strangers*, W. W. Norton, 2006.

———. "Cosmopolitan Patriots." *Critical Inquiry*, vol. 23, no. 3, Spring 1997, pp. 617–39. *JSTOR*, https://www.jstor.org/stable/1344038?seq=1.

———. "Cosmopolitan Reading." *Cosmopolitan Geographies: New Locations in Literature and Culture*, edited by Vinay Dharwadker, Routledge, 2001, pp. 199–225.

———. *The Ethics of Identity*. Princeton UP, 2005.

———. "Making Sense of Cosmopolitanism: A Conversation with Kwame Anthony Appiah." *Hedgehog Review*, vol. 11, no. 3, Fall 2009, pp. 42+. *Gale Academic OneFile*, https://link.gale.com/apps/doc/A214206457/AONE?u=otta77973&sid=AONE&xid=bb2cb099.

Areco, Macarena, and Jorge Volpi. "Sobre el enigma del compromiso del intelectual en el lado de allá y en el de acá." *Revista Iberoamericana*, vol. LXXIII, no. 218, 2007, pp. 299–311.

Aristotle. "Poetics by Aristotle." MIT, 1994. *The Internet Classics Archive*, classics.mit.edu/Aristotle/poetics.2.2.html.

Baynes, Kenneth. "The Hermeneutics of Situated Cosmopolitanism." *Philosophy and Social Criticism*, vol. 33, no. 9, May 2007, pp. 301–8.

Bencomo, Anadeli. "Geopolíticas de la novela hispanoamericana contemporánea: en la encrucijada entre narrativas extraterritoriales e internacionales." *Revista de crítica literaria latinoamericana*, vol. 35, no. 69, January–March 2009, pp. 33–50. *JSTOR*, https://www.jstor.org/stable/27944642?seq=1.

Bett, Richard. "Stoic Ethics." *A Companion to Ancient Philosophy*, edited by Mary Louise Gill and Pierre Pellegrin, Blackwell, 2006, pp. 530–48.

Bhabha, Homi. *The Location of Culture*. Routledge, 1994.

Bletz, May E. *Immigration and Acculturation in Brazil and Argentina: 1890–1929*. Palgrave Macmillan, 2010.

Bloch, Ernst. *L'esprit de l'utopie*. Gallimard, 1977.

Bloom, Harold. *The Anxiety of Influence: A Theory of Poetry*. Oxford UP, 1973.

Bolívar, Simón. "Contestación de un Americano Meriodional a un caballero de esta Isla (Carta de Jamaica)." *Obras completas I*, edited by Vicente Lecuna, Editorial Lex, 1950, pp. 159–74.

———. "Discurso pronunciado por el Libertador ante el Congreso de Angostura el 15 de febrero de 1819, día de su instalación." *Obras completas III*, edited by Vicente Lecuna, Editorial Lex, 1950, pp. 674–97.

Booker, M. Keith. *Vargas Llosa among the Postmodernists*. U of Florida P, 1994.

Borges, Jorge Luis. *Discusión*. 1932. Alianza Editorial, 1980.

———. "El escritor argentino y la tradición." *Obras completas*, Emecé, 1974, pp. 267–74.

———. "Tema del traidor y del héroe." *Literatura.us*, https://www.literatura.us/borges/tema.html.

Breckenridge, Carol A., et al. *Cosmopolitanism*. Duke UP, 2000.

Browitt, Jeffrey, and Werner Mackenbach, editors. *Rubén Darío: Cosmopolita arraigado*. IHNCA, 2010.

Brown, Eric. "Hellenistic Cosmopolitanism." *A Companion to Ancient Philosophy*, edited by Mary Louise Gill and Pierre Pellegrin, Blackwell, 2006, pp. 549–58.

Brown, Garrett Wallace, and David Held. *The Cosmopolitanism Reader*. Polity, 2010.

Caballero Wangüemert, María. "La Flor de Lis." *América sin nombre*, 11–12, 2008, pp. 79–86. https://americasinnombre.ua.es/article/view/2008-n11-12-la-flor-de-lis.

Calhoun, Craig. "The Class Consciousness of Frequent Travelers: Toward a Critique of Actually Existing Cosmopolitanism." *South Atlantic Quarterly*, vol. 101, no. 4, Fall 2002, pp. 869–97. *Project Muse*, doi:10.1215/00382876-101-4-869.

Camín, Héctor Aguilar. "Mario Vargas Llosa: La realidad y la utopía." *Nexos*, 3 November 2012. https://www.nexos.com.mx/?p=13998.

Carmen, Mari, and Héctor Olea. *Inverted Utopias: Avant-Garde Art in Latin America*. Yale UP, 2004.

Carpentier, Alejo. "Conciencia e identidad de América." *Visión de América*. Seix Barral, 1999, pp. 173-83.

Casanova, Pascale. *The World Republic of Letters*. Harvard UP, 2004.

Castillo Pérez, Alberto. "El *Crack* y su manifiesto." *Revista de la Universidad de México*, no. 31, 2006, pp. 83-7. http://www.revistadelauniversidad.unam.mx/3106/pdfs/83-87.pdf.

Catelli, Nora. "La élite itinerante del boom: seducciones transnacionales en los escritores latinoamericanos (1960-1973)." *Historia de los intelectuales en América Latina—Los avatares de la ciudad letrada*, edited by Carlos Altamirano, Ketz Editores, 2010, pp. 712-32.

Chávez Casteñada, Ricardo, and Celso Santajuliana. "Diccionario Volpi." *En busca de Jorge Volpi—Ensayos sobre su obra*, edited by José Manuel López de Abiada et al., Verbum, 2004, pp. 72-99.

Cheah, Pheng. "Cosmopolitanism." *Theory, Culture & Society*, vol. 23, May 2006, pp. 486-96. *Scholars Portal*, doi:10.1177/026327640602300290.

———. "What Is a World? On World Literature as World-Making Activity." *Daedalus: Journal of the American Academy of Arts and Sciences*, vol. 137, no. 3, Summer 2008, pp. 26-38. JSTOR, https://www.jstor.org/stable/40543795?seq=1.

Cobb, Russell. "The Politics of Literary Prestige: Promoting the Latin American 'Boom' in the Pages of *Mundo Nuevo*." *A Contracorriente*, vol. 5, no. 2, Spring 2008, pp. 75-94. *A Contracorriente Archive*, acontracorriente.chass.ncsu.edu.contracorriente/article/view/942/1577.

Coll, Pedro-Emilio, et al. "Charloteo." *Cosmópolis: Revista Universal*, vol. 1, no. 1, 1894, pp. 1-5.

Cornejo-Polar, Antonio. "Mestizaje e hibridez: los riesgos de las metáforas. Apuntes." *Revista Iberoamericana*, vol. LXVIII, no. 200, June-September 2002, pp. 867-70.

———. *The Multiple Voices of Latin American Literature*. Doe Library, University of California, 1994.

Corral, Wilfrido H. "La prosa/cultura no ficticia según Leonardo Valencia y Jorge Volpi." *MLN*, vol. 126, no. 2, 2011, pp. 366-89. JSTOR, https://www.jstor.org/stable/23012654?seq=1.

Corral, Wilfrido H., et al. "Jorge Volpi." *The Contemporary Spanish-American Novel: Bolaño and After*. Bloomsbury, 2013, pp. 97-105.

Cortázar, Julio. "Acerca de la situación del intelectual latinoamericano." *Último round*. Siglo XXI, 1969, pp. 265-80.

———. "Algunos aspectos del cuento." *Literatura.us*, https://www.literatura.us/cortazar/aspectos.html.

Couture, Jocelyne. "Qu'est-ce que le cosmopolitisme?" *Le cosmopolitisme: enjeux et débats contemporains*, edited by Ryoa Chung and Geneviève Nootens, Presses de l'Université de Montréal, 2010, pp. 15-35.

Dallmayr, Fred. "Cosmopolitanism: Moral and Political." *Political Theory*, vol. 31, no. 3, June 2003, 421–42.

Darío, Rubén. "Dilucidaciones." *Obras completas*. Ediciones Anaconda, 1948, p. 274.

De Abiada, José Manuel López, and Jorge Volpi. "Entre los meandros de la memoria y el dilema fáustico. Entrevista a Jorge Volpi." *Revista Iberoamericana*, vol. 1, no. 4, December 2001, pp. 149–54. *JSTOR*, https://www.jstor.org/stable/41672745?seq=1.

De Castro, Juan E. *The Spaces of Latin American Literature: Tradition, Globalization, and Cultural Production*. Palgrave Macmillan, 2008.

De Castro, Juan E., and Nicholas Birns. *Vargas Llosa and Latin American Politics*. Palgrave Macmillan, 2010.

Domínguez Michael, Christopher, and Lisa Dillman. *Critical Dictionary of Mexican Literature (1955–2010)*. Dalkey Archive, 2012.

Donoso, José. *Historia personal del "boom."* Anagrama, 1972.

Dravasa, Mayder. *The Boom in Barcelona: Literary Modernism in Spanish and Spanish American Fiction (1950–1974)*. Peter Lang, 2005.

Dudgeon, Jeffrey. *Roger Casement. The Black Diaries—With a Study of His Background, Sexuality, and Irish Political Life*. Belfast Press, 2002.

Erskine, Toni. *Embedded Cosmopolitanism: Duties to Strangers and Enemies is a World of "Dislocated Communities."* Oxford UP, 2008.

Fabian, Johannes. *Time and the Other: How Anthropology Makes Its Object*. Columbia UP, 1983.

Fernández Retamar, Roberto. *Calibán: Apuntes sobre la cultura en nuestra América*. Editorial Diógenes, 1974.

Fojas, Camilla. *Cosmopolitanism in the Americas*. Purdue UP, 2005.

Fuentes, Carlos. *El espejo enterrado*. Taurus, 1997.

———. *Geografía de la novela*. Alfaguara, 1993.

———. *La nueva novela hispanoamericana*. Joaquín Mortiz, 1974.

———. "Situación del escritor en América latina." *Mundo Nuevo*, vol. 1, no. 1, July 1966, pp. 5–21.

Fuguet, Alberto, and Sergio Gómez. *McOndo*. Grijalbo Mondadori, 1996.

Fukuyama, Francis. "The End of History?" *Quadrant*, vol. 33, no. 8, August 1989, pp. 15–25.

———. *The End of History and the Last Man*. Perennial, 1992.

García Canclini, Néstor. *Culturas híbridas: estrategias para entrar y salir de la modernidad*. Grijalbo, 1990.

Giudicelli, Christian. "Mario Vargas Llosa et le démon de l'histoire—Entre histoire et narration." *De Flora Tristan à Mario Vargas Llosa*, edited by Stéphane Michaud, Presses de la Sorbonne Nouvelle, 2004, pp. 187–200.

Glantz, Margo. "Las hijas de la Malinche." *Literatura mexicana hoy: del 68 al ocaso de la revolución*, edited by Karl Kohut, Verveurt, 1995, pp. 121–9.

———. "Las hijas de la Malinche." *La palabra contra el silencio*, edited by Nora Erro-Peralta and Magdalena Maiz-Peña, Ediciones Era, 2013, pp. 72–90.

Gónzalez Echevarría, Roberto. "La razón recobrada." *En busca de Jorge Volpi—ensayos sobre su obra*, edited by José Manuel López de Abiada et al., Verbum, 2004, pp. 145–8.

Goodlad, Lauren M. E. "Cosmopolitanism's Actually Existing Beyond; Toward a Victorian Geopolitical Aesthetic." *Victorian Literature and Culture*, vol. 38, no. 2, September 2010, pp. 399–411. *Scholars Portal*, doi:10.1017/S1060150310000070.

Gowan, Peters. "The New Liberal Cosmopolitanism." *Institut für die Wissenschaft von Menschen Working Papers*, no. 2, 2000. http://www.geocities.ws/gennarolasca/liberalcosmopolitanism.pdf.

Gramuglio, Maria Teresa. "*Sur*. Una minoría cosmopolita en la periferia occidental." *Historia de los intelectuales en América Latina*, edited by Carlos Altamirano, Katz, 2008, pp. 192–210.

Grünfled, Mihai H. "Cosmopolitismo modernista y vanguardista: Una identidad latinoamericana divergente." *Revista Iberoamericana*, vol. 55, no. 146–7, Enero–Junio 1989, pp. 33–41.

Gruzinski, Serge. *The Mestizo Mind: The Intellectual Dynamics of Colonization and Globalization*. Routledge, 2002.

———. *La pensée métisse*. Fayard, 1999.

Gutiérrez Mouat, Ricardo. "Cosmopolitismo y hospitalidad en *El Paraíso en la otra esquina*, de Mario Vargas Llosa." *MLN*, vol. 123, no. 2, March 2008, pp. 396–414. *JSTOR*, https://www.jstor.org/stable/30133936?seq=1.

Hallman, J. C. *In Utopia: Six Kinds of Eden and the Search for a Better Paradise*. St. Martin's Press, 2010.

Hannerz, Ulf. "Two Faces of Cosmopolitanism: Culture and Politics." *Statsvetenskaplig tidskrifts*, vol. 10, no. 3, 2005, pp. 199–213. https://journals.lub.lu.se/index.php/st/article/view/3534/0.

Hass, Ingrid, and Jorge Volpi. "Jorge Volpi: Quiero dedicarme a la música." *Pro Ópera*, vol. 17, no. 6, November 2009, pp. 32–5. https://www.yumpu.com/es/document/view/25531432/jorge-volpi-pro-apera.

Hernández Arregui, Juan José. *Imperialismo y cultura. La política de la inteligencia argentina*. Editorial Amerindia, 1957.

Hobsbawm, Eric. *The Age of Extremes: A History of the World, 1914–1991*. Peter Smith, 2000.

Hoyos Ayala, Héctor. *Beyond Bolaño: The Global Latin American Novel*. Columbia UP, 2015.

Hurley, Teresa M. "Mother/Country and Identity in Elena Poniatowska's *La 'Flor de Lis.'*" *Mothers and Daughters in Post-revolutionary Mexican Literature*. Támesis, 2003, pp. 151–88.

Ibarra, Néstor. "Préface." *Fictions*. 1951. Gallimard, 1974, pp. 7–30.

Inglis, David. "Alternative Histories of Cosmopolitanism." *Routledge Handbook of Cosmopolitanism Studies*, edited by Gerard Delanty, Routledge, 2012, pp. 11–24.

Jaimes, Héctor, ed. *The Mexican Crack Writers: History and Criticism*. Palgrave Macmillan, 2017.

Jitrik, Noé. *Historia e imaginación literaria*. Biblos, 1995.

Kanev, Venko. "El salvajismo institucionalizado en *El sueño del celta* de Mario Vargas Llosa." *América* 50, July 2017, pp. 85–94. https://doi.org/10.4000/america.1850.

Kant, Immanuel. "Idee zu einer allgemeinen Geschichte in weltbürgerlicher Ansicht." *The Cosmopolitanism Reader*, edited by Garrett Wallace Brown and David Held. Polity, 2010, pp. 17–26.

Kirsch, Adam. *The Global Novel: Writing the World in the 21st Century*. Columbia Global Reports, 2017.

Köllmann, Sabine. "The Return of the Grand Design: *La Fiesta del Chivo* (2000), *El Paraíso en la otra esquina* (2003) and *El sueño del celta* (2010)." *A Companion to Mario Vargas Llosa*. Támesis, 2014, pp. 223–75.

Krauze, Enrique. "Conversación con Mario Vargas Llosa. Utopías." *Letras Libres* 62, January 2004. https://www.letraslibres.com/mexico/utopias-conversacion-mario-vargas-llosa.

Kristal, Efraín Samuel. "From Utopia to Reconciliation: *The Way to Paradise*, *The Bad Girl*, and *The Dream of the Celt*." *The Cambridge Companion to Mario Vargas Llosa*, edited by Efraín Kristal and John King, Cambridge UP, 2012, pp. 129–47.

———. *The Temptation of the Word: The Novels of Mario Vargas Llosa*. Vanderbilt UP, 1998.

Kurasawa, Fuyuki. "Cosmopolitanism's Theoretical and Substantive Dimension." *Routledge Handbook of Cosmopolitanism Studies*, edited by Gerard Delanty, Routledge, 2012, pp. 301–11.

Kymlicka, Will, and Kathryn Walker. *Rooted Cosmopolitanism: Canada and the World*. UBC Press, 2012.

Lefort, Daniel. "Mario Vargas Llosa, de *la Fête* au *Paradis*: fiction de l'histoire et pouvoir de l'écrivain." *Esprit*, vol. 11, no. 299, November 2003, pp.65–75. JSTOR, https://www.jstor.org/stable/24249051?seq=1.

Lemus, Rafael. "Lo que todo lectora (no) quisiera saber del siglo XX." *Letras Libres*, December 2006, pp. 74–83.

Leprohon, Pierre. *Flora Tristan*. Éditions Corymbe, 1979.

Loss, Jacqueline. *Cosmopolitanisms and Latin America: Against the Destiny of Place*. Palgrave Macmillan, 2005.

Lukács, Georg. *The Historical Novel*. Merlin, 1962.

Mariátegui, José Carlos. *Siete ensayos de interpretación de la realidad peruana*. Ocean, 2007.

Martí, José. *Nuestra América*. Fundación Biblioteca Ayacucho, 2005.

Menton, Seymour. *Latin America's New Historical Novel*. U of Texas P, 1993.

Michaud, Stéphane. "Arabesques: Mario Vargas Llosa et Flora Tristan." *De Flora Tristan à Mario Vargas Llosa*, edited by Stéphane Michaud, Presses de la Sorbonne Nouvelle, 2004, pp. 201–16.

Michaud, Stéphane, and Albert Bensoussan. "Histoire et fiction: entretien avec Albert Bensoussan et Stéphane Michaud." *De Flora Tristan à Mario Vargas Llosa*, edited by Stéphane Michaud, Presses de la Sorbonne Nouvelle, 2004, pp. 217–36.

Mignolo, Walter D. *The Darker Side of Western Modernity: Global Futures, Decolonial Options*. Duke UP, 2011.

———. "De-colonial Cosmopolitanism and Dialogues among Civilizations." *Routledge Handbook of Cosmopolitanism Studies*, edited by Gerard Delanty, Routledge, 2012, pp. 85–100.

———. *The Idea of Latin America*. Blackwell, 2005.

———. "The Many Faces of Cosmo-polis: Border Thinking and Critical Cosmopolitanism." *Public Culture*, vol. 12, no. 3, September 2000, pp. 721–48. *Scholars Portal*, doi:10.1215/08992363-12-3-721.

Miller, Marilyn Grace. *The Rise and Fall of the Cosmic Race: The Cult of Mestizaje in Latin America*. U of Texas P, 2004.

Millington, Mark. "Transculturation: Contrapuntal Notes to Critical Orthodoxy." *Bulletin of Latin American Research*, vol. 26, no. 2, April 2007, pp. 256–68. *Scholars Portal*, doi:10.1111/j.1470-9856.2007.00223.x.

Nobel Foundation. "Mario Vargas Llosa: Facts." Nobel Foundation, 2010. https://www.nobelprize.org/prizes/literature/2010/vargas_llosa/facts/.

Nussbaum, Martha. "Cultivating Humanity." *Liberal Education*, Spring 1998, pp. 38–45.

———. *For Love of Country: Debating the Limits of Patriotism*. Beacon, 1996.

———. "Kant and Stoic Cosmopolitanism." *Journal of Political Philosophy*, vol. 5, no. 1, March 2002, pp. 1–25. *Scholars Portal*, doi:10.1111/1467-9760.00021.

———. "The Worth of Human Dignity: Two Tensions in Stoic Cosmopolitanism." *Philosophy and Power in the Graeco-Roman World: Essays in Honour of Miriam Griffin*, edited by Gillian Clark and Tessa Rajak, Oxford UP, 2002, pp. 31–50.

Olivier, Florence. "La 'pensée 68' française et l'intellectualité mexicaine: satire et parodies dans *El fin de la locura* de Jorge Volpi." *América: Cahiers du CRICCAL*, vol. 34, no. 1, 2006, pp. 257–65. *Persée*, doi:10.3406/ameri.2006.1768.

Ortiz, Fernando. *Contrapunteo cubano del tabaco y el azúcar: advertencia de sus contrastes agrarios, económicos, históricos y sociales, su etnografía y su transculturación.* Cátedra, 2002.

———. *Cuban Counterpoint: Tobacco and Sugar.* Translated by Harriet de Onís, Duke UP, 1995

Ó Síocháin, Séamas. "Roger Casement's Vision of Freedom." *Roger Casement in Irish and World History*, edited by Mary E. Daly, Royal Irish Academy, 2005, pp. 1–10.

Padilla, Ignacio. "Jorge Volpi: Almografía imposible." *En busca de Jorge Volpi—Ensayos sobre su obra*, edited by José Manuel López de Abiada et al., Verbum, 2004, pp. 218–19.

Pageaux, Daniel-Henri. *Littératures et cultures en dialogue.* L'Harmattan, 2007.

Palou, Pedro Ángel. "Pequeño diccionario del *Crack*." *Crack: instrucciones de uso.* Mondadori, 2005, pp. 193–205.

Palou, Pedro Ángel, et al. "Manifiesto Crack." *Crack. Instrucciones de uso.* Mondadori, 2005, pp. 207–24.

Parks, Tim. "The Dull New Global Novel." *New York Review of Books*, 9 February 2010, https://www.nybooks.com/daily/2010/02/09/the-dull-new-global-novel/.

Paz, Octavio. "El caracol y la sirena." *Los signos en rotación y otros ensayos.* Alianza Editorial, 1971. pp. 88–102.

———. "*El laberinto de la soledad.* 1950. Cátedra, 1993.

———. *The Labyrinth of Solitude.* Translated by Lysander Kemp, Grove Press, 1961.

———. *El ogro filantrópico, historia y política 1971–1978.* Editorial Joaquín Mortiz, 1979.

Perilli, Carmen. "Retrato de familia." *Catálogo de ángeles mexicanos: Elena Poniatowska.* Beatriz Viterbo Editora, 2006, pp. 21–39.

Pizarro, Ana. *El sur y los trópicos.* Universidad de Alicante, 2004.

Plutarch. *Parallel Lives.* University of Chicago, 2019. http://penelope.uchicago.edu/Thayer/E/Roman/Texts/Plutarch/Lives/home.html.

Pollock, Sheldon. "Cosmopolitan and Vernacular in History." *Public Culture*, vol. 12, no. 3, September 2010, pp. 591–625. *Scholars Portal*, doi:10.1215/08992363-12-3-591.

Poniatowska, Elena. "Box y literatura del *crack*." *La Jornada*, 26 June 2003. https://www.jornada.unam.mx/2003/06/26/03aa1cul.php?origen=index.html&fly=1.

———. "Discurso Premio Cervantes." 24 April 2014, Alcalá de Henares, pp. 1–8. http://www.mecd.gob.es/prensa-mecd/dms/mecd/prensa-mecd/actualidad/2014/04/20140423-cervantes/poniatowska-cervantes.pdf.

———. *La "Flor de Lis."* Ediciones Era, 1988.

———. *Me lo dijo Elena Poniatowska: su vida, obra y pasiones.* Ediciones del milenio, 1997.

———. *Nada, nadie. Las voces del temblor.* Ediciones Era, 1988.

———. *La noche de Tlatelolco.* Ediciones Era, 1971.

———. "A Question Mark Engraved on My Eyelids." *Mexican Writers on Writing*, edited by Margaret Sayers Peden, Trinity UP, 2007, pp. 96–109.

———. "Sobre castas y puentes." *Sobre castas y puentes: conversaciones con Elena Poniatowska, Rosario Ferré y Diamela Eltit*, edited by Walescka Pino-Ojeda, Editorial Cuarto Propio, 2000, pp. 21–76.

———. *Tinísima*. Ediciones Era, 1992.

———. *Tinísima*. Translated by Katherine Silver, U of Mexico P, 1995.

Pons, María Cristina. *Memorias del olvido: del Paso, García Márquez, Saer y la nueva novela histórica en América latina*. Siglo Veintiuno Editores, 1995.

Poot Herrera, Sara. "La '*Flor de Lis*': Códice y huella de Elena Poniatowska." *Mujer y literatura mexicana y chicana: culturas en contacto*, edited by Aralia López González et al., Colegio de México, 1990, pp. 99–105.

Pratt, Mary Louise. *Imperial Eyes: Travel Writing and Transculturation*. Routledge, 2008.

Rama, Ángel. "El *boom* en perspectiva." *Más allá del boom. Literatura y mercado*. Folios, 1984, pp. 51–110.

———. *La ciudad letrada*. Ediciones del Norte, 1984.

———. *Las máscaras democráticas del Modernismo*. Fundación Ángel Rama, 1985.

———. *Rubén Darío y el Modernismo—circunstancia socioeconómica de un arte americano*. Ediciones de la Biblioteca de la Universidad central de Venezuela, 1970.

———. *Transculturación narrativa en América Latina*. Siglo Veintiuno Editores, 1982.

Rangel, Dolores. "Los extremos de la sexualidad en la caracterización literaria de Vargas Llosa: El chivo, Gauguin y Flora Tristán." *Hispanet Journal*, vol. 1, 2008, pp. 1–24. http://www.hispanetjournal.com/LosextremosdelasexualidadEDITADO.pdf.

Reyes, Alfonso. "Alfonso Reyes, escritor civilizatorio." *El universal*, 16 June 2015. https://www.eluniversal.com.mx/articulo/cultura/letras/2015/06/16/alfonso-reyes-escritor-civilizatorio.

Rodó, José Enrique. *Ariel*. Cátedra, 2000.

Rojas, Ricardo. "Nota Preliminar." *Facundo: Civilización y barbarie*. Libreria "La Facultad," 1901, pp. 9–24.

Rosenberg, Fernando J. "Afecto y política de la cosmópolis latinoamericana." *Revista Iberoamericana*, vol. 72, no. 215–16, April–September 2006, pp. 467–79.

———. *The Avant-Garde and Geopolitics in Latin America*. U of Pittsburgh P, 2006.

———. "Cultural Theory and the Avant-Gardes: Mariátegui, Mario de Andrade, Oswaldo de Andrade, Pagu, Tarsila do Amaral, César Vallejo." *A Companion to Latin American Literature and Culture*, edited by Sarah Castro-Klein, Blackwell, 2008, pp. 410–25.

———. "Derechos humanos, comisiones de la verdad, y nuevas ficciones globales." *Revista de Crítica Literaria Latinoamericana. Cuadernos de Literatura*, vol. 35, no. 69, January–March 2009, pp. 141–65. *JSTOR*, https://www.jstor.org/stable/27944645?seq=1.

Russek, Dan. *Textual Exposures: Photography in Twentieth Century Latin American Narrative Fiction*. U of Calgary P, 2015.

Said, Edward W. *Orientalism*. Vintage, 1979.

———. *Representations of the Intellectual: The 1993 Reith Lectures*. Vintage, 1994

———. *The World, the Text, and the Critic*. Harvard UP, 1984.

Santodomingo, Roger. "El fin de la locura." *BBC Mundo*, 24 September 2004. http://news.bbc.co.uk/hi/spanish/misc/newsid_3685000/3685372.stm.

Sanzana Inzunza, Isaac. "Consideraciones sobre el *cosmopolitismo* en Rubén Darío." *Borradores* X–XI, 2009–10, pp. 1–10. https://www.unrc.edu.ar/publicar/borradores/Vol10-11/pdf/Consideraciones%20sobre%20el%20cosmopolitismo%20en%20Ruben%20Dario.pdf.

Sarlo, Beatriz. *Borges, un escritor en las orillas*. Siglo XXI, 2007.

———. *Una modernidad periférica: Buenos Aires 1920 y 1930*. Nueva Visión, 2003.

———. "Vanguardia y criollismo: La aventura de 'Martin Fierro.' " *Revista de crítica literaria latinoamericana*, vol. 8, no. 15, 1982, 39–69. *JSTOR*, https://www.jstor.org/stable/4530040?seq=1.

Sarmiento, Domingo Faustino. *Facundo: civilización y barbarie*. Cátedra, 1990.

———. *Viajes*. Editorial de Belgrano, 1981.

Scheffler, Samuel. "Conceptions of Cosmopolitanism." *Utilitas*, vol. 11, no. 3, November 1999, pp. 255–76. *Cambridge UP Digital Archives*, doi:10.1017/S0953820800002508.

Schoene-Harwood, Berthold. *The Cosmopolitan Novel*. Edinburgh UP, 2009.

Schuessler, Michael K. *Elena Poniatowska: An Intimate Biography*. U of Arizona P, 2007.

Shaw, Donald. "The Post-Boom in Spanish American Fiction." *Studies in 20th Century Literature*, vol. 19, no. 1, Winter 1995, pp. 11–27. https://newprairiepress.org/cgi/viewcontent.cgi?article=1359&context=sttcl.

Shea, Louisa. *The Cynic Enlightenment: Diogenes in the Salon*. Johns Hopkins UP, 2010.

Siskind, Mariano. *Cosmopolitan Desires: Global Modernity and World Literature in Latin America*. Northwestern UP, 2014.

———. "El cosmopolitismo como problema político: Borges y el desafío de la modernidad." *Variaciones Borges: revista del Centro de Estudios y Documentación Jorge Luis Borges*, vol. 24, July 2007, pp. 75–92. *Academic OneFile*, https://link.gale.com/apps/doc/A171139037/AONE?u=otta77973&sid=AONE&xid=8f028c6d.

Sommer, Doris. *Foundational Fictions: The National Romances of Latin America*. U of California P, 1991.

Spitta, Silvia. *Between Two Waters: Narratives of Transculturation in Latin America*. Rice UP, 1995.

Steinberg, Samuel. "'Tlatelolco me bautizó': Literary Renewal and the Neo-liberal Transition." *Mexican Studies/Estudios Mexicanos*, vol. 28, no. 2, Summer 2012, pp. 265–86. *ProQuest*, doi:10.1525/msem.2012.28.2.265.

Trigo, Abril. "De la transculturación (a/en) lo transnacional." *Revista de investigaciones literarias y culturales*, vol. 6, no. 11, January–June 1998, pp. 61–76.

———. "On Transculturation: Toward a Political Economy of Culture in the Periphery." *Studies in Latin American Popular Culture*, vol. 15, January 1996, pp. 99–117.

de Valdés, María Elena. "Identity and the Other as Myself." *The Shattered Mirror: Representations of Women in Mexican Literature*. U of Texas P, 1998, pp. 114–43.

Valera, Juan. *Cartas americanas: Primera serie*. Fuentes y Capdeville, 1889.

Van Hooft, Stan. *Cosmopolitanism: A Philosophy for Global Ethics*. McGill-Queen's UP, 2009.

———. "Cosmopolitanism as Virtue." *Journal of Global Ethics*, vol. 3, no. 3, December 2007, pp. 303–15. *Scholars Portal*, doi:10.1080/17449620701728014.

Vargas Llosa, Mario. *Aunt Julia and the Scriptwriter*. Translated by Helen R. Lane, Farrar, Straus and Giroux, 1982.

———. *Cartas a un joven novelista*. Ariel/Planeta, 1997.

———. *Cinco esquinas*. Alfaguara, 2016.

———. "Conferencia inaugural." Congreso Internacional "El canon del boom," 5 November 2012. *Biblioteca Virtual Miguel de Cervantes*, http://www.cervantes virtual.com/obra/conferencia-inaugural-del-congreso-el-canon-del-boom/.

———. "Confessions of an Old Fashioned Liberal." *AEI Annual Dinner Address 2005*, 2 March 2005, Washington DC. https://www.aei.org/articles/confessions-of-an-old-fashioned-liberal/.

———. "*El corazón de las tinieblas*—Las raíces de lo humano." *La verdad de las mentiras: Ensayos sobre literatura*. 1992. Punto de lectura, 2011, pp. 60–70.

———. "La corrección política es enemiga de la libertad." Entrevista con Maite Rico. *El País*, 25 February 2018. https://elpais.com/elpais/2018/02/15/eps/1518713349_374841.html.

———. "The Culture of Liberty." *Foreign Policy*, no. 122, January–February 2001, pp. 66–71. *JSTOR*, https://www.jstor.org/stable/3183227?seq=1.

———. *Desafíos a la libertad*. Aguilar, 2007.

———. "Discurso Nobel: Elogio de la lectura y la ficción." 7 December 2010, Oslo, pp. 1–13. https://www.nobelprize.org/prizes/literature/2010/vargas_llosa/25185-mario-vargas-llosa-discurso-nobel/.

———. *Dream of the Celt*. Translated by Edith Grossman, Farrar, Straus and Giroux, 2012

———. *La fiesta del chivo*. Alfaguara, 2000.

———. *La guerra del fin del mundo*. 1981. Alfaguara, 2000.

———. *El héroe discreto*. Alfaguara, 2013.

———. *Historia de Mayta*. Seix Barral, 1984.

———. *Lituma en los Andes*. Planeta, 1993.

———. *Mon itinéraire intellectuel/My Intellectual Journey/Mi trayectoria intelectual*. Institut économique de Montréal, 2014.

———. *El Paraíso en la otra esquina*. Alfaguara, 2003.

———. "El Perú soy yo." *La República*, 7 October 2010. https://larepublica.pe/politica/501689-el-peru-soy-yo/.

———. *El pez en el agua: Memorias*. Seix Barral, 1993.

———. "The Power of Lies." *Encounter*, vol. 69, no. 5, December 1987, pp. 28–9. http://www.unz.org./Pub/Encounter-1987dec-00028.

———. *El sueño del celta*. Punto de lectura, 2010.

———. *La Tía Julia y el escribidor*. 1977. Alfaguara, 2000.

———. *Travesuras de la niña mala*. Alfaguara, 2006.

———. *Touchstones: Essays on Literature, Art, and Politics*. Translated and edited by John King, Farrar, Straus and Giroux, 2007.

———. *La verdad de las mentiras: Ensayos sobre literatura*. 1992. Punto de lectura, 2011.

———. *The Way to Paradise*. Translated by Natasha Wimmer, Farrar, Straus and Giroux, 2003.

———. *Wellsprings*. Harvard UP, 2008.

Vasconcelos, José. *Qué es la revolución*. Ediciones Botas, 1937.

———. *La raza cósmica*. Espasa-Calpe Mexicana, 1966.

Vieira, Fátima. "The Concept of Utopia." *The Cambridge Companion to Utopian Literature*, edited by Gregory Claeys, Cambridge UP, 2010, pp. 3–27.

Volpi Escalante, Jorge. *En busca de Klingsor*. 1999. Editorial Seix Barral, 2008.

———. "Código de procedimientos literarios del Crack." *Crack: instrucciones de uso*, edited by Ricardo Chávez et al., Mondadori, 2005, pp. 175–88.

———. "El fin de la conjura." *Letras libres*, October 2000. https://www.letraslibres.com/mexico/el-fin-la-conjura.

———. *El fin de la locura*. Editorial Planeta Mexicana, 2003.

———. "El fin de la narrativa latinoamericana." *Revista de crítica literaria latinoamericana*, vol. 30, no. 59, January–March 2004, pp. 33–42. *JSTOR*, https://www.jstor.org/stable/4531302?seq=1.

———. *La imaginación y el poder: una historia intelectual del 1968*. Ediciones Era, 2001.

———. *El insomnio de Bolívar: cuatro consideraciones intempestivas sobre América Latina en el siglo XXI*. Debate, 2009.

———. *No será la Tierra*. Alfaguara, 2006.

———. "Política y literatura." *El correo digital*, April 2003. http://servicios.elcorreo.com/auladecultura/volpi1.html.

———. *Season of Ash*. Translated by Alfred MacAdam, Open Letter, 2009.

———. "Yo soy una novela." *Nexos*, 1 March 2011, https://www.nexos.com.mx/?p=14167.

Volpi Escalante, Jorge, et al. "Postmanifiesto del Crack, 1996–2016." *El Boomeran(g)*, 7 February 2016. http://www.elboomeran.com/blog-post/12/17117/jorge-volpi/postmanifiesto-del-crack/.

Walford, Lynn. "Vargas Llosa's Leading Ladies." *Leading Ladies: mujeres en la literatura hispana y en las artes*, edited by Yvonne Fuentes and Margaret Parker, Louisiana State UP, 2006, pp. 70–82.

Weldt-Basson, Helene Carol, ed. *Redefining Latin American Historical Fiction: The Impact of Feminism and Postcolonialism*. Palgrave McMillan, 2013.

Werbner, Pnina. "Vernacular Cosmopolitanism." *Theory, Culture & Society*, vol. 23, no. 2–3, May 2006, pp. 496–8.

Zanetti, Susana. "Elegía a la ilusión cosmopolita en un singular poema dariano de sus últimos años." *Rubén Darío: cosmopolita arraigado*, edited by Jeffrey Browitt and Werner Mackenbach, IHNCA, 2010, pp. 56–81.

Zea, Leopoldo. *El regreso de las carabelas*. Universidad Nacional Autónoma de México, 1993.

# Index

acculturation, 33–34, 112
Achebe, Chinua, 226n23
aesthetic cosmopolitanism, 8–11, 13, 22–23, 72, 210–11
*afrancesamiento*, 31, 167
Africa, 100–101, 103, 128, 226n23; colonization of, 105–9, 193, 227n25
Aguilar Camín, Héctor, 177
Allende, Salvador, 138, 160, 202
Althusser, Louis, 138, 159, 161, 164–66
*Amauta*, 219n5
Ancient Greece, 2, 16
Anderson, Benedict, 119, 123, 185
anglophilia, 141
anti-globalization movement, 139, 184
*antropofagia*, 5, 13
*A pesar del oscuro silencio* (Volpi), 228n1
Appiah, Anthony Kwame, 2–3, 16–19, 75, 95, 205, 220n9; on narrative, 21–22, 220n11
Arequipa, Peru, 65, 83–84, 86, 223n5, 224n7
Argentina, 9, 14, 144, 154, 219n5, 230n8
Aristotle, 102
*arritmia temporal*, 10, 12, 15, 25, 220n8
Asturias, Miguel Ángel, 223n4
Auckland, New Zealand, 193, 198
authoritarianism, 170, 190, 200, 202
autobiographical novel, 6–7, 28, 30, 59
autofiction, 7, 30, 70
Avant-Garde, 13, 219n5. See also *Vanguardias*

*Balún Canán* (Castellanos), 222n9
Barthes, Roland, 138, 159, 161
Battle of Seattle, 184, 200
Belgian Congo, 100, 102–4, 108–11, 129. See also Congo Free State
Belgium, 108
Berlin, 122, 185

Berlin, Isaiah, 74–75
Berlin Wall, 8, 138, 172, 174, 178
Bhabha, Homi, 34, 105
*Bildungsroman*, 28, 221n2
Bolivia, 65, 154
Boom, 4, 9, 12–13, 25, 63, 68; and cosmopolitanism, 209, 216; criticism of, 14–15, 229n6; influence of, 140–41, 144, 149; and nationality, 153–54, 219n6; in Spain, 219n7. See also Crack movement; *novelas totales*; Post-Boom movement
borders, 9, 73, 76, 156, 161, 168–69, 187–88. See also nation-state; sovereignty
Borges, Jorge Luis, 9, 24, 69, 143–49, 216, 219n5, 226n21. See also "El escritor argentino y la tradición" (Borges)
Brazil, 103
Britain, 37–38, 100, 103; influence of, 209. See also British Empire; England
British Empire, 101, 104, 106, 110–11, 113–16; and Home Rule, 119, 121. See also Britain; England

Camus, Albert, 73–74, 224n8
capitalism, 73, 128, 184, 189, 199; as broken, 196; as ideology, 190–91, 200; in Russia, 197, 202. See also neo-liberalism
Carpentier, Alejo, 77
*Cartas a un joven novelista* (Vargas Llosa), 223n2
Casement, Roger, 7, 64, 67–68, 79, 215; as a colonizer, 104–8, 226n23, 227n25; as a cosmopolitan, 112, 128, 213–14; fanaticism of, 103–4; nationalism of, 99–100, 113–22, 128–29, 133–35, 211; as tragic hero, 102–3; transformation of, 100–101, 109–11, 125–27, 130, 132, 226n21; writings of, 131. See also *El sueño del celta* (Vargas Llosa)

*247*

Castellanos, Rosario, 222n9
Castro, Fidel, 74, 99, 138, 160, 170, 202
Catalonia, 134
Chernobyl disaster, 8, 138, 183, 196
Chiapas, 171, 200
Chile, 14, 138, 160
Christianity, 107–8, 121–22, 124
*Cinco Esquinas* (Vargas Llosa), 223n5, 224n7
citizenship, 2, 4–5, 18, 26; cosmopolitan, 212, 215; global, 68–70, 72, 126, 139, 211, 213; and literature, 143, 151
*ciudad letrada*, 42. *See also* republic of letters
class, 3, 29–30, 32; and belonging, 41, 43–44, 47, 53–56; and culture, 37–38, 51; equality, 82, 89–90, 98; and language, 39. *See also* elitism; Eurocentrism
Clinton, Bill, 197
Cold War, 5, 14, 73, 177
colonialism, 3, 8, 227n25; and cosmopolitanism, 17, 19–20, 24–25, 82; and cultural hybridity, 34, 96; exploitation of, 128–29; and imitation, 159; and language, 39; modern, 193–94; and nationalism, 115; rejection of, 108–9, 111; undoing of, 12–13, 23, 79, 99, 114, 200, 220n10. *See also* Africa; colonized peoples; decoloniality; imperialism; Latin America; neo-colonialism
colonized peoples, 99, 106–8, 110–11, 115, 211; saving of, 117–18. *See also* Africa; Indigenous people; Ireland; subaltern cultures
communism, 74, 178, 184, 186–91, 199; failure of, 202–3; fall of, 197, 200. *See also* USSR
Communist Bloc, 138, 185
Communist Party, 187, 189
Congo Free State, 109, 226n21, 226n23. *See also* Democratic Republic of the Congo
Conrad, Joseph, 108, 226n23
*Contrapunteo cubano del tabaco y el azúcar* (Ortiz), 33
Cortázar, Julio, 228n2
cosmopolitanism, 2–7; and belonging, 28, 60; concept of, 16–21, 23–24, 81–82, 90, 220n11; criticism of, 14–15, 141, 182, 216–17; exclusionary, 32, 60; and humanism, 179–80; and identity, 36, 143; ideology of, 189; as imperial, 39–40, 216; *versus* individualism, 92–93, 187–88; liberal, 73, 75–76, 99, 135; in literature, 25–26, 64–65, 148–49, 157, 200, 204–5, 209–11;

and modernity, 8–12; and narrative, 22–23; and nationalism, 115, 139; and the Other, 95–96, 128; and patriotism, 101–2, 112, 117, 127; politics of, 212–15; and utopia, 79, 85, 98, 203. *See also* aesthetic cosmopolitanism; cosmopolitan reading; decolonial cosmopolitanism; globalization; political cosmopolitanism; rooted cosmopolitanism; travel; universalism; Western cosmopolitanism
cosmopolitanism studies, 212
cosmopolitan reading, 22–23, 210, 214
"cosmopolitics," 4
Crack movement, 12, 15, 138, 140–43, 146, 152; cosmopolitanism in, 217; and public intellectuals, 178; and readers, 156; universalism of, 203–4, 206. *See also* "Manifiesto Crack"; "Postmanifiesto del Crack"; Volpi, Jorge
Cuba, 73, 138, 160, 169–70. *See also* Castro, Fidel; Cuban Revolution
Cuban Revolution, 74, 158, 169–70, 177, 224n8
Cuesta, Jorge, 145, 148, 228n1
cultural studies, 4
Cynic school, 16, 93, 97

Darío, Rubén, 9, 11
decolonial cosmopolitanism, 20–21, 216–17. *See also* decoloniality; rooted cosmopolitanism
decoloniality, 3, 11, 18, 21, 220n10. *See also* colonialism; decolonial cosmopolitanism; decolonization
decolonization, 35, 60. *See also* decoloniality
democracy, 133, 190
Democratic Republic of the Congo, 193–94, 197. *See also* Congo Free State
*deseo de mundo. See* "desire for the world"
"desire for the world," 4–5, 28, 209–10
developing world, 3. *See also* Third World
*Días de ira* (Volpi), 228n1
Díaz, Porfirio, 31. *See also* Porfiriato
Díaz Ordaz, Gustavo, 181, 221n3
Diogenes of Sinope, 16. *See also* Cynic School
"displacement," 4–5
Domínguez, Michael Christopher, 145
*Don Quijote* (Cervantes), 159, 231n12

Earth First, 194
Easter Rising, 100, 107
education, 32, 37, 42, 55, 220n8

"El escritor argentino y la tradición" (Borges), 143, 146
"El fin de la conjura" (Volpi), 176–77
*El fin de la locura* (Volpi), 5, 7–8, 138, 140, 157–59, 196; and cosmopolitanism, 214, 231n11; and *Don Quijote*, 231n12; failure in, 202–3; as historical and global novel, 180, 182, 198–200, 204, 207; and intellectual history, 160–61; intellectual passions of, 201; as political novel, 178
"El fin de la narrativa latinoamericana" (Volpi), 143–46, 156, 229n5
*El hablador* (Vargas Llosa), 223n5
*El héroe discreto* (Vargas Llosa), 223n5, 224n7
*El insomnio de Bolívar* (Volpi), 137, 150, 230n9
elitism, 2–3, 14, 24; and cosmopolitanism, 31, 38–40, 42, 212; in the Crack movement, 142. *See also* class
Elizondo, Salvador, 228n1
*El laberinto de la soledad* (Paz), 27, 34–35
*El ogro filantrópico* (Paz), 35
*El Paraíso en la otra esquina* (Vargas Llosa), 5, 7, 61, 64, 78–79, 129; as cosmopolitan, 67, 213–14; individualism in, 224n7; meaning of, 131–33, 135; and the search for utopia, 85, 96, 112, 114. *See also* Gauguin, Paul; Tristán (Tristan), Flora
*El reino de este mundo* (Carpentier), 77
*El sueño del celta* (Vargas Llosa), 5, 7, 61, 64, 66, 78–79; as cosmopolitan, 213–14; meaning of, 131–33, 135; and nationalism, 99, 113, 127; plot of, 67, 100–101, 103–4, 130. *See also* Casement, Roger
*En busca de Klingsor* (Volpi), 1, 151–52, 197
"end of history," 8, 139, 178
England, 42, 89, 163. *See also* Britain
English (language), 145
*Estridentistas*, 219n5
Eurocentrism, 2, 7, 19–20, 86; and class, 53; and colonialism, 104; as cosmopolitan, 32, 36–39, 60
Europe: as colonial power, 20, 106–7; as cultural model, 32, 37, 42, 52–53, 164; emancipation from, 179; inequality in, 88–90, 93; literature of, 9–12; as metropole, 70–72, 171; publishing in, 13
extremism, 67, 74, 79, 98–99, 129; dangers of, 133. *See also* fanaticism; ideology

fanaticism, 67, 107, 122, 129, 175, 226n18; ideological, 190. *See also* extremism; ideology; nationalism
Faulkner, William, 66
fiction, 3, 113–14, 143, 158, 204–5. *See also* autobiographical novel; autofiction; global novel; historical novel; narrative; novel
Foucault, Michel, 138, 159, 161, 171, 175
France, 11, 29; as literary metropole, 46, 56, 68–69, 163, 170, 180, 209, 228n2; literature of, 13; as model, 31, 37, 41–42, 52; as setting, 79–81, 83, 90, 96, 158, 161. *See also afrancesamiento*; May 1968; Paris
free market, 73, 75. *See also* capitalism; neoliberalism
French (language), 56, 108, 145
French Polynesia, 67, 79–81, 92–93, 95
Fresán, Rodrigo, 153, 230n8
Fuentes, Carlos, 145, 149, 177, 216, 231n14. *See also Geografía de la novela* (Fuentes)
Fuguet, Alberto, 15, 144, 146, 220n8. *See also* McOndo; *McOndo* (Fuguet and Gómez)
Fujimori, Alberto, 65, 223n5
Fukuyama, Francis, 8, 139, 178

Galbraith, John Kenneth, 183
García Márquez, Gabriel, 146, 151–52, 223n4, 229n6
Gauguin, Paul, 7, 64, 67, 79–82, 99, 225n13; and cosmopolitanism, 127–28, 214; nationalism of, 130, 134–35; search for paradise of, 92–97, 131, 133, 226n19; utopianism of, 98, 112, 129. *See also El Paraíso en la otra esquina* (Vargas Llosa)
gender, 3, 32, 82, 89, 98, 221n2
*Geografía de la novela* (Fuentes), 149
Germany, 103, 121
*Glasnost*, 202
global consciousness, 6, 178, 181, 207, 212, 215
globality, 139, 157, 180, 182, 197, 200; in literature, 207; and the local, 191, 209, 228n2
globalization, 2, 4–5, 8, 76; and colonialism, 220n10; and cosmopolitanism, 25, 88, 209; and culture, 135, 146; and identity, 203–4, 213; as ideology, 189; and literature, 14, 78, 130, 133–34, 145, 154, 215, 231n11; and McOndo, 220n8; resistance to, 214. *See also* global consciousness; globality; global novel; neoliberalism

global novel, 146, 155–56, 180, 182, 198–200, 207. See also *El fin de la locura* (Volpi); *No será la Tierra* (Volpi); rooted cosmopolitanism; Volpi, Jorge
Gómez, Sergio, 15, 146, 220n8. *See also* McOndo; McOndo (Fuguet and Gómez)
Gorbachev, Mikhail, 189–90, 202
Greenpeace, 194
Gulag, 184, 188

*Heart of Darkness* (Conrad), 108, 226n23
*hibridismo* (Paz), 5, 34–35, 61. *See also* hybridity; transculturation (Ortiz)
*Historia de Mayta* (Vargas Llosa), 78
historical novel, 64, 76–78, 100, 130–32, 135, 197; cathartic, 178–80; genre of, 201–3, 207, 215, 224n11–224n12; as literature, 228n27. *See also* Latin America; Vargas Llosa, Mario; Volpi, Jorge
humanism, 77, 187–88
human rights, 67, 99–100, 108, 115, 117
Hungary, 185
hybridity, 4, 47, 213; and belonging, 51; and class, 53; of identity, 57–58, 60–61; Indigenous-European, 31–34. See also *hibridismo* (Paz); identity; transculturation (Ortiz)

identity, 4–7, 15; and cosmopolitanism, 19, 143, 216; cultural, 13, 27–28, 134–35; debates on, 10, 179; and education, 37; erasure of, 203, 206; exploration of, 35–36, 157; hybrid, 47, 51, 53; individual, 55, 191; intellectual, 198; Latin American, 141, 165–68; literary, 147–48; national, 9, 12, 145, 180, 184, 210–11, 215; transformation of, 42, 44, 56–58, 60, 72. *See also* class; ideology; Latin America; Mexico; nationalism(s)
ideology, 6–7, 75, 103, 127, 143, 214; collectivist, 132; and cosmopolitanism, 24; danger of, 206; end of, 157, 178, 183; excesses of, 182, 189–91, 198–99, 202–3; rejection of, 99, 142, 214. *See also* capitalism; communism; extremism; fanaticism; liberalism; nationalism(s); revolution; universalism; utopianism
"imagined community," 119
imperialism, 2–3, 19, 24, 100, 112; American, 193; and cosmopolitanism, 39, 210, 213. *See also* British Empire; United States

Indigenous people, 27, 99, 128–29; colonization of, 115–16; and hybrid identity, 31–32, 34–35, 45; languages of, 222n9; in literature, 130; in Mexico, 51, 61, 200. *See also* Africa; colonialism; colonized peoples; *hibridismo* (Paz); hybridity; subaltern cultures
individualism, 15, 65, 98, 130, 190–91
intellectual history, 8, 138, 158–59, 171, 212; Latin American, 179; Mexican, 152
intellectualism, 65, 180
intellectuals, 8, 16, 66, 133, 138; and colonialism, 159–61; end of, 178; global, 179–80, 216–17; of Latin America, 140, 158, 171–72; and power, 176–78, 203; revolutionary, 169–70. *See also* intellectual history; Latin America; Mexico
internationalism, 79–80, 129, 132, 141. *See also* globalization; socialist internationalism
International Monetary Fund (IMF), 138, 184, 192–93, 197
Ireland, 109–13, 121–23, 211–12; nationalist cause of, 100–103, 113–21, 127–29, 133–34. *See also* Casement, Roger; Easter Rising; *El sueño del celta* (Vargas Llosa)

Joyce, James, 66

Kipling, Rudyard, 106
Krauze, Enrique, 177
Kymlicka, Will, 16

Lacan, Jacques, 138, 159, 161, 166–67
*La fiesta del Chivo* (Vargas Llosa), 78, 224n11, 225n14, 226n18
*La "Flor de Lis"* (Poniatowska), 5–6, 28–30, 221n2; as allegory, 31, 51, 59–60; and cosmopolitanism, 60–61; and Mexican identity, 33–34, 212–13. *See also hibridismo* (Paz); hybridity; transculturation (Oritz)
*La guerra del fin del mundo* (Vargas Llosa), 66, 78, 99, 226n18
La Malinche, 222n9–222n10
language: and belonging, 37, 72, 145; and colonization, 108, 111, 113, 116; and identity, 56, 69, 156, 230n9; and nation, 39; universal, 64. *See also* English (language); French (language); Spanish (language)
*La paz de los sepulcros* (Volpi), 228n1

*La tía Julia y el escribidor* (Vargas Llosa), 70, 79, 219n6
Latin America: Avant-Garde in, 13; cosmopolitanism in, 17–18, 20–21, 28, 60, 65; cosmopolitan writers of, 23–25, 63; cultural models for, 42, 164; decolonization of, 220n10; in global context, 8, 128, 138–39, 142, 180, 203–4, 216, 228n2; global novel of, 155; historical novels of, 7, 64, 66, 131–32, 201, 215–16; identity in, 1–2, 6, 12, 14, 137–38, 143, 168–69; inequality in, 90; intellectuals of, 158, 160–61, 178–79, 181; and language, 39; literature of, 15, 22, 69–70, 76–77, 141–42, 145–55, 209–11; and modernity, 32; politics of, 9, 73–74. *See also* Indigenous people; Mexico; Peru; Spanish America
Leopold II, 103, 108, 226n21
*L'homme révolté* (Camus), 224n8
liberalism, 7, 65–66, 73, 75–76, 130; double standard of, 192; triumph of, 178; in Vargas Llosa's novels, 132–33, 224n8. *See also* individualism; neo-liberalism
*Lilus Kikus* (Poniatowska), 30
Lima, Peru, 88, 128, 223n5, 224n7
*literatura light*, 156
literature, 21–22, 64, 215; as cosmopolitan, 137, 204; history of, 212; Latin American, 140–43; national, 179; and nationalism, 123; as product, 156; universal language of, 69. *See also* Boom; Crack movement; fiction; global novel; historical novel; Latin America; magical realism; "Manifiesto Crack"; McOndo; *Modernismo*; narrative; novel; Post-Boom movement; Spanish America
*Lituma en los Andes* (Vargas Llosa), 78
Livingstone, David, 105
London, 11, 88–89

magical realism, 15, 141–42, 147, 150–52, 229n3, 229n6
"Manifiesto Crack," 15, 140–41, 146, 203–4, 229n3, 231n13. *See also* Crack movement; "Postmanifiesto del Crack"
Maples Arce, Manuel, 219n5
Maoism, 160
Mariátegui, José Carlos, 219n5
Marquesas Islands, 94, 129
martyrdom, 122–23

Marxism, 51, 56, 74, 132, 160
May 1968, 8, 138, 158, 160–62, 166, 181
McOndo, 15, 142, 144, 146, 151, 217
*McOndo* (Fuguet and Gómez), 15, 220n8
*mestizo*, 32, 35, 51
Mexican Revolution, 32, 38, 41, 45, 60–61, 219n5; novel of, 229n6
Mexico, 1, 15, 27–28; authors of, 147; belonging to, 42–43, 47–50, 54, 56–57, 59–60, 137–38, 164–65, 198; as colonial, 180, 193, 197; in global context, 204, 216; history of, 221n3; intellectuals in, 171–72, 176–77, 179, 181; in literature, 29–30; literature of, 140, 142, 151–52; national identity of, 6–7, 31–36, 46, 60–61, 154, 166–71; nationalism in, 36, 60, 212; perceptions of, 37–38, 222n8; politics of, 158, 160, 213; rural, 41. *See also El fin de la locura* (Volpi); Indigenous people; *La "Flor de Lis"* (Poniatowska); Mexican Revolution; Partido Revolucionario Institucional (PRI); Poniatowska, Elena; Tlatelolco massacre; Volpi, Jorge
Mexico City, 46, 59; massacre of the Plaza de las Tres Culturas, 165–66. *See also* Tlatelolco massacre
Mignolo, Walter, 3, 17–18, 20–21, 217, 220n10
miscegenation, 5, 23, 60
Mistral, Gabriela, 223n4
modern art, 82, 94
*Modernismo*, 4, 9–12, 25, 209
*Modernistas*, 10–11, 216
modernity, 9–11; and the Avant-Garde, 12–13; and colonialism, 20; and cosmopolitanism, 23, 211; and Mexico, 32; and Spain, 219n7
More, Thomas, 85
*Mundo Nuevo*, 219n6
muralism, 32

narrative, 21–22, 25, 113, 204–6. *See also* fiction; novel
nationalism(s), 2, 4, 7; as anachronistic, 155; and colonial emancipation, 32; and cosmopolitanism, 8–9, 12, 16, 19–20, 23–25, 64–65, 126–27; *versus* cosmopolitanism, 82, 97–99, 139, 203, 213, 215–16; and culture, 111–14, 135; ethnic, 112; and exclusion, 151, 153; and fanaticism, 117–24, 182, 190; in literature, 79, 148, 206; new, 217, 232n18; as a pathology, 185–86; rejection of, 61, 66,

99–101, 142–43, 150; rise of, 67; turn to, 103, 128–29. *See also* identity; ideology; Ireland; Mexico; patriotism
nationality, 49–50, 66, 145, 181; of authors, 1, 153; and language, 56; and literature, 151, 206, 230n7. *See also* identity
nation-state, 5; creation of, 67; decline of, 25, 73, 209, 213; in global context, 215; limits of, 90; rejection of, 9. *See also* borders; sovereignty
neo-colonialism, 10, 17, 19, 24, 39
neo-liberalism, 8, 73, 75, 157, 203, 209; deterritorialization of, 214; in Mexico, 172, 181; resistance to, 192, 200
Neruda, Pablo, 223n4
New World Order, 8, 139, 159
New York, 190
New Zealand, 197–98
Nobel Prize for Literature, 1, 63–64, 68, 223n4
Norway, 103
*No será la Tierra* (Volpi), 5, 7–8, 138–40, 182–85; as an opera, 231n16, 232n17; and cosmopolitanism, 214; and death, 196; failure in, 203; as a global novel, 198–200, 204, 207, 213; intellectual passions of, 201–2; as metafiction, 196–97; as universalist, 197–98. *See also* ideology; rooted cosmopolitanism; Volpi, Jorge
novel, 6–7, 15, 22–23, 141, 203; Hispanic tradition of, 145; social function of, 206, 210; as universal, 214. *See also* autobiographical novel; Boom; Crack movement; global novel; historical novel; narrative; *novelas totales*; political novel; universalism
*novelas totales*, 100, 103, 141

Oceania, 93, 97. *See also* French Polynesia
Orozco, José Clemente, 32
Orthodox Church, 189
Ortiz, Fernando, 31, 33–34. *See also* transculturation

Padilla, Heberto, 73
Padilla, Ignacio, 140, 203
Padilla Affair, 73–74, 99, 224n8. *See also* Cuban Revolution
Palestine, 193–94, 197–98, 200
Palou, Pedro Ángel, 141
*Parallel Lives* (Plutarch), 80, 129–30, 132

Paris, 8, 11, 28, 58–59, 65; as cultural model, 164; as literary metropole, 70, 72, 159–61, 219n6; in literature, 168–69. *See also* France; May 1968
Partido Revolucionario Institucional (PRI), 172, 177, 221n3
patriarchy, 79–80, 128
patriotism, 7, 101–2, 111, 117–18; extreme, 119–20
Paz, Octavio, 11, 27, 69, 148–49, 216, 223n4; on hybridity, 31, 34–35; as public intellectual, 177, 231n14. See also *El laberinto de la soledad* (Paz); *El ogro filantrópico* (Paz); *hibridismo*
Pearse, Patrick, 121–22
*Pérégrinations d'une paria* (Tristan), 63, 131, 226n17
Perestroika, 189, 202, 232n18
Peru, 1, 65–66, 68–72; as literary setting, 78, 80, 86, 134, 223n5; literature of, 219n5–219n6; Putumayo district of, 102–3, 115, 128–29, 227n25. *See also* Arequipa, Peru; Lima, Peru
Pinochet, Augusto, 14
Plunkett, Joseph, 122–24
Plutarch, 80, 129–30, 132
*Poetics* (Aristotle), 102
political cosmopolitanism, 4–5, 8, 10, 23, 210, 214; criticism of, 15
political novel, 178
Poniatowska, Elena, 1–2, 4, 177, 210, 216; autobiographical novel of, 6, 215, 222n8; as a chronicler, 221n3, 223n11; cultural identity of, 27–29; discovery of Mexico, 222n10. See also *La "Flor de Lis"* (Poniatowska)
Popper, Karl, 74
Porfiriato, 31, 61
Post-Boom movement, 14–15, 141, 154
post-colonialism, 19–21, 99–100, 220n10
"Postmanifiesto del Crack," 141, 206. *See also* "Manifiesto Crack"
Premio Cervantes, 1, 27
psychoanalysis, 160, 167, 171, 199

race, 3, 32
racism, 42, 53, 96, 129, 227n25
*Rainbow Warrior*, 198
Rama, Ángel, 10
realism, 14

252  Index

*realismo mágico. See* magical realism
religion, 123, 189–90. *See also* Christianity
republic of letters, 15, 72, 143. See also *ciudad letrada*
revolution, 73, 92, 95–96, 158–59, 162, 169–75; end of, 178, 201; failure of, 224n8; international, 198–99. *See also* Cuban Revolution; ideology; Mexican Revolution
Revueltas, José, 231n14
Reyes, Alfonso, 24, 66, 143, 149, 216
Rivera, Diego, 32
rooted cosmopolitanism, 2–3, 5–6, 8, 16–19, 21, 220n9; challenges of, 211, 215; and connection to home, 102, 143, 182–83, 213–14; and human needs, 203, 207; in Latin American literature, 24–25, 210, 216–17; in Vargas Llosa novels, 67–68, 112, 127–28, 135; in Volpi novels, 139–40, 155, 181, 198–200. *See also* cosmopolitanism; universalism
Rulfo, Juan, 145
Russia, 193, 196–97, 202

Said, Edward, 105, 179–80, 195–96
Salinas de Gortari, Carlos, 138, 157, 171–72, 181
Sartre, Jean-Paul, 224n8
Scotland, 134
setting, 15, 70; global, 142, 156–57, 215–16; and identity, 138; in *La "Flor de Lis,"* 35, 47; national, 223n5, 224n7; in Vargas Llosa novels, 7, 66, 76; in Volpi novels, 8. *See also* France; Mexico; Peru
Siqueiros, David, 32
socialism, 74, 82, 134, 186
socialist internationalism, 7
sovereignty, 19, 112, 116, 139. *See also* nation-state
Soviet Union. *See* USSR
Spain, 1, 8, 10–11, 65, 137, 151; independence from, 31; influence of, 209; as literary metropole, 13, 68, 219n6–219n7
Spanish (language), 37, 39, 56, 204; as language of literature, 145; Mexican, 156
Spanish America, 2, 4–5; authors of, 14, 145–46, 216–17; literature of, 6–8, 19, 25–26, 64–65, 135, 138–41, 209–10; and modernity, 10–11, 17. *See also* Latin America; magical realism
Spanish Ultraist movement, 219n5
Stalin, Joseph, 197, 202

Stanley, Henry Morton, 105, 107–8
Stoics, 16–17, 90
structuralism, 159, 161
subaltern cultures, 20–21, 29, 128, 200, 221n3

Tahiti, 95
*testimonio*, 7
third space (Bhabha), 4, 34
Third World, 192, 199–200, 227n25. *See also* developing world
Tlatelolco massacre, 1, 165–66, 181, 221n3, 231n14
tragic hero, 7, 102–3
transculturation (Ortiz), 5–6, 31, 33–34, 213, 216; and identity, 42, 60–61; in *La "Flor de Lis,"* 36, 59–60; rejection of, 40. *See also* hybridity
travel, 6, 23, 81–82, 85, 157; of authors, 69, 137; of characters, 79–80, 86–87, 90, 93–97, 103–5, 109, 126, 128; as cosmopolitan, 161, 182, 211–12, 228n26
*Travesuras de la niña mala* (Vargas Llosa), 223n5, 228n26
Tristán (Tristan), Flora, 7, 63–64, 67–68, 79–81, 130, 215, 225n13; as cosmopolitan, 82, 96–98, 112, 127–29, 213–14; and liberalism, 134; transformation of, 86–92, 133; writings of, 225n14, 226n17. See also *El Paraíso en la otra esquina* (Vargas Llosa); *Pérégrinations d'une paria*

Ukraine, 138
United Kingdom. *See* Britain
United States, 8, 10, 103, 185, 197; as colonial power, 20; as ideology, 190–91; imperialism of, 193, 195, 199–200; influence of, 209; and Mexico, 32; and nationalism, 217
universalism, 3, 13, 16–19; and cosmopolitanism, 81–82, 182–83, 211; in Crack literature, 141; criticism of, 14, 200; of culture, 135; and equality, 89; as Eurocentric, 39; as ideology, 189, 199; and intellectuals, 180; in literature, 25, 64, 66, 139–40, 154, 204–6; and the local, 193, 195, 203; of narrative, 21–22, 210; and nationalism, 118–19. *See also* ideology; novel
USSR, 8, 74, 183–90, 196–97, 199–200. *See also* communism; Russia
*Utopia* (More), 85

Index   253

utopianism, 64–65, 67–68, 79; and cosmopolitanism, 82, 85, 96–99, 188; end of, 172–74; and equality, 89; as ideology, 186, 193, 203; and individualism, 92–93; and love, 90–91; project of, 94–95; of Roger Casement, 100

Vallejo, César, 219n5
*Vanguardias*, 9, 12, 25, 229n6. *See also* Avant-Garde
*Vanguardistas*, 13, 216, 219n5
Vargas Llosa, Mario, 1–2, 4, 7, 61; cosmopolitanism of, 65–66, 68, 70–71, 101–2, 127, 210, 213–14; criticism of, 216–17, 224n10, 225n14; historical novels of, 6, 67, 76–79, 103–4, 130–33, 215, 224n11, 228n27; on literature, 63–65, 223n2; on nationalism, 99–100, 111–15, 119–20, 123–24, 127; politics of, 72–76, 134–35, 178, 224n8; settings of, 223n5; on utopias, 91, 98. See also *El Paraíso en la otra esquina* (Vargas Llosa); *El sueño del celta* (Vargas Llosa); *Historia de Mayta* (Vargas Llosa); historical novel; *La fiesta del Chivo* (Vargas Llosa); *La guerra del fin del mundo* (Vargas Llosa); *La tía Julia y el escribidor* (Vargas Llosa); *Lituma en los Andes* (Vargas Llosa); rooted cosmopolitanism; *Wellsprings* (Vargas Llosa)
Vasconcelos, José, 32
Venezuela, 168
Videla, Jorge Rafael, 14

Volpi, Jorge, 1–2, 4, 6–8, 137–38, 196–97, 200–201; cosmopolitanism of, 139–40, 143–49, 155–57, 200, 204–5, 207, 210, 213–14; criticism of, 216–17; historical novels of, 224n12; on ideologies, 182–83; on Latin American intellectuals, 163, 176–79, 181; on Latin American literature, 150–55, 228n1, 229n6; national allegiance of, 230n7; on *No será la tierra*, 231n16; *novelas ensayos* of, 215–16, 231n11; politics of, 203. *See also* Crack movement; "El fin de la conjura" (Volpi); *El fin de la locura* (Volpi); "El fin de la narrativa latinoamericana"; *El insomnio de Bolívar* (Volpi); *En busca de Klingsor* (Volpi); global consciousness; global novel; *No será la Tierra* (Volpi); rooted cosmopolitanism; "Yo soy una novela" (Volpi)

*Wellsprings* (Vargas Llosa), 111, 120
Western cosmopolitanism, 20, 24
World Trade Organization (WTO), 184

Yeltsin, Boris, 189
"Yo soy una novela" (Volpi), 204

Zaid, Gabriel, 177
Zaire. *See* Democratic Republic of the Congo
Zapatistas, 200
Zócalo, 46–47

www.ingramcontent.com/pod-product-compliance
Lightning Source LLC
Chambersburg PA
CBHW041311240426
43661CB00065B/2900